© 2022 PostScripts Productions
Rise of the Prison Planet
Earth Gulag
And the Great Escape

BY LUIS B. VEGA
vegapost@hotmail.com
www.PostScripts.org

Category: Religion & Spirituality

Publisher: Lulu
www.lulu.com

Binding: Paperback
Interior: Color
Dimensions: US Trade (6 x 9 in / 152 x 229 mm)

Publication Date: Jun 24, 2022
Language: English

ISBN: 9781387845910

PRISON PLANET

EARTH GULAG

AND THE GREAT ESCAPE

LUIS BERNARDINO VEGA

Comprehensive Studies showing the possible start
of Daniel's 70th Week of Years 'Prison Sentence', based on
Contributing Factors of Signs in the Sun, Moon and the Stars
Above and Geo-Political Events Below.

SETTING THE PRISONERS FREE

The Scroll of the Prophet Isaiah was handed to Him.
Unrolling it, He found the place where it was written:

The Spirit of the LORD is on Me, because He has Anointed
Me to preach Good News to the Poor.

He has sent Me to proclaim Liberty to the Captives and
Recovery of Sight to the Blind, to Release the Oppressed,
to Proclaim the YEAR of the LORD'S Favor'.

-Luke 4:17-19

DEDICATED TO

Council of Foreign Relations
Council of World Churches
International Monetary Fund
Rockefellers
Rothschilds United Nations
Trilateral Commission
World Bank
World Economic Forum
World Health Organization
Lucis Trust
Anthony Fauci
Lucifer
Bill Gates

May you all Reap what you have helped to Sow.

TABLE OF CONTENTS

PROLOGUE
Great Deception

'The Totalitarian State sets-up unquestionable Dogmas, and it alters them from Day-to-Day. It needs the Dogmas, because it needs Absolute Obedience from its Subjects, but it cannot avoid the Changes, which are dictated by the Needs of Power Politics. Almost certainly we are moving into an Age of Totalitarian Dictatorships – an Age in which Freedom of Thought will be at first a Deadly Sin and later on a Meaningless Abstraction. The Autonomous Individual is going to be stamped out of Existence'.
-George Orwell

How do you Imprison all the Humans on Planet Earth? You Lie to them by making them believe they are believing in the Truth. It is called the Great Delusion, the Great Lie. Where is this coming from? The purpose of this Book is to chronicle the Events, Places, People and Issues that are making Earth into a Prison Planet. In fact, it already is. It started with Fallen Angels. The Bible, in Genesis 6 speaks about an Infringement upon Humanity that took place on Earth. The Creation Account speaks about how YHVH created certain Species of Being after their own 'Kind' and that Species were not to cross each other.

It was sort of the 'Prime Directive' that is suggested in the original Star Trek TV Series. It stipulated that the Crew of the Enterprise would not interfere with or Infringe upon the Civilizations of Being encountered in their Space Travels. One could look at the Star-Fleet Command Crew as 'Angels' or in some cases as the 'Gods' that came down from the Sky or Space. This is how early Human civilization considered them. In fact, this is the prevailing Thesis and Theme of the History Channel's Ancient Alien TV Series from the USA. The aim is to condition the World for a Soft Disclosure that in fact, they believe Beings other than Humans are the 'Gods' from other Planets.

They are said to come from distant Star Clusters and/or Galaxies that created Human Beings on Planet earth. The issue, from a Biblical Narrative is that this Theory is 'half-right'. How so? The Book of Enoch teaches this very Fact, that 'Gods' or Angels are Stationed around the Universe as Sentinels and for the Purpose of YHVH, who the Bible identifies as the Creator. It so happens that 1 Angel Cherub decided to be GOD, in place of YHVH's Power and Authority.

Fall of the Anointed 4-Winged Angelic Being called Lucifer. Dore.

This 4-Winged Angelic Creation was and is called Lucifer. He is the true 'God', the Light Bearer to his Followers. Lucifer is the Original Rebel, according to Saul Alinsky, who wrote Rules for Radicals and in fact dedicated the Book to Lucifer. And the Problem? This Rebel Angel instigated a Heavenly Insurrection against YHVH. One might not realize but the notion that 'Heaven' is a place of Fluffy Clouds and Fat Babies with Wings playing the Harp is not the case. There is to the contrary, an Angelic War, full-on that is raging and in the midst is Humanity, as this War is not just contained within Heaven. So, the point is that, according to 1 account, recorded in the Book of Enoch, about 200 Fallen Angels that joined the Rebellion.

They sided with Lucifer and made a Secret Pack to come down to Earth, on Mount Hermon. And for the purpose? It was to cross Species with Humanity as to defile what makes Humanity different and Special. How so? Humanity is the only known type of Being that is created in what the Bible states is the 'Image and Likeness' of the Creator Himself, thus Adam and Eve. Humanity are the 'Image Bearers'. And more so, that they will 1 Day be elevated to a Higher Rank and Purpose than Angels.

This is 1 Notion why perhaps Lucifer rebelled, realizing that Humans, being lower and weaker, having Flesh would assume their Thrones, Dominions and Power 1 Day. Moreover, because of their Insurrection and violation of YHVH's 'Prime Directive', Lucifer and his Cadre of Fallen Angels would be defeated and castigated to suffer the Eternal Judgment of the Lake of Fire.

And by the Hands of whom? A mere Mortal Man. But this Mortal Man was no mere Mortal in part. This Man was Jesus Christ, Mortal in the sense that Jesus was born of a Human Mother but is GOD the Sun who came in the Flesh to save Humanity from the Infringement of Lucifer and his Fallen Angels. And how does this Preface play into the Prison Planet on Earth of this Book? Both in the Bible and the Book of Enoch, it teaches that such Angels that came down on Mount Hermon did defile Humanity by taken Women

They also were teaching them Forbidden Knowledge and Sexually producing Angelic-Human Hybrids that became the Giants and Gods of Mythology. For this Infringement upon Humanity, YHVH condemned them and sentenced the 200 Angels to Prison, on Earth, within Earth. This place is later identified as Tartarus. This word is only found once in the entire Bible, used by the Apostle Peter in how he Teaches that the Old World was Judged and destroyed by the Flood because of this violation of the Prime Directive.

In part, such Fallen Angels left their Estate and came down to Earth to deliberately Defile Humanity and violate the 'Prime Directive'. And for this reason, the Earth became a 'Prison Planet'. Both the Apostle Peter and Enoch explain that 1 of the reasons why these Angels are in Prison is that YHVH has reserved them to be used as Instruments of Judgment to be released in the Last Generation on Earth to execute Judgement upon the Humans at that time. This Narrative corroborates with the teachings of the Apostle John in how in the Book of Revelation, there is a Place and Time, wherein the Bottomless Pit or the Abyss is opened by a Fallen Angel, Apollyon, the Name in the Greek.

Mount Hermon where 200 Watcher Class of Angels came.

He is the Leader of this Rebel Contingency and the 200 will be released, but only when Christ Jesus commands. In a sense, there will be a Jail-Break, but it will not be accomplished by Lucifer, but by YHVH. What a horrific time that will be as no doubt, they will have vengeance upon Humanity for the time spent in the Prison Planet, Earth. But realize that, fast-forward to this Last Generation before Jesus returns, there is in the works another type of a 'Great Escape' also. Of whom? The Bride of Christ. There is going to be a sort of 'Prisoner Escape' occurring. In this case, it is called the Rapture event, etc. For the Fallen Angels in Earth's Prison of Tartarus, the Jail-Break is exactly what Lucifer and his Fallen Angels, on the other side of the Prison Planet have attempted to do. Evidence? One suggested that 1 way they are doing it is with CERN.

On the outset, CERN in Switzerland might seem all that Scientific, Intriguing, Cutting-Edge and it all is. It is the most sophisticated and largest 'Machine' ever built by Humanity. But like NASA in the USA, the Agency is run by Luciferians at the very top. The aim is not to find the 'God Particle'; that is the Cover. No, the aim is to pierce the Dimensions to the Prison and release their Fellow Angelic Gods from Tartarus. Why?

Realize again that Heaven is in a State or War, and so is Earth. The very Souls of every Human Being are in the Balance and being fought over. Thus, Lucifer and his Fallen Angels realize they are out-numbered, 3 to 1. So, their Odds are not in their favor. Solution? Jail-Break their 'Comrades' in Tartarus for the coming Fight, Armageddon. And to this end, throughout the Millennia since Adam and Eve, Lucifer and his Fallen Angels have beguiled Humanity into joining their Cause, their 'Gospel'.

And this has been, 'The Lie'. And this is how you Enclave Billions of Humans on Earth. What is worse is that certain portions of Humanity have bought the Lie and have actively joined Lucifer's Cause in destroying Humanity. The aim of Lucifer is to Enslave Humanity on Earth and has converted it into a Prison Planet. Examine all the major Human Institutions and those who are at the Helm. These are the 'Wardens' that rule the Prison Planet on their behalf.

These are the Clause Schwab's of the World, etc. Examples? Consider the United Nation, the World Health Organizations, the various Governments and Ideological Movements like Marxism, Communism, Socialism, Feminism, Nazism, etc. All such apparatuses have attempted to Enslave Humanity and keep it from its true Potential. There is a War for the Human Mind. Also such Institutions as Education, the Military, Societal Norm and through False Religions has Lucifer used and uses to Imprison Humanity.

And as Lucifer took the God-Given Dominion, Power and Authority away from Adam in the Garden, through the Deception believed by Eve, Lucifer grants such positions to those on Earth that become his Prison Wardens. And what does that look like? Lucifer lends his Power, though temporal to the Captains of Industry, Media, the Banks, Medicine, etc. For example, take the concept of a Bank Mortgage. The very meaning comes from the French word for Death. Humans are imprisoned by Mortgages for Life, from Financial Debt, Health Mandates now, by an Indoctrination of the Youth now starting in Kindergarten.

Transvestites are Men pretending to be Women. FreePik.

The objective is to reject the Truth about Biological Sex and embrace Moral Relativism, etc. People are imprisoned, Psychologically in their mind through the Mass Psychosis that was and is COVID, for example. Humanity is imprisoned by Narcotic and become Slaves and Prisoners on Earth, bound to Satan and his Minions due to Sin and Humanity's natural inclination for Power and Lust. Here are some examples of how this Present Imprisonment looks like, practically. This is evidence that the Prison Planet on Earth is run by the Tyrants of Tartarus. It mostly deals with occurrences in the USA.

-A Christian Teacher is suspended for not referring to a Student's Preferred Pro-Nouns.

-In the case of the Texas School Shooting, Parents report the Police stopping them from intervening.

-Canadian Pastor Artur Pawlowski is repeatedly Arrested for voicing protest at Trudeau's Tyranny.

-During COVID, the Governments admitted that Cell Phone information was monitored and gathered.

-In the USA, the Homeland Security sets up 'Disinformation Governance Board' to fight 'Misinformation'.

-USA Homeland Security issues Terrorism Bulletin over those that believe in 'Conspiracy Theories'.

-USA Justice Department investigates Mothers at local School Boards as being 'Domestic Terrorists'.

-The FBI, after more than 30 Fire-Bombings of Pro-Life Centers finally open-up an Investigation.

-Drag Queen Story Hours are promoted in Public Libraries across the USA.

-Dangerous COVID mRNA Experimental Shots are now authorized to be given to Babies.

-Employment, Shopping and Travel will soon be tied to one's Vaccination Status, i.e., Vaccine Passports.

-The CDC took down from their website how to Prepare for the Coming Zombie Apocalypse. Seriously.

-The Female Supreme Court Nominee cannot define what a Woman is. That only a Biologist is qualified to do so. And when they do, and a Woman is said to be a Female, that is bigoted.

The List continues and the focus is on the USA, as that is the Nation that leads all the Trends and types of Legislation that often affects or in this case 'Infects' the rest of the World. All that to say, that the USA has lost its Mind. It is now a foregone Conclusion of an Experiment. It tried to 'Free' Humanity from the Tyranny of oppressive Government 'Wardens'. It tried to Free the African Slaves during its Civil War, but it is emblematic of the Prison Planet Humanity is really in. So, yes, the Earth is a Prison Planet, for now. But there is Good News.

The 200 Watcher Angels were imprisoned in Tartarus. Tissot.

Jesus has changed all that. He has now secured the 'Jail Break' to come 1 Day in that the present Prison Planet Conditions that are a Reality will revert back to when Earth was Garden of Eden instead. This is why the Biblical Narrative is full of innuendos and Language about, 'Setting the Captives Free'. Jesus came to Jail-Break all of Humanity subject to the Bondage of Sin and Death. And how when Jesus Died and went to the Place of the Dead, the Prison where in some sort of Close Proximity to those Imprisoned Spirits were, there and then Jesus proclaimed His Victory and it says that he then 'Lead Captivity Captive'.

Theologically, upon Jesus' Resurrection and being Free from the Bondage of Death, rose to also bring all those Dead in Christ, that were in Abraham's Bosom, or Sheol, the Place of the Dead and take all those Souls to Heaven with Jesus. They await their Glorified Bodies as the Soul and Spirit of such People will then be given at the Resurrection-Rapture event.

This Resurrection-Rapture event is what is next on the Prophetic Time Clock on Earth. And what is amazing to consider is that the Last Generation of all those that are putting their Faith and Trust in Jesus, that are alive will not see Death. They will be those that will experience the 'Great Escape' from Earth's Prison Planet. It is the only Generation of Human Beings that will never experience Death nor its Power.

And to this end, this Book will thus present various chapters of Topics, Events and or Occurrences that deal with Geo-Politic, Astronomical Nuances and Theological Constructs that show how the Prison Planet will be moving in a direction where Lucifer will have the Upper Hand, momentarily and truly convert the entire Earth into a Prison Planet. In fact it will be for 7 Years and specifically the last 3.5 years or 42 Months will be how Lucifer's Warden of the Prison Planet, that being Earth will enslave every Human Being. How so?

This will be done through the False Prophet and AntiChrist's Beast System that will be tied to the Medical Health Apparatus. In that all who wish to Buy and Sell, or basically live must accept and receive into or on their Bodies the Mark that is associated with Lucifer's AntiChrist or False Messiah Savior of the World. It will be either an Image, a Number or his Name. And this 'Savior' will have help as the 'Alien Gods', the Fallen Angles that are now imprisoned in Tartarus will show-up to lend their support and assistance to Lucifer's False Messiah.

Their 'Beast' System will enable them to control what will become a Mass Concentration Camp on Earth. Of course, all that is to come can be averted and will be based on the Great Escape. How so? It is very simple. Salvation and the Truth are easy concepts to Understand. It is not 'Rocket Science' as it is said. One remembers when one 1st got Saved in the 8th Grade. One read Revelation 1st and then Daniel 2nd. The 3rd Book was Proverbs. And that is how one understood that there is Freedom in Jesus Christ.

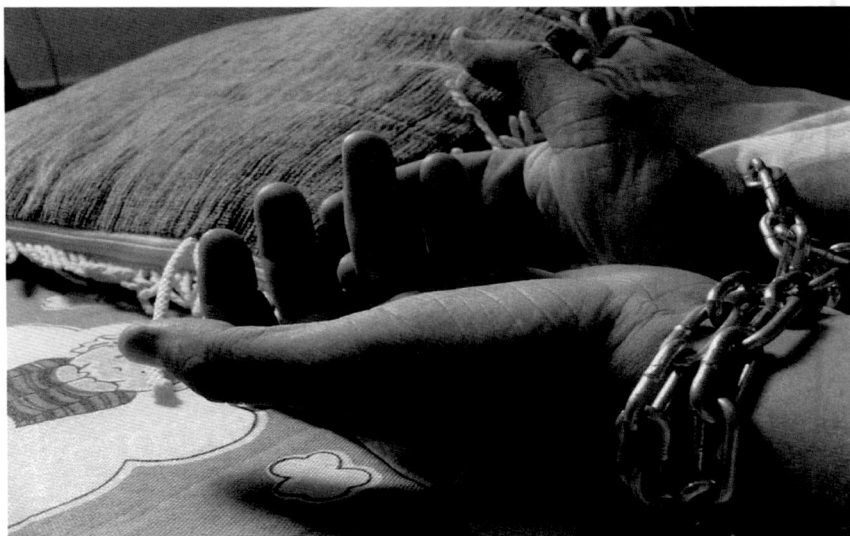

The Enslavement of Humanity began with Eve. PxHere.

No matter one's Level of Intelligence, it is Christ Jesus that bestows Knowledge and Understanding. One realized that Information is Power and why Jesus said, 'If you know the Truth, the Truth will set you Free. This is why 'Truth Matters'. This is to be Free: Know the Truth, Truth is Freedom. But that the Ultimate Truth is Jesus. Jesus said that of Himself, 'I Am the Truth'. It is why it is so important that Absolutes be sustained, maintained. Or else? Well, as the saying goes, 'If one cannot Stand for Something, One will Fall for Anything'. That is what is happening now on Planet Earth, the Prison Planet.

How are Billions of Humans being Imprisoned? Believe the Lie instead. Suspend what is Truth, etc. Destroy all that is True or points to Truth, like Jesus and His Followers. Presently, the Prison Planet is laughing at the Christians. Such are increasingly becoming Hostile and Intolerant. They are now basically labeling Followers of Jesus as 'Racists, Bigoted, Stupid, Backward, you name it. It is so easy to just make a typical Stereotypical Blanket Statement.

And that sure, many Christians are not the High Class of the World or the Celebrated Intelligentsia. That most are just hard working Common People. But it is such People that realize their Faults and need of a Savior. Jesus is not looking for 'Perfect People' to then Call to come into the Fold, the Light, the Truth. And as one told a Students at one's University, who was thinking of going into Full Time Ministry, one reiterated what one's Mentor taught, 'Jesus does not Call the Qualified, he Qualifies the Called'.

Realize that throughout History, it has been the 'Less Than' People, for the most part that have come to Jesus. It is seen in the Gospels; the Thieves, Prostitutes, Beggars, Outcasts, Lepers, Slaves, the IRS People, are the ones who saw their Need and came to Jesus. They were then Transformed, changed and changing from what they were, etc. It says in the Bible that YHVH sought Fellowship or a Relationship with Humanity.

And after being Rejected by Adam and Eve, He searched and found Abraham. He wanted to be 'Friends' and thus they made a 'Blood Brother' Pack. But it was unilateral as YHVH sealed the Deal on behalf of Abraham. And the point was that YHVH said that He used Wisdom and Knowledge for those in the World to convince them. Did that do it? No. Then for the Jews, YHVH said that He used Signs and Wonders to convince them. Did that work? No.

So, YHVH said, oversimplifying it here…Ok, I am going to go to the Less Than People and I will give them Wisdom and Understanding, and Signs and Wonders. They will Receive me gladly and I will show them my Wisdom and Wonders through them. And for what? To lift up Jesus, and have People be Saved to escape the Earth's Prison Planet run by Lucifer and his Fallen Angels, Demons and Demented People. It is because only then are the Scales of Humanity's Spiritual Blindness taken off to see and understand the Truth. It is by this Truth of the gospel that Human beings are truly set Free.

Tartarus is believed to be the Prison of the Titan Angels. PxHere.

Only in Jesus is Wisdom, Understanding and Signs and Wonder given for the purpose to draw all of Mankind to Redemption and Release just as the Hebrews were set Free from the Bondage of Pharaoh, etc. Realize that it is Jesus that has also masterminded a 'Great Escape' from the Prison Planet that is Earth. It is called the Rapture. It is called the Blessed Hope in the anticipated Appearing, in the Sky, in the Clouds of Jesus that is coming for only those that the Bible calls, 'The Bride'. It is made-up of all those Human Beings that have put their Faith and Trust in what Jesus did at the Cross of Calvary.

Jesus essentially, 'Went to Prison' in one's Stead to pay for the Infringement of Sin that condemns all of Humanity to the Prison of Eternal Death. As a Willing Substitutionary Offering, Jesus paid with His Perfect and Sinless Life. This was the Price to 'Ge out of Jail' Card. And that Card is now being offered to every Human 'Prisoner' on this Prison Planet. One just needs to receive it and play it.

One just has to present that 'Card' to the Warden of this Earth, Lucifer. It is what the Card represents, the Payment in Blood to set every Human Prisoner Free as the Cell Doors of one's Prison will be open, metaphorically speaking. As to the structure of the Book, Numbers 1-10 will be numerated for emphasis. Not all the Proper Grammar Rules will be adhered to.

The Narration will be in the 3rd Person. In certain places, parts of the paragraphs, phrases or words will be bold to highlight the idea or thought. All Graphics as in Charts are one's own work. All Pictures have been taken from the Public Domain or by Permission. If any Image is believed to be Copyrighted, please inform this Author to either remove the Image or give due Credit and Citation, etc.

German Nazi Concentration Prison are here again. PxHere.

Those who refuse the New Reset will be Beheaded. PxHere.

During the COVID Lock-Downs, People were sent to Camps. FreePik.

THE GULAG
RUSSIAN: ГУЛАГ

Acronym for Гла́вное Управле́ние Лагере́й
Glávnoje Upravlénije Lageréj
Chief Administration of the Camps

A 'Gulag' was the Government Agency in charge of the Soviet Network of Forced Labor Camps set-up under Vladimir Lenin. It reaching its peak during Joseph Stalin's Rule but were still implemented up to the Fall of the Soviet Union. They were no better than NAZI Concentration Camps, these were the Left's Version.

The Gulag was used as a tool to Politically Repress any form of protest to the Mighty Soviet Union. The Soviet Concentration Camps were used to deal with 'Soviets' involved in Petty Crime to those that were Political Dissidents and or Religious. The Convictions were large based on Hear-Say and Suspicion. It is estimated that the Population of the Gulag Camps were in the Millions, as much as 14 Million 'Soviets' went through the System.

Usually such statistics are usually at least double in reality. The Living Conditions were Sub-Human and the Gulags were usually in out-of-the-way Locations, not easily viewed by the General Population. However, in Major Cities like Moscow, ag Gulag, could be a single Apartment Block, for example hidden in plain sight.

It is reported that it was Nikita Khrushchev that on January 25, 1960, dismantled the Gulag System but it continues to exist in the Russian Federation to this Day. It was the famous Russian Aleksandr Solzhenitsyn, Winner of the Nobel Prize in Literature, who survived eight years of Gulag incarceration, that gave the term, Gulag its international Recognition by publishing, The Gulag Archipelago in 1973.

He described the Gulag as a System where People were Worked to Death. He was 1 among many who demonstrated that the Gulag as an Instrument of Governmental Repression against its own Citizens on a Massive Scale. This is how Governments, both on the Right and the Left, once in Power will see to it that a Gulag Type of System is in place to essentially convert the Citizenry into a Prison Planet.

It is how it maintains Control, Surveillance and Autonomy over its People, not seen as Citizens but as Prisoners. The only Purpose of People it to 'Work' for and Worship the State. How is this Gulag Type of System introduced? It came out of a Revolution in Czarist Russia. In other Nations, it comes out of Calamites, Man-Made like COVID-19.

In the USA, for example, after 3 Years of the Original Strain of COVID-19 the prolonging Narrative is that 'Variants' and New Types of Pandemics will require the USA to still be under FEMA Rule and the Emergency Status, of which former President Trump made, will never be withdrawn now. In fact, for such a Purpose, the CDC had come up with its Operation Shielding Approach in which, essentially, it has designed, created and identified Locales in their Gulag Type of Facilities to house the 'Quarantined'. This State Apparatus of Repression and Enslavement is now already in place in the West.

But it has a different Name, 'Quarantine Facilities', thanks to their new-found way of implementing their State Totalitarianism; Declare a Plandemic. For example, in Australia, such COVID Gulag Camps were constructed and administered. Mass COVID Injection of Adolescents in a Stadium took place with Armed Police that prohibited Parents from withdrawing their Children form this Forced Injection of the State. In Shanghai, China, the entire Metropolitan City was Quarantined-off.

China has been the Beta Test in how once the Luciferian Globalists take over the entire World with their New World Order, the China Model will be implemented worldwide. The COVID0-19 was just the initial Gulag 1.0 version. It came the Globalist a lot of feedback to know how to improve the System when it goes Wholesale. How will that look like? Rations.

It will be based on the China Social Credit Score System. Due to Modern Technology, now a State can have total Surveillance and Control of People. It has been done through the guise of a Medical Preclusions, etc. On the contrary, the façade of a Medical Mandate to 'Protect' People, for their 'Safety' will result in the State forcing People to take Dangerous mRNA Injection.

The Disease or any Manufactured Plandemic will do and it is. The ultimate goal is to have the Modern Technology of Total Surveillance withing the Body. This is why the mRNA. Why? The Biological System will be fused at the DNA Level in Humans that will be tied to Block-Chain type of Infrastructure to then Track and Trace one's Digital Wallet of Currency issued by the State.

It will also serve to follow the 'Carbon Footprint' of People to restrict types of Foods, like Meat, Poultry and Beef, etc. Such a Total Spectrum Dominance will also restrict a Person's Movement and ability to Buy, Sell and Travel. This is the stuff of the Book of Revelation. The World has arrived. The Prison Planet is ready.

SOVIET GULAG

IMAGES OF THE PRISON PLANET

It is estimated that at least, 18,000,000 'Soviets' passed through the Gulag Camps System. There were 53 Gulag Camp Directorates and 423 Labor Colonies in the Soviet Union just before World War 2 broke out. According to research, the tentative consensus in contemporary Soviet historiography is that roughly ~2 Million Soviets Died due to Detention in the Gulag Camps.

Petty Crimes and Jokes about the Soviet Government and Officials were punishable by Imprisonment. It is estimated that about half of Political Prisoners in the Gulag Camps were imprisoned without a Trial. Official Data suggest that there were over 2.6 Million Soviets sentences to Imprisonment on cases investigated by the Secret Police, the KGB.

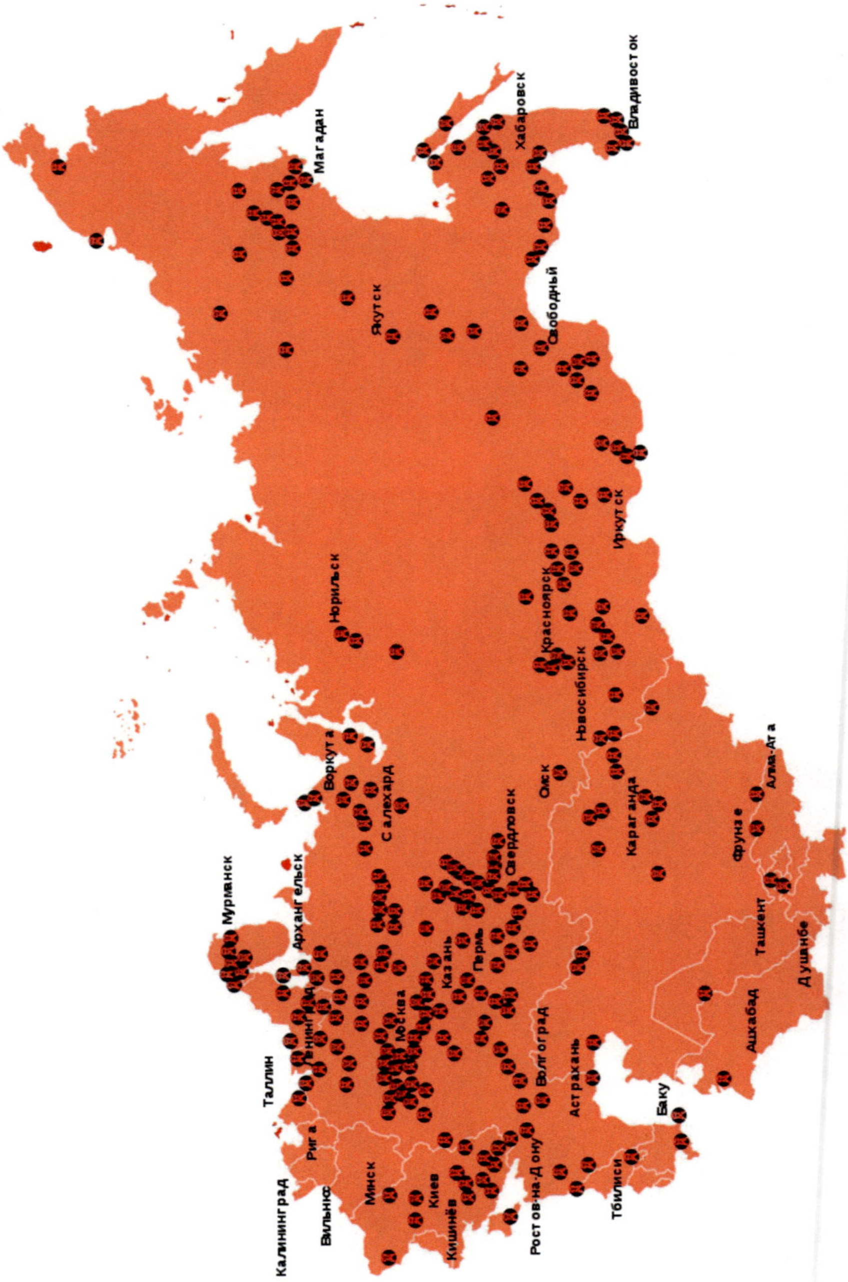

Магадан

Хабаровск

Владивосток

Якутск

Свободный

Иркутск

Норильск

Красноярск

Новосибирск

Омск

Караганда

Алма-Ата

Воркута

Салехард

Свердловск

Пермь

Казань

Фрунзе

Ташкент

Душанбе

Ашхабад

Мурманск

Архангельск

Москва

Ленинград

Рига

Таллин

Калининград

Вильнюс

Минск

Киев

Кишинёв

Ростов-на-Дону

Волгоград

Астрахань

Баку

Тбилиси

W.H.O. GULAGS
World Health Organization

IMAGES OF THE PRISON PLANET

According to Research, in the midst of the Russian Civil War, Lenin and the Bolsheviks established a 'Special Prison' Camp System. They were separate from the Traditional Prison System and under the control of the Chelates Camps, as Lenin envisioned them, had a distinctly Political Purpose.

The main purpose of the camps within the GULAG System was to Isolate and Eliminate Class-Alien, Socially Dangerous, Disruptive, Suspicious, and other Disloyal Elements, whose Deeds and Thoughts were not contributing to the Support of the Dictatorship of the Soviet Proletariat or Ruling Oligarchy.

Forced Labor as a 'Method of Re-Education'. It was applied in the Gulag Camps based on Trotsky's Experiments with Forced Labor Camps for Czech War Prisoners from 1918. He then introduced the 'Compulsory Labor Service'.

Australia

Coronavirus evacuees expected to arrive at NT workers' camp near Darwin.

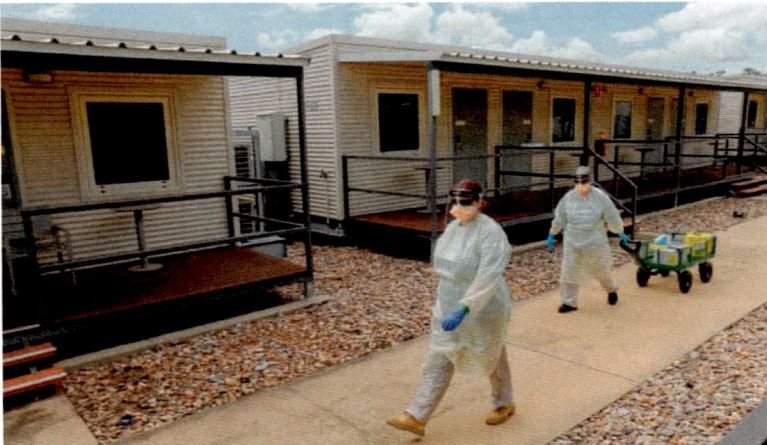

Australia Hotel Quarantine: Calls for more Remote Facilities over Mutant COVID Strains.

Nations like Australia and Canada have implemented COVID Travel Restrictions.

Now Children are dying after being herded into Australian Arena for Jabs without their Parents' Consent.

Peoples Republic of China
CCP

IMAGES OF THE PRISON PLANET

Although the term Gulag was originally used in reference to a Government Agency, the Acronym acquired the qualities of a Common Noun, denoting a State System of Prison-Based, Unfree Labor. Even more broadly, 'Gulag' has come to mean that the State itself is a Repressive System. It involves a set of Procedures that Prisoners once called the 'Meat-Grinder'.

It starts with the Arrests, the Interrogations, the Transport in unheated Cattle Cars, the Forced Labor, the Destruction of Families, the years spent in 'Detention, the Early and Unnecessary Deaths, etc.

The term's contemporary usage is no longer just directly related to the former USSR. The Expression is used now to denote Repressive and Totalitarian States, like North Korea's Gulags who operate camps today.

42

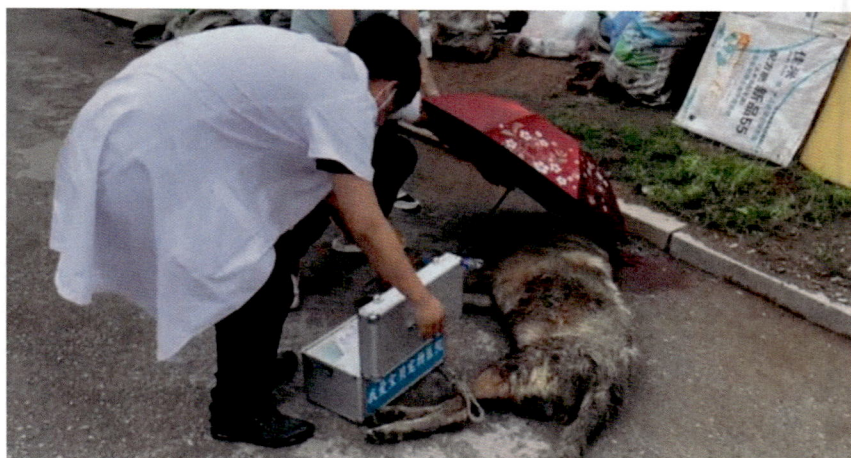

UNITED STATES OF AMERICA

IMAGES OF THE PRISON PLANET

Various Categories of Prisoners were defined during the Gulag Years in the former Soviet Union. They included Petty Criminals, POWs, Officials accused of Corruption, Sabotage and Embezzlement, Political Enemies, Dissidents and other People deemed Dangerous for the State. This included the Clergy.

At first the Gulag System did not distinguish between Criminal Prisoners, Religious and Political or 'Special Prisoners'. The judicial and penal systems were neither unified nor coordinated. The State had total Power to Detain any person for any Reason, even on a suspicion or False Accusation.

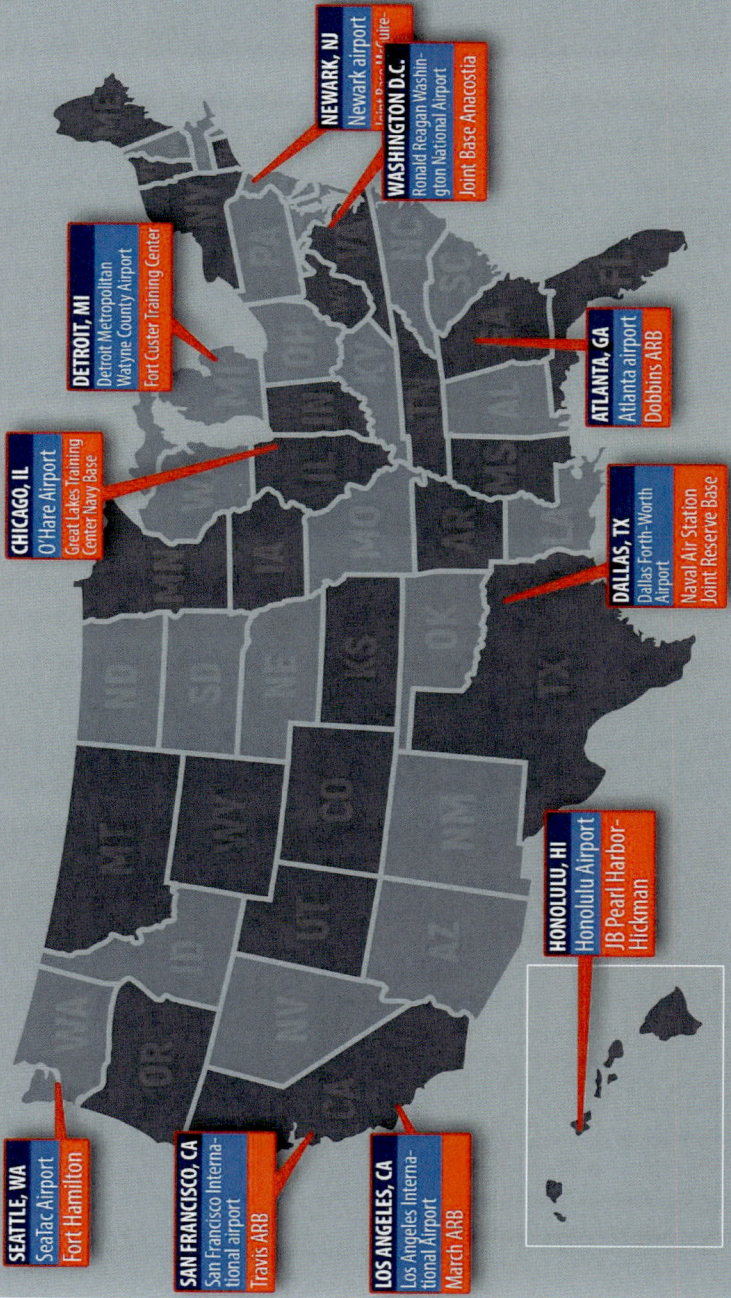

APPROVED COVID-19 QUARANTINE CAMPS NEAR MAJOR US AIRPORTS

NEWARK, NJ
Newark airport
Joint Base McGuire

WASHINGTON D.C.
Ronald Reagan Washington National Airport
Joint Base Anacostia

DETROIT, MI
Detroit Metropolitan Watyne County Airport
Fort Custer Training Center

ATLANTA, GA
Atlanta airport
Dobbins ARB

CHICAGO, IL
O'Hare Airport
Great Lakes Training Center Navy Base

DALLAS, TX
Dallas Forth-Worth Airport
Naval Air Station Joint Reserve Base

HONOLULU, HI
Honolulu Airport
JB Pearl Harbor-Hickman

SEATTLE, WA
SeaTac Airport
Fort Hamilton

SAN FRANCISCO, CA
San Francisco International airport
Travis ARB

LOS ANGELES, CA
Los Angeles International Airport
March ARB

49

U.S. State and Federal Prison Population, 1925-2016

2016: 1,458,173

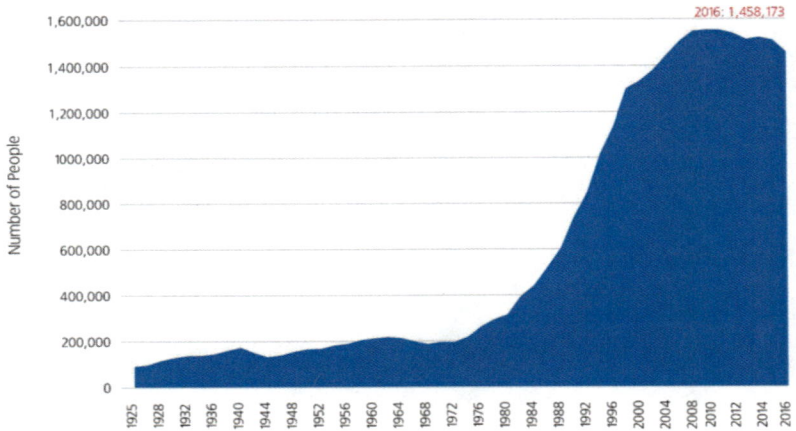

U.S. prison population by offense

Drug offenders account for nearly half.

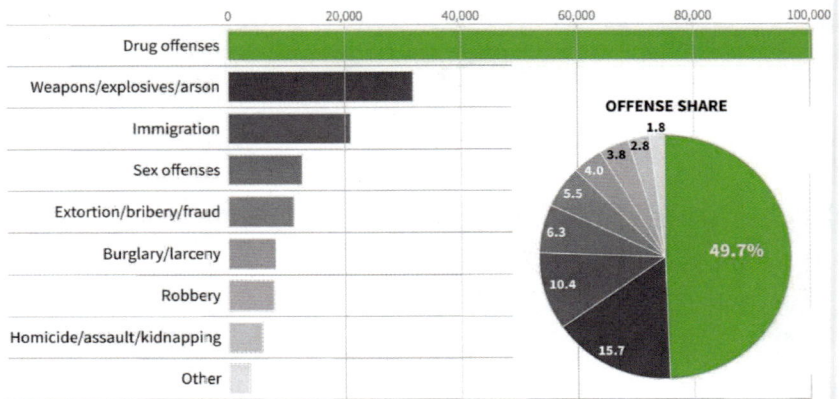

	0	20,000	40,000	60,000	80,000	100,000
Drug offenses						
Weapons/explosives/arson						
Immigration						
Sex offenses						
Extortion/bribery/fraud						
Burglary/larceny						
Robbery						
Homicide/assault/kidnapping						
Other						

OFFENSE SHARE

49.7%

15.7

10.4

6.3

5.5

4.0

3.8

2.8

1.8

Source: U.S. Federal Bureau of Prisons

S. Culp, 03/09/2014

LOCKED UP: **INCARCERATION RATES**

After being the country with the highest incarceration rate in the world for years, the United States slipped to rank no. 2 in 2012, behind Seychelles, a tiny island nation with a total population of less than 100,000. Here are the 50 most populous countries in the world, in order of incarceration rate:

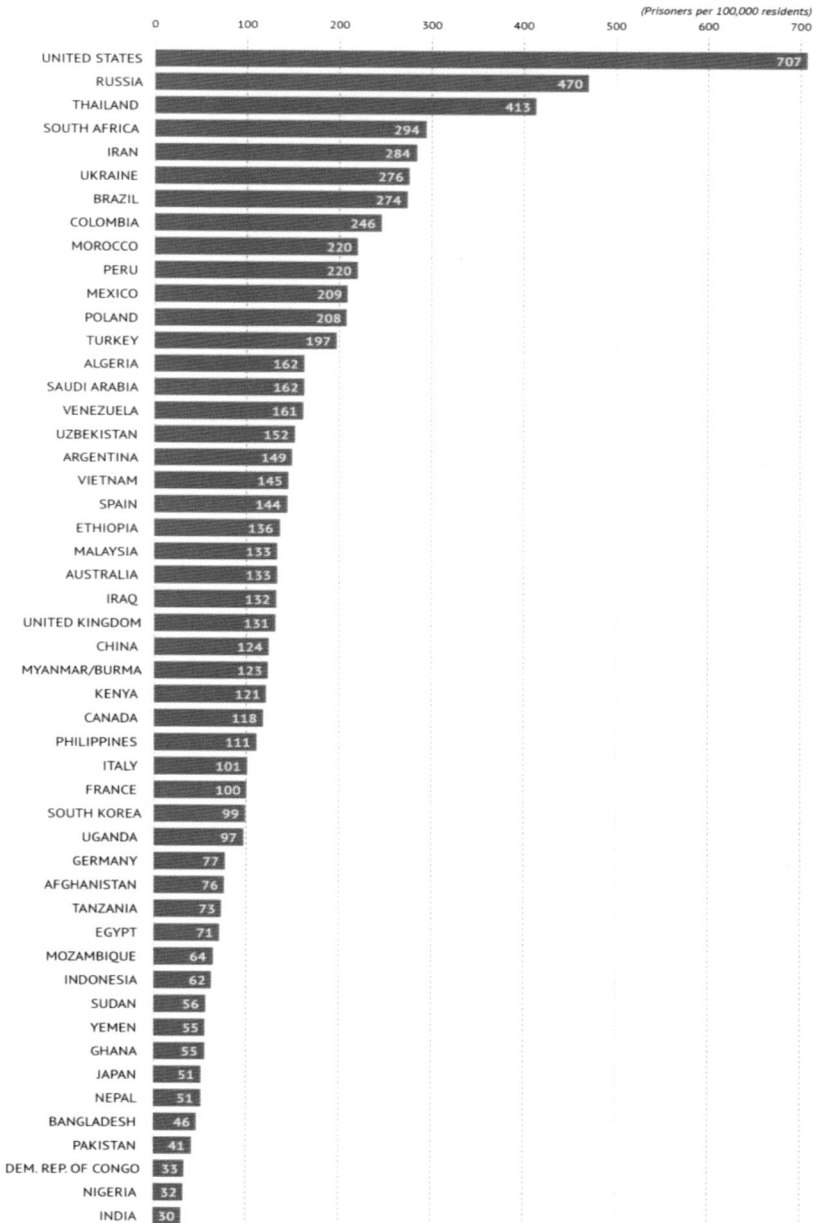

(Prisoners per 100,000 residents)

UNITED STATES	707
RUSSIA	470
THAILAND	413
SOUTH AFRICA	294
IRAN	284
UKRAINE	276
BRAZIL	274
COLOMBIA	246
MOROCCO	220
PERU	220
MEXICO	209
POLAND	208
TURKEY	197
ALGERIA	162
SAUDI ARABIA	162
VENEZUELA	161
UZBEKISTAN	152
ARGENTINA	149
VIETNAM	145
SPAIN	144
ETHIOPIA	136
MALAYSIA	133
AUSTRALIA	133
IRAQ	132
UNITED KINGDOM	131
CHINA	124
MYANMAR/BURMA	123
KENYA	121
CANADA	118
PHILIPPINES	111
ITALY	101
FRANCE	100
SOUTH KOREA	99
UGANDA	97
GERMANY	77
AFGHANISTAN	76
TANZANIA	73
EGYPT	71
MOZAMBIQUE	64
INDONESIA	62
SUDAN	56
YEMEN	55
GHANA	55
JAPAN	51
NEPAL	51
BANGLADESH	46
PAKISTAN	41
DEM. REP. OF CONGO	33
NIGERIA	32
INDIA	30

By Lisa Mahapatra for International Business Times; Source: International Centre for Prison Studies, Prison Population Rate

51

MONKEY POX EXERCISE 2021
WORLD DEATH PROTOCOLS
A Cover-Up for COVID VAIDS

The purpose of this chapter is to consider the March 2021 Bio-Weapon Mock Attack Exercise on the Planet with Monkey Pox. And when was that release of Monkey Pox supposed to have occurred? May 15, 2022. And amazingly, the Monkey Pox suddenly appeared as an 'Outbreak in 82 counties. And from that time, it has been reported as a New Virus and next Potential Pandemic or is it another of their Plandemic.

It is rather stunning that in all prior major Human Turning Points that have affected the entire Globe, such Transitional Times have been preceded by an 'Exercise'. It so happened in 2000, that just months prior to 9-11, there was a Pentagon Simulated Exercise called, Operation Dark Winter. It simulated an Attack on the USA and what would be the response. And guess what was the Outcome and Recommendation? The USA must have a 'Department of Homeland Security'.

See Article here: https://www.postscripts.org/ps-news-428.html

Take for example, 9-11. On the very Day of the Attack on the World Trade Center Buildings, there was a U.S. Air Force Exercise exactly simulating Commercial Airliners being used as Bombs to ram into Skyscrapers in New York City. Astonishingly, the Fighter Pilots requested confirmation if the Exercise was real. A Commercial Plane was detected on their Radar and asked to intercept. Guess what happened? The Stand Down Order came from the then Vice President Cheney, the 'Real' U.S. President at the time.

Then, in 2010, there was another Report released by the Rockefeller Foundation. It was called Scenarios for the Future. And guess what the Scenario looked like? They predicted that there would be a COVID-Like Virus Outreach coming from where? China. And that World Governments had to declare 'National Emergency' to curtail the 'Spread' and suspend Civil Liberties. That Mask Mandates would be implemented as well as forced Lock-Down, etc.

See Article here: https://www.postscripts.org/ps-news-423.html

Then behold, in the month of October of 2019, the Bill and Melinda Gates Foundation along with John Hopkins University, and the World Economic Forum, the 'Usual Suspects' undertook a Simulation Exercise where a Pandemic, a Virus was released. The Outcomes? Secure the Narrative by controlling Information and the News Outlets. Censor any Information and/or Data that contradicts the 'Official Scientific Narrative'. Give greater power to the Centralized Government, and require 'Vaccinations', etc.

The Scenario further prescribed Lock-Downs, Mask Mandates, Social Distancing and compliance, primarily enforced, not by Government, but by Corporations. And that an easement would follow but only to then secure more Centralized Power to suspend Civil Right. This is exactly what occurred in Canada with Fidel Castro's Bastard Son, Justin. He suspended the Truckers Bank Accounts, ceased their Rig/Trucks, Fuel. He Character Assassinated them as being Nazis and Confederates. All the while his Globalist Police Force stomped over Grandmothers and Trudeau's Deputy, Chrystia Freeland who is a Director at World Economic Forum.
Her Grandfather was a Nazi, made his Emergency Powers Permanent. It is they who are the Nazis.

See Article here: https://www.postscripts.org/ps-news-627.html

The End Result of Event 201 would have required all Humans on the Planet to not only get 'Vaccinated' but that it would be interwoven into one's Digital Vaccine Passport and eventual Block-Chain Digital Wallet. All this, by the way, has not gone away. Hello Monkey Pox. According to Dr. Karen Kingston, who has appeared in Talk Shows like Stew Petters, has come out on the Record to state that Monkey Pox is a 'Cover-Up' for all those People that are now developing 'VAIDS''. What is VAIDS?

It is essentially the result of taking these Dangerous COVID mRNA Shots that have Monkey and Swine Cell Lines. But they also destroy one's Immune System, to the point that People are no better than AIDS Patients. And as a result, with each 'Booster' Shot, there is an approximate 25% diminishing of one's Natural Immune System. And Skin Outbreaks like Shingles, Skin Rashes and/or Blister-Like 'Poxes' will be intentionally Diagnosed as 'Monkey Pox'. Why?

This will ensure a Consistent Scare and Infection Rates to justify the coming Mandatory Testing and Lock-Down as well as Mask Mandates. It will call into question all those Injection Hesitant or Resisters that will now be Forcibly Injected. And now the Globalists have had their Monkey Pox corresponding 'Exercise' that exactly predicted when the Outreach was to be released, May 15, 2022.

No, not a mere Coincidence. Now, one considers that all those Scientists, Doctors, and Specialists that were involved in the Monkey Pox Experiment are not 'All in it'. In most cases, at this level, People are Compartmentalized. And in fact, most would consider what they are working on as a Good Thing for Humanity. One is talking in terms of the 'Black Hand', the 'Invisible Hand', those in Power 'Behind the Curtain' that are the true Arbitrators of Life and Death on this Planet Earth, currently, The 'Gods of Earth', etc.

Usual Suspects

These are the Self-Proclaimed 'Gods of Earth' that seek to subjugate Humanity and 'Erase' the 'Image and Likeness' of YHVH, with, 1 Injection at a time. Why? Genetically, every Human Being is endowed with YHVH's Name, in the ACTG Sequence. And so, what was the Nuclear Threat Initiative all about and why? The following is taken directly from their Public Website on the Subject and will be said in paraphrase form. The Nuclear Threat Initiative NIT partnered-up with the Munich Security Conference MSC. It brought 19 Global Leaders, via Zoom on March 15 of 2021.

Nuclear Threat is once again real and menacing. PxHere.

Interestingly, the NTI is a Non-Profit, co-founded by Ted Turner and the Munich Security Conference. Ted Turner is the Founder of CNN and who is on Record stating that there are 'Too many Humans' and that the 'ideal' level should be less than 2 Billion People on Earth. They meet once a Year to discuss International Security Policy. They have been meeting since 1963. The Monkey Pox Mock Bio-Attack was discussed under the topic entitled: Strengthening Global Systems to Prevent and Respond to High-Consequence Biological Threats.

https://www.nti.org/wp-content/uploads/2021/11/NTI_Paper_BIO-TTX_Final.pdf

The Goals and Intention of the International Think-Tank might seem Ultraistic, Noble and Commendable, but. As they gather the Global Leaders from Governments, Industry, and Civil Society, their aim is Global Governance. It is not about 'Reducing the Risks' of Catastrophic Biological Events. They are the ones who foment all that.

They are using the Failures they precise from COVID-19 and are now ensuring they are closing the 'Gap' on perceived 'Vulnerabilities', or in other words, 'Tightening the Noose'. They use the Terms, 'Future Biological Events could exceed COVID', etc. Their Luciferian Plan is precisely what they seek to prevent. In this case, it is not about any concern over Lost Lives, Economic Damage and Political Disruption.

The Scenario, much like Dark Winter, Lock-Step, Event 201, test the 'Resolve' both Nations and their People will have, or not. They want to know what type of Response will occur once they implement their Disruption in the Supply and Food Chains, Public Services, Cyber-Security, and control of the Narrative.

The Monkey Pox, for this Exercise, occurred in the Fictitious Nation of Andoriban. The release is intentional with the aim at crippling the Nation's Economy. Funny, but is that not what COVID did? And still is doing? This next Plandemic will surely be the Proverbial 'Last Nail in the Coffin'. And the Outcome? They seek to justify a Global Government, to have a Global Response.

This 'Response' will dictate the Medieval Protocols for every Human Being on the Planet. This will inevitably set-up the New World Order Beast System, otherwise called the Return of the Babylonian Whore System in the Last Days, during the 7-Year Tribulation Period. They seek to justify having the WHO take over as most Nations are too poor to respond in the way they want.

MONKEYPOX IN THE UK

793 cases

SCOT 18
N.IRE 3
WAL 6
ENG 766

WORLD'S CURRENT HOTSPOTS
CONFIRMED SUSPECTED

UK:		793
SPAIN:		497
GERMANY:		412
PORTUGAL:		297
FRANCE:		183

COUNTRIES SPOTTED IN
53

WHEN CASES WERE REPORTED

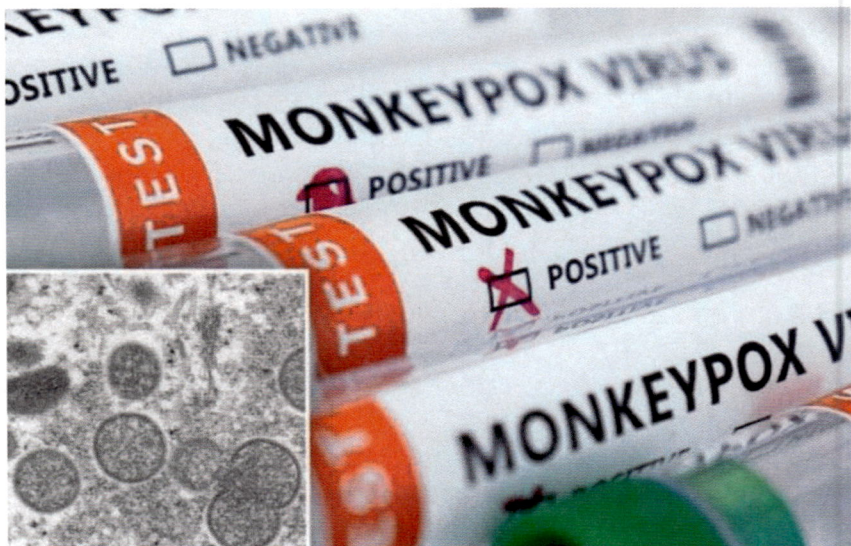

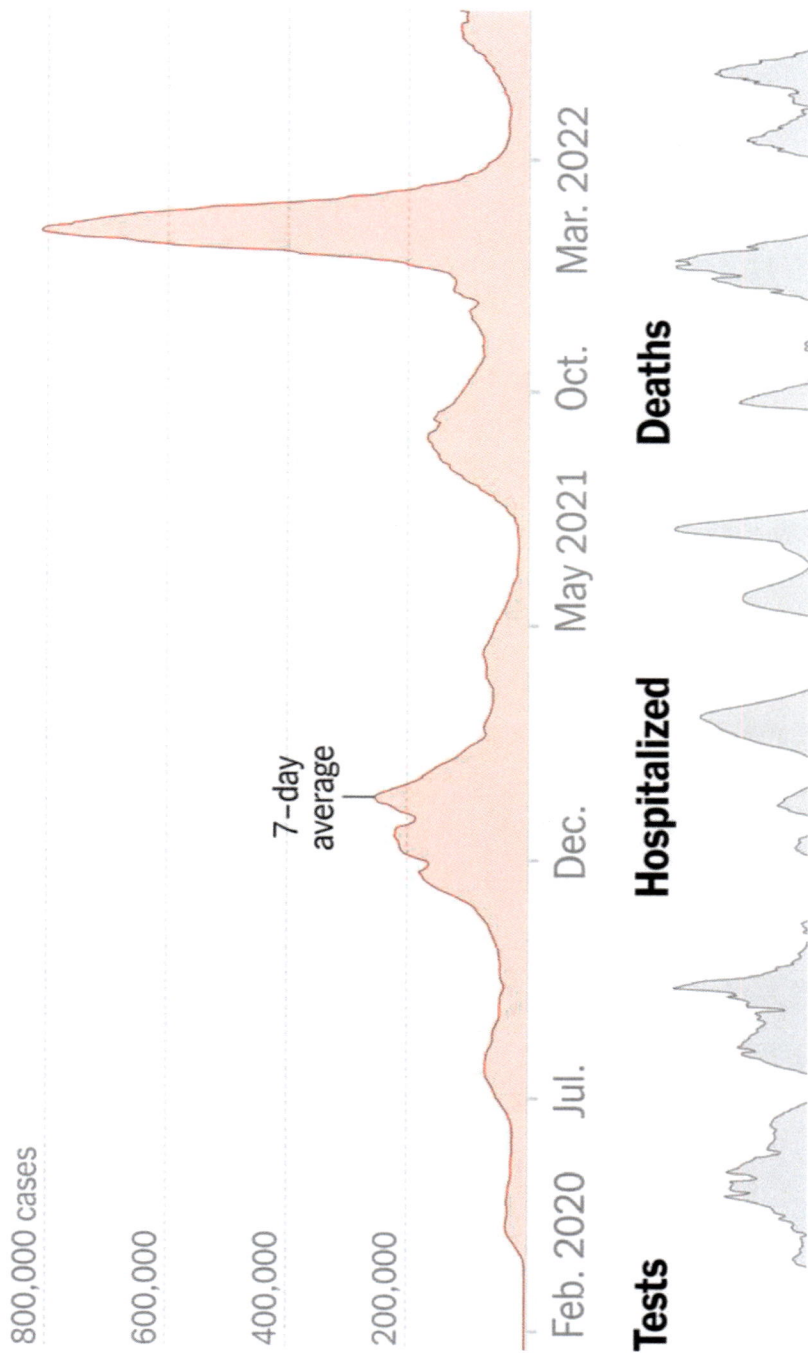

800,000 cases

600,000

400,000

200,000

7-day
average

Feb. 2020   Jul.   Dec.   May 2021   Oct.   Mar. 2022

Tests   **Hospitalized**   **Deaths**

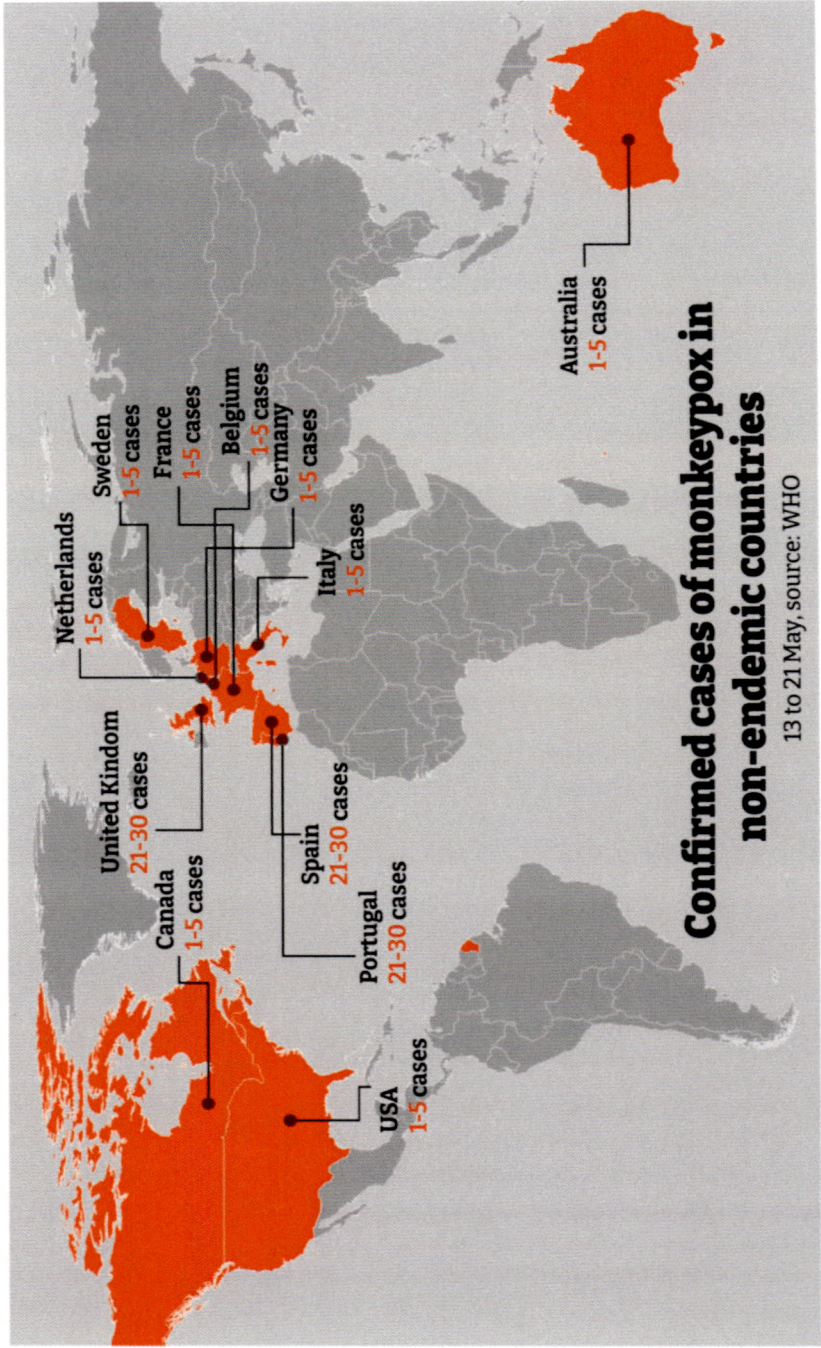

Confirmed cases of monkeypox in non-endemic countries

13 to 21 May, source: WHO

Sweden — 1-5 cases
France — 1-5 cases
Belgium — 1-5 cases
Germany — 1-5 cases
Netherlands — 1-5 cases
Italy — 1-5 cases
United Kindom — 21-30 cases
Spain — 21-30 cases
Canada — 1-5 cases
Portugal — 21-30 cases
USA — 1-5 cases
Australia — 1-5 cases

MONKEYPOX

SYMPTOMS

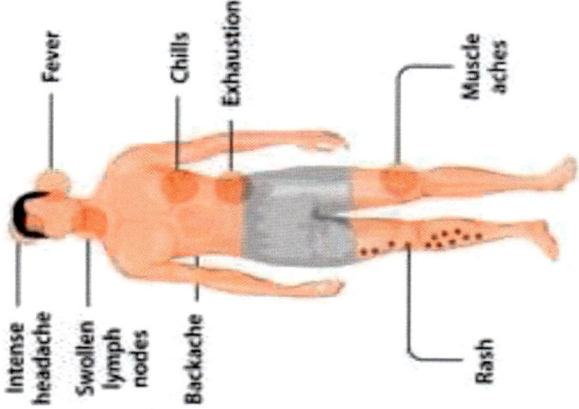

- Fever
- Chills
- Exhaustion
- Muscle aches
- Intense headache
- Swollen lymph nodes
- Backache
- Rash

Illness lasts for 2-3 weeks

HOW IT SPREADS

Primarily animals, typically rodents

Bites   Scratches   Consumption of bush meat

Human-to-human transmission is possible, but limited

Through close contact with infected respiratory tract secretions or skin lesions

Monkeypox Cell

And why not with the Trillions given by the USA, Communist China and Bill Gates. And the Scare Tactic? Monkey Pox. The Narrative will argue that most Nations lack Coordination. And as a result, astonishingly, they predict, based on their Exercise, that there will be up to 2 Billion Humans infected with Monkey Pox and about 120 Million will Die. Where has one heard of such Parabolic Mortality Rates and Statistics? Oh yes, COVID.

The initial Scare for COVID was that if the World did not Lock-Down, Mask-Up and Social Distance, 3 Million People in the USA alone would die. In reality it is these Numbers that are being broadcast that they want Dead. The Luciferians want less than 500 Million consuming 'Their' Resources. So, eventually having over 2 Million People Dead from their Bio-Engineered Attack against Humanity would be a Victory in their War against Humanity and ultimately, Jesus Christ, the Savior of Humanity.

The Exercise had a Mock News Outlet Video that that NTI put out as part of their Outbreak Scenario. It portrayed a News Broadcast of the Monkey Pox Outbreak. But those who study Communications, Speech and/or Propaganda, will easily be pick-up on the Brain-Washing Techniques. The Mock Newscast starts out by showing the words, 'This is a Fictitious Scenario'. It then leads into a False 'GNN' News Anchorwoman that opens the Broadcast by saying, 'There are New Questions today about the New Deadly Outbreak of ...

Then a Blank Screen appears with the words, 'Another Global Outbreak'. But this time, it Is different'. Then the Anchorwoman states, 'Scientists that studied this have determined that this is Monkey Pox...was Engineered'. The Screen cuts to the words, 'Biological Terrorism in 1 Region'...'Unleased on the rest of the World... Billions of Cases... Hundreds of Millions Dead'.

Sabotage Scenarios

Then the Anchorwoman appears saying, 'With limited Anti-Viral Drugs and no known Effective Treatments, countries around the World are struggling to Control and Pandemic, with already devastating effects''. The Video cuts to the words, 'Poor Oversight and Gaps in Global Governance'… 'Leave us Vulnerable to Catastrophic Biological Threats'.

The Mock News Video then goes on to question, 'Can the International Community act quickly enough?' Then the Video cuts to a supposed 'International Correspondent, named Philip Romano. Who states, 'We are seeing far fewer Cases in countries where they took Early and Decisive Actions'.

Then another Individual appeared, a 'Science the Health Correspondent' who said, 'Some International Experts are urging the WHO to adopt a Phased Approach towards to Warnings'. Then the Video cuts to more words against a Black Screen that says, 'The Time to Prepare for the Next Global Pandemic'…'Is Now'. As one can assess, the real Terrorists are the Luciferian Globalists, bent on Population Reduction and their Great Reset U.N. Agenda.

Yes, there are Questions being asked, why was such a Germ Warfare Scenario played-out in March of 2021, on the 1 Year Anniversary of the COVID-10 Plandemic? Why was the Simulation plainly stated that Monkey Pox was Bio-Engineered and released? This is exactly the Scenario in which COVID, their prior Plandemic Virus has been found to have been 'Leaked' from a Bio Lab in China.

Then there is the Debacle with Fauci in his Gain of Function Research. It is a Global Attack, and it is being perpetrated again on Humanity by these Satanists Blood Sucking Vampire Wizards and Warlocks. And they even plainly tell the World that 'This Time is Different'. True. COVID 19 was the Test Run.

Now that the Preliminarily 'Weak Points' are known, this next Plandemic of theirs will be used to usher in the Global Government they have sought out and needed to implement their Globalist and Luciferian Agenda. And that is? To Inject as many People with their Serum. Why? It is not about a Virus but what is in the Shots.

Is it any coincidence that the Mock Exercise conducted by the NTI 'arbitrarily chose the Month of May in 2022 for the release? And behold, that is when the 'Outbreak' of Monkey Pox has been 'Discovered' and now been reported? Then mysteriously, there were 13-19 Million Doses against Monkey Pox were readily available?

How is it that, out of nowhere, there are now enough Monkey Pox Doses, that Biden of the USA purchased 13-19+ 'Vaccines' Monkey Pox? Those Injections are not going to be sitting around to be stored. No, these mRNA Shots are to go into the Arms of as many Humans as possible. Why? Based on 3 Years of COVID Research, one has come to conclude that it is for 3 main Purposes. 1. To Contaminate. 2. To Cull. And 3. To Control all of Humanity in such a Global Scenario.

It is found in the Book of Revelation with the Mark of the Beast System. It is coming. The Video Mock Scenario is truthful, in how it is mocking People with the prior COVID-19 Plandemic. It was Unleashed into the World as a Bio-Weapon. What is noticeably different is the planned scope of the Contamination. They use 'Billions of Cases' and '100s of Millions Dead'.

This will truly be an Apocalyptic End Time Scenario. And they are not wrong on this account. They are Deadly Serious about such Parameters and Protocols. But so is the Bible. Monkey Pox, now unleashed, is to further Control People and force Compliance on every Human possible in preparation for their New Medial Order.

Contaminate, Cull, Control, Repeat…
It is astonishing that they are using the same 'Scientific Narrative' that was used for COVID. How so? That it is a 'Deadly Virus' and there are, 'No Known Treatments'. This is a Lie. With COVID, there were and are Preventative Treatments and it does not need to end in a Death of a Patient.

In fact, Scientists like Dr. McCullough of Texas in the USA, have argued and fought for Early Treatment of COVD. But Fauci, the WHO, the CDC, FDA have banned such Preventative Protocols. What Hypocrisy. When such Evil Luciferians think of when they say, 'There are no Preventative Treatments', they mean they want more forced Lock-Downs, Mask Mandates, etc. This is despite Monkey Pox does not spread like COVID.

A person basically has to go to the Congo in Africa to come in direct Skin Contact to get the Monkey Pox. Yet, all of a sudden, right-on Time, in May of 2022, the Monkey Pox Virus Break-Out occurred in over 28 Nations and climbing. And guess what type of People have contracted Monkey Pox? It is only those People who have received the Dangerous New mRNA COVID Shots. Why?

Based on Research done by a few Doctors and Scientists, that one researched, the COVID 19 Shots have Monkey and Swine Cell Lines, aside from Aborted Fetal Tissue and a host of other Toxic Ingratiates.

The assumed Narrative is that individual Nations are at a loss to be able to control and address such a Pandemic of this Proportion. So, Send in the WHO, to the rescue! Yes, the Narrative calls for the WHO to be given the Power and Authority to orchestrate their Phased Approach, or really, their Death Protocols. What this really will mean and result in, is that their long-awaited Global Government has arrived.

It will be run by Luciferians who are Eugenicists and their Beast System is essentially here, now. Contrary to their Narrative that they want to 'Save' People. No. It is a Pretext and Mock Posterity. The Luciferians want to kill Humanity, reduce it to less than 500 Million. They want to Contaminate, Cull and Control Humanity. At this level, using Bio-Engineered Viruses from their Labs, Humanity can be Tagged, Surveilled and its Reproduction controlled, entirely. Hello China. This type of 'New Humanity 2.0' will be the Subservient Class like in the Book, The Brave New World. Consider what the Pfizer CEO Albert Bourla, stated at a World Economic Forum Conference concerning the New Technology in their Shots.

Screenshot of Zoom Meeting of the NTI led by Ernest Moniz.

He said the following ...'Basically, [a] Biological Chip that is in the Tablet and once you take the Tablet and dissolves into your Stomach, it sends a Signal that you took the Tablet. So, imagine the Applications of that Compliance'... The coming Luciferian and Eugenicist World Order will have the Gods of Earth, the Luciferian Elite at the top. They think they have achieved it to regain their lost Golden Age where Lucifer was their LORD. Consider that once the WHO takes over the Sovereignty of all the Nations of the World, all 194 of them, they will then hand over this Power and Authority to the 1st Beast.

This Beast Ruler will be the Luciferian and Biblical AntiChrist. It is coming. This Monkey Pox Scenario, unsuspectingly is a Biblical one that is being realized in this Last Generation, hidden in plain view. The Narrative they will be selling and peddling to the World Government is that there are, 'Gaps in Global Governance'. Why? It is because such contrived 'Scientific' Narratives work on Humanity. They plainly have said it and mean it. It is that the World is vulnerable to Biological Threats.

Ture. But the Biological and Nuclear as well as Chemical Threats come from them to make these Deadly Poison and have used them against Humanity. It was rather interesting that in the Mock News Narrative, their 1st Interviewee had a Last Name of Romano. Could this be a Freudian Slip, an intentional one in how the coming AntiChrist will be a 'Roman' per 1 interpretation of the Prophecies of the Book of Daniel? Interesting.

So, the Mock Scenario using Monkey Pox as the latest Deadly Virus is to get the WHO to basically take over the Nations' ability to Respond to such Pandemics or rather their Plandemics. Is it also no coincidence that in every dialog that is broadcast about needing more Global Government, has it been noticed how they emphasize, 'In the Next Pandemic'? How would they know? Are they like Fauci who in early 2017 stated, 'for a fact, a surprise Pandemic' was going to be unleashed during Trump's Administration? He is a Medical Prophet or 'For Profit.

It has been reported that Fauci has bought-up all the Small Pox Virus Injections. One wonders why. It is tiring to see the 'Usual Suspects; behind such Genocidal Attempts to Contaminate, Cull and Control Humanity. You have the Gates, the WHO, the CDC, FDA, the Klaus Schwab's, and the Noah Harari's of the World who have taken upon themselves, the 'Gods of Earth' to determine the Fate of the rest of Humanity.

Monkey Pox is a Mild Contagious Disease and Survivable with Early Known Treatments. It is not a Pandemic. It is just another Phase in their Orchestrated Plandemics that will be leading an Unsuspecting Humanity to the Mark of the Beast System and subsequently to their Eternal Doom.

Main Sources
SecurityConference.org
Nuclear Threat Initiative
Wikipedia.com

2021 NTI WITH THE MUNICH SEC. CONF. CONDUCTED AN EXERCISE SIMULATING A GLOBAL MONKEYPOX
https://brandnewtube.com/watch/2021-nti-with-the-munich-sec-conf-conducted-a-exercise-simulating-a-global-quot-monkeypox-quot_z9VCTcQczGCD5qT.html

March 2021 NTI Conducted Tabletop Exercise with Munich-Security-Conference to Simulate Monkeypox Pandemic
https://ho1.us/2022/05/march-2021-nti-conducted-a-tabletop-exercise-with-the-munich-security-conference-to-simulate-a-monkeypox-pandemic/

NTI and Munich Security Conference Convene Global Leaders for Fourth Annual Tabletop Exercise on Reducing High-Consequence Biological Threats
https://www.nti.org/news/nti-and-munich-security-conference-convene-global-leaders-for-fourth-annual-tabletop-exercise-on-reducing-high-consequence-biological-threats/
NTI Holds a Monkeypox Tabletop Exercise March 17, 2021
https://pandemictimeline.com/2021/03/nti-holds-a-monkeypox-tabletop-exercise/

Trudeau's Deputy, Whose Grandfather Was Nazi, to Make Emergency Powers Permanent
https://neonnettle.com/news/18357-trudeau-s-deputy-whose-grandfather-was-nazi-to-make-emergency-powers-permanent

Video

Event 201 Pandemic Exercise: Highlights Reel
https://www.youtube.com/watch?v=AoLw-Q8X174

Stew Peters Network
https://rumble.com/c/StewPeters
https://rumble.com/embed/v13mw1b/?pub=4

Articles

#625: PLANETARY PARADE 2022
https://www.postscripts.org/ps-news-625.html

#624: W.H.O. IS IN CHARGE
https://www.postscripts.org/ps-news-624.html

#623: AMERICA'S UKRAINE
https://www.postscripts.org/ps-news-623.html

Resources

Free COVID Related Webpage
https://www.postscripts.org/covid.html

HERCULID METEOR SHOWER
HERO MOTIF MESSAGE TO THE CHURCH
A Comprehensive Connection to Prophetic Events

'As it is written: For Your sake we face Death all Day long; we are considered as Sheep to be Slaughtered. No, in all these things we are more than Conquerors through Him who Loved us. For I am convinced that neither Death nor Life, neither Angels nor Principalities, neither the Present nor the Future, nor any Powers, neither Height nor Depth, nor Anything else in all Creation, will be able to Separate us from the Love of GOD that is in Christ Jesus our Lord.'
-Romans 36-39

The purpose of this chapter is to consider the Herculid Meteor Shower at the end of May 2022. It will depend on the circumstances if it will materialize. The event is coming from the Constellation of Hercules, and thus the Name. The reason why this is a topic to consider is that in the online Bible Prophecy Watch Blog, Revelation 12 Daily, Brad, the Site Administrator highlighted the event as a possible Celestial Sign, pointing to the Rapture.

Such Online Communities are Vigilant, wanting to be on the Look-Out for such Signs in the Sun, Moon and the Stars. One was a bit puzzled as to why such an assertion of a mere Meteor Shower could have any possible Prophetic Implications. With that in mind, one was reminded that one is trusting the Holy Spirit to lead the Topic Discussions. And to perhaps discern what the 'Message' is that Christ would have been, as a possible 'Sign', because the End of the Church Age is fast approaching. Granted, for the Christian, the Final Revelation and 'Message' is found in the Bible.

ARECIBO MESSAGE ALIEN TO HUMANITY

HERCULES

The Hero - Motif of Jesus Christ

Nasak (Marsic)
The Wounding

Caiam
Treading Under Foot

Kornephoros
The Branch, Kneeling

Ras al Gethi
The Head of Him who Bruises

Sirius

Corona Borealis

Maasym
Sin Offering

M13

τ-Herculids

DRACO

M13 GALAXY CLUSTER QUADRANT

MESSAGE FROM HERCULES THE STRONG MAN

There is no debating that. What one is discussing is the 'Signs' that accompany, given the Times. This Vigilance and Disposition to 'Watch' such things is like how it was with the Sons of Issachar. The Bible says that although they knew the Torah and the Prophets, no doubt, it is noted how they 'Watched' in a complimentary and exemplary fashion, from 1 Chronicles 12:32-33. 'From Issachar, Men who understood the Times and knew what Israel should do: 200 Chiefs with all their Kinsmen at their Command'.

How would they have known 'what to do', if they did not know how and what to Watch for? And that is the Purpose of a Watchman and Watchwoman. They are Vigilant, they See, Watch and report to the others in their Community and/or Family, etc. With this in context, the following Prophetic Observations will be made. Indeed the Herculid Meteor Shower, that is coming from the Constellation of Hercules, perhaps is 'Signaling' the Message of what the Motif stands for and 'says'. How so? Note that this Prophetic Interpretation of the Constellation is based on how the 'Witness of the Stars' conveys a facet of the Redemptive Work of Jesus Christ. It is the 'Gospel' displayed above for all to see in a 'Picture' Storyline. Thus, one was intrigued as it became clear why this Motif of Hercules, at this Time and Place is perhaps something to consider. Why?

Here is the Key. The Herculid Meteor Shower originates close to the Galaxy Cluster called M13 there as well, in the Constellation. And? This has then profound Prophetic Implications that will be discussed further down in the study. Before then, here is the latest consideration of what the Herculids are and how they come about for context. It has been reported that the Herculid Meteor Shower will start around May 29-31, 2022, which the 29th is interestingly, Jerusalem Day. They will only be able to be seen in the Western Hemisphere, starting from Baja California and on-down towards the Equator.

ARECIBO MESSAGE

TRANSMISSION ANSWER FROM THE STARS

ALIEN

- ← Decimal Numeration
- ← Main Elements
- ← DNA Code & Structure
- ← Height & Population
- ← Habitation of Planet Position
- ← Type of Transmission Used

HUMAN

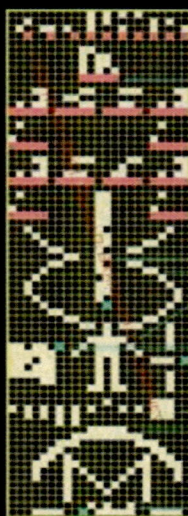

- ← Decimal Numeration
- ← Main Elements
- ← DNA Code & Structure
- ← Height & Population
- ← Habitation of Planet Position
- ← Type of Transmission Used

Where do Meteor Showers come from? Most Meteor Showers come from the Debris of broken-up Comets. As the Earth passes through the Space Field of these Fragmented Comet Particles, the Night Sky lights-up with streaks of those Fragments and burn-up as they enter Earth's Atmosphere. The Effect is a 'Shooting Star', literally. In this case, the Comet has been identified. It is due to Comet 73P/Schwassmann-Wachmann, or SW3 for short. Now to the study. In thinking about why Brad posted this Herculid Meteor Shower, one wondered if the Holy Spirit is wanting to draw the Bride's attention to this area of the Astronomical Sky and why? One will see why.

Since the Shower takes place near the Messier 13 or M13 Galaxy Cluster, it involves an array of many Prophetic 'loose ends' that only looking back in Hind-Sight make sense, or more sense. It involves the Topics of: Planet X, Sabbath Cycles, the AntiChrist Persona or the 'Hero' Hercules that the Bride of Christ is waiting for, Crop Circles, Aliens, Disclosure, Contact, a Mars Connection, DNA Manipulation, Mayan Calendar Dooms Day, etc. So with all that, here is one's best attempt to tie it all together and set the Background to what this 'Herculid' Sign is 'Messaging' at this Time and might imply.

It starts back in 2008, just before the start of the 2 prior Sabbath Cycles. On July 16, 2008, there was a famous Planetary Alignment construed in a Crop Circle in Avebury, England. And? It occurred in one of the UK's Occult Ley-Lines. So, one is treading on the Territory, Spiritually Speaking, of the Enemy, so be warned. Avebury is an Ancient Circle Mount itself but part of a Triangulation with the other famous Occult and Druid Landmarks. There is Salisbury Hill or Mount and then an Open Field with other Monolithic Markers, next to the small Hamlet towards the West. These are all within 1 Mile of each other. This Ancient Monolithic Triangulation matches, topographically the Ley-Lines of Cydonia, Mars Star Gate.

ARECIBO ALIEN MESSAGE TO HUMANITY

MESSAGE FROM HERCULES THE STRONG MAN

M13 GALAXY CLUSTER QUADRANT

HERCULES
The Hero Motif of Jesus Christ

Nasak (Marsic)
The Wounded

Caiam
Treading Under Foot

Kornephoros
The Branch Kneeling

Ras al Gethi
The Head of Him who Bruises

Sirius

Maasym
Sun Offering

M13

Planet X?

VEGA

DRACO

CROP CIRCLE
DECEMBER 21, 2012

Avebury
Crop Circle Depiction

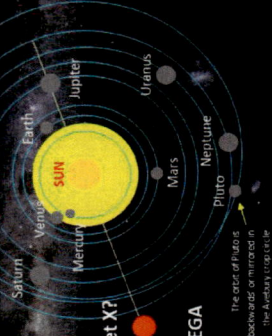

SUN

Mercury
Venus
Earth
Mars
Jupiter
Saturn
Uranus
Neptune
Pluto

The orbit of Pluto is
backwards or mirrored in
the Avebury crop circle

SOLAR SYSTEM
DECEMBER 21, 2012

3D Model
Computer Software

SUN
Mercury
Venus
Earth
Mars
Jupiter
Saturn
Uranus
Neptune
Pluto

Nibiru?
Sun's Binary Star
System

Face of Mars
ALA-LU

Neptune

Chilbolton Crop Circles - 2001

'Face on Mars'
Answer from Stars
CODEX

Chilbolton
Observatory

Winchester Crop Circle - 2002

Alien 'GREY'

'CD' of Binary
ASCII Message

ORION'S BELT STARS

Avebury Crop Circle - 2008

Coming to a Solar System Near You

So, this is a 'Hot Spot' for Fallen Angel conduits, to use in coming-and-going from their Dimensions, etc. And as one has a running Theory about Earth's Ancient Mars Connection, it is that all Ancient and Modern Sites of Power, Religion and Commerce are Spiritually or in this case Luciferian Charged. Not good. And? This is one connection. The connection is what happened there, in July of 2008. If one believes there is something to the Crop Circles Phenomena, then all this will make sense. There are clear Hoaxes, but many appear overnight, and People have witnessed and video-taped glowing Spheres of Light hovering over the Fields as Patterns emerge instantaneously.

What distinguishes these 'Real Ones' from the Fake Ones is how the Reeds are Bent by Heat, etc. So, a Crop Circle of the Solar System there in Avebury. What was unique about the Planetary Alignment or Depiction is that it nearly matched to what the Planet's positions would be. When? On the Mayan Doomsday End of the Calendar, of December 21, 2012. Does anyone remember all that? So, the Crop Circle Depiction occurred 4 Years prior. What was also very unique is that the Depiction had what many were and are convinced was also a Depiction of a 2nd Sun System approaching the Solar System, hello Planet X.

At that time, this other Phenomena of the Planet X, the Red Dragon took off. Ok and? It so happened that 1 Sabbath Cycle prior to 2008, in August of 2001, a Crop Circle emerged that shocked many Watching Communities, Christian and Non-Christian alike. So the Sabbath Cycles are Periods of 7 Years: 1994, 2001, 2008, 2015, 2022, etc. It is believed by some that this Cycle of Time is how the Creator, YHVH reckons Time and Prophecy, etc. What appeared right next to England's largest Radio Tower was the Crop Circle of the 'Face of Mars'.

From Avebury, it was 42 KM or 26 Miles south, next to the Chilbolton Observatory. Then amazingly, 3 days later, a Genetic Code Strip appeared in a Crop Circle within eyesight. This 'Code' or Message appeared to answer the Human Code that was transmitted by the USA's largest Radio Telescope, at the time, the Arecibo Telescope in Puerto Rico. Sadly a recent Hurricane destroyed it.

But, if one has seen the Movie with Jodie Foster, named 'Contact', it tracks this Narrative. What Narrative`? The movie is a bit 'Cheesy' but for its time, interesting, especially if one was into Ufology, Aliens, etc. It is about 'Alien' Contact. The movie came out in1997. It is an American Science Fiction Drama Film directed by Robert Zemeckis. It is based on the 1985 novel by Carl Sagan.

Sagan and his wife Ann Druyan wrote the Story Outline for the film. It stars Jodie Foster as Dr. Eleanor 'Ellie' Arroway, a SETI Scientist who is chosen to make first contact. She finds Evidence of Extraterrestrial Life based on a Transmission Message sent from a Star named Vega. And where is Vega located at? Right next to the Constellation of Hercules, the 'Hero-Strong Man', etc.

The connection is that in the Sabbath Cycle of 1973-74, Carl Sagan formulated a Binary Code Message that was used to Transmit to Outer Space that depicted Code of who Human Being are, where and what they are made out of, Genetically. Where did NASA send it? Precisely in the Constellation of Hercules, the Hero in the Galaxy Cluster called M13.

It is right at the side of Hercules's Torso area, anthropomorphically. And? Well, 27 years later in the Sabbath Cycle of 2001, the 'Answer' was received in the form of a Crop Circle, Binary Code. This is where the DNA comes into play in that based on some study of the Message, it is an Alien Deception.

78

'Alien' Contact

It is an attempt to trick Humanity and especially its Scientists into believing that the 'Alien Gods', the Herculeans of Old, the 'Men of Renown' the Bible speaks of, have established 'Contact' and Dialog. Then the next Connection occurred 1 Year on August 15, 2002, 5 or 6 miles further Southwest, is the Chilbolton Radio Observatory. A Gray Alien Face with Disk appeared in a Crop Circle. It formed in a Wheat Field and was 250 Feet wide by 360 Feet long. This depiction was at Vale Farm, next to Crabwood Forest in the village of Pitt near Winchester, Hampshire, U.K.

This was another 'Alien Message', but this time the Code that appeared to be in the Disc was in the Computer Language of ASCII Binary Code. This Disc Motif has been observed in other Pictographs where Aliens and UFO are also depicted. And? All this is connected. And the 'Message'? *'Beware of the Bearers of False Gifts and their Broken Promises. Much Pain but still Time. There is Good out there. We oppose Deception. Conduit closing'.* The Luciferians are preparing the World for their Arrival. When? Right after the Resurrection-Rapture event. It will serve to explain-away the Disappearance of Millions around the Rapture. Humanity is now desensitized enough to accept such 'Beings' that will be literally manifesting in Space and Time. Why have they not prior?

They have and do, but in a limited scope and opportunity. Due to a large extent, it is because of the Body of Christ presently on Earth. It has served as the 'Restrainer' of Full-On Evil, as that is the source of who and what these Fallen Angels are, masquerading as 'Beings of Light', etc. Pertaining to the Motif of Hercules, according to EW Bullinger, here is the Biblical Inferences. 'Hercules is the Mighty Man kneeling on 1 Knee. It symbolizes the Vanquisher seeming being humbled in the Conflict.

But holding aloft the Tokens of Victory, with his Foot on the Head of the Dragon'. 'Hercules is seen engaged in destroying some Malignant Foe: now it is the Nemean Lion. Then it is the slaying of the Boar of Erymanthus. Again, it is the Conquest of the Bull of Crete. Then the killing of the 3-Headed Hydra, by whose venom Hercules afterwards Died. In the Belly of the Sea Monster, he is said to have remained 3 Days and 3 Nights.

We can understand how the original Star-Picture must have been a Prophetic Representation of Him who shall destroy the Old Serpent and open the way again, not to fabled Apples of Gold, but to the Tree Of Life itself. He it is who though suffering in the Mighty Conflict, and brought to His Knee, going down even to the Dust of Death, shall yet, in Resurrection and Advent Glory, wield His Victorious Club, subdue all His Enemies, and plant His Foot on the Dragon's Head'. The Stars of Hercules.

-The Brightest Star, α in the head, is named Ras al Gethi, which means 'Head of Him who Bruises'.

-The next Star, β in Right Arm-Pit, is named Kornephorus, and means 'The Branch, Kneeling'.

-The Star κ in the Right Elbow) is called Marsic, 'The Wounding'.

-The Star λ in the upper part of the Left Arm is named Ma'asyn, 'The Sin-Offering'.

-Star ω in the lower part of the Right Arm is Caiam, 'Punishing'. in Arabic, 'Treading Under Foot'.

For those that ascribe to Biblical Astronomy, the Depiction of Hercules is a clear Motif of the Work and Mission, Ministry of Jesus Christ, the Son of the Creator. Jesus came to Destroy the 3 Evil Works of Lucifer: Sin, Satan and Death like Hercules. Jesus, is the Branch that came, Wounded to Death by the Cross of Calvary.

80

Jesus' was the Sin Offering that took on the Substitutionary Judgment for a Human Race bound to Eternal Separation from the Life of the Creator. That is the real Definition of Hell. Jesus came to fulfil the 1st Prophecy given and promised to Humanity in Genesis 3:15. It is that although Lucifer, the Serpent Seed would 'Bruise' the Heel of Jesus, i.e., at the Cross with Death, through Death, Jesus would destroy and Crush the Head of the Serpent, Lucifer, etc.

Thus, this is the Message, the Holy Spirit is perhaps giving to the Church, the Body of Christ, the Bride of Christ at this Point in Time based on the Herculid Meteor Shower event. It is a somber reminder in the final closing moments of the End of the Church Age. And it would be an appropriate one. The Purpose and Promise of Jesus still stands and reverberates, even down to the Last Days before the Resurrection-Rapture event occurs.

It is a reminder that although the World is collapsing, by design as a Controlled Demolition, and it appears Evil is now rampant and increasing by the Day, Jesus' Message for His Beloved is that He is the Hero, He is the Victor over the 3 major Herculean Enemies that sought to Destroy the Human Race: Death, Satan and the World.

Main Sources
Wikipedia.com

Article

Alien Crop Circles – The Arecibo Message
#48 https://www.postscripts.org/ps-news-48.html

Chart

Avebury Cydonia Mars Star Map
https://onedrive.live.com/?cid=F18D5BF95B5644F2&id=F18D5BF95B5644F2%2112329&parId=F18D5BF95B5644F2%216864&o=OneUp

Everything to Know About 2022's Tau Herculid Meteor Shower, Including When It Peaks and How to Watch
https://people.com/human-interest/tau-herculid-meteor-shower-everything-to-know/

Tau Herculid Meteor Shower May See 1,000s of Shooting Stars From Comet SW3
https://www.newsweek.com/comet-sw3-tau-herculid-meteor-shower-next-week-1710298

New Tau Herculids Meteor Shower May Dazzle – or Disappoint
https://science.howstuffworks.com/tau-herculids-meteor-shower-news.htm
SETI Institute - Arecibo Message
https://www.seti.org/seti-institute/project/details/arecibo-message

Arecibo Message Decoded
https://www.youtube.com/watch?v=5V2KuClix_k

ALIENS ANSWERED THE ARECIBO MESSAGE MAKING CROP CIRCLES
https://www.youtube.com/watch?v=2Q0NjXqAy8M

Crop Circle Response To Arecibo Message Images Result
https://design.onmedianet.com/

Movie: Contact – Alien Message from Vega
https://www.imdb.com/title/tt0118884/plotsummary

University Mathematician Decodes Crop Circle Binary Code & Extraterrestrial Face
https://exonews.org/university-mathematician-decodes-the-crop-circle-with-a-binary-code-extraterrestrial-face/

Winchester, Hampshire Circular Code
http://www.teaserville.com/pile/hmm/crabwood2002/

2002 'Alien Face' Formation
https://www.cropcircleresearch.com/articles/alienface.html

X-FILES PROPHECIES?
VIRUS PREDICTIVE PROGRAMMING
When Fiction Meets Reality

'Those who can make you believe Absurdities can make you commit Atrocities'. -Voltaire

The purpose of this chapter is to consider the main Conspiratorial Narratives that ran through the very popular American Science Fiction TV Series called the X-Files. The 'Conspiracies' will be examined if, indeed, there was enough Predictive Programming that constituted a credible correlation from Science Fiction to Reality. Specifically, the study will examine Key Dialogs of the Series of Episode that alluded to the 'Conspiracy Theory' of a Virus and Vaccine to be injected into every Human Being Possible.

The Question is, was that all Predictive Programming or has it all become a Reality? If what the Dialog between the Main Characters was a Fore-Shadowing and perhaps a Warning of coming Worldwide Pandemics, i.e., COVID, Monkey Pox, it would make sense. One would not be surprised, as often is the case, that there is Truth in Conspiracy Theories. As one who studies the Occult, Luciferianism, Freemasonry and the New World Order, it is exactly what they were doing.

This study is a result of prior Articles that first considered the significance of the Herculid Meteor Shower of Late May of 2022. The reason why that study was composed was how it was in the Constellation of Hercules, in that Messier 13 (M13) was where the 1st Human Radio Transmission was sent. And then 27 Years later from 1974, the Arecibo Message was 'Answered'. The 'Answer' was in the form of Crop Circles found near England's Sacred Megalithic Stone Circles.

Tell A Lie Enough Times...
The Message was interpreted to have been from 'Aliens' that are keeping themselves at a distance but have been involved with Humans since Creation. When discussing the Article, a Contributor at Revelation 12 Daily Blog, Archangel sarcastically noted that she was going to 'Call Fox Mulder this instant!' It was the stuff of the X-Files apparently. And Fox who? One had to look that up. Fox? Well, that started to become interesting, as those who study the Occult would realize that 'Fox' is Code for 666. As many know, it is a 'cryptic' 666 where the Letters F=6, O=60, and X=600 = 666, etc.

Why this Assessment of the X-Files? It is because the Biblical Prophecies appears to parallel this sort of X-Files Genre and Conspiracy Narrative. Thus, the X-Files 'Prophecies' as one calls the Evaluation of the Conspiratorial Narrative that will be based on the Biblical Perspective. Why this might be different than most, is that one has not seen an entire Episode, in all its run. Why not? One must divulge that during the 1990 and presently, one does not have a TV. If one ever remembers the phrase, 'Kill Your TV', it was taken seriously and for good reason. The rationale behind not having a TV is also based on keeping a 'Clear and Sober' Mind from Worldly 'Programming.

It is also because, having studied the Occult, Luciferianism, Brain-Washing Techniques through Psychology, Political Science and Biology in College, one was and is convinced enough that TV is used as a Device to control the Prevailing Narratives and Thoughts of the People. Sure, there is a lot of 'Good' TV and the Internet is no different. It just depends on how one utilizes it. But with the Internet, one has more Control. At the onset of TV 'Channeling', there were only 3 in the USA, for example. There was ABC, CBS and NBC. And? Not many choices and basically, only 3 versions of the same story.

The point is that there have been many Scientific Studies on People that watch TV and/or see Movies. It is well documented that within mere Seconds, People are induced into a State of Hypnosis. The Blood-Flow decreases to the Frontal Lobe where Cognitive Thinking is made within the Brain. This then allows for any Suggestive Thoughts, Images and Narratives to saturate the Psyche of a person. Or in other words, a person can be easily Brain-Washed. That is what TV does. And whoever Controls TV, that is its 'Programs' or Broadcasting, as in Spells-Cast, can and do Control the People.

TV, Movies and Radio can influence People as one is already predisposed into believing Figures of Authority. And that is what those who own the TV Programs bank on accomplishing. For example, this notion of Controlling the Masses through Media Propaganda was highly effective during the Nazi Regime of Germany. Paul Joseph Goebbels was the German Nazi 'Gauleiter' or Chief Propagandist. It was all about Image and Show, Performance, etc. He coached Hitler in how to Speak, but in such a way that it made Women faint like at a Rock Concert. It is also no coincidence that the Root Word for 'Media' comes from Medium as in a State of Possession in which Entities can take over.

In the Bible, Lucifer is called the Prince of the Power of the Air, as in Air Waves. And the TV, Radio Broadcasting is done in Frequencies. This is not to say that just by listening to a good Song on the Radio or watching a Program on TV will result in a Demonic Possession. But, it has been studied and shown that Music, Vibration, Sound pierces the Soul of Humans, etc. So, the Point is that one must 'Guard' the Doors of one's Senses and know what is being allowed in, into the Deepest Recesses of one's Consciousness. The Luciferian Globalists know the Power of Persuasion and use this Medium to Control the Masses with.

Age of Conspiracies

This is why they have made it sure that they own all the Means of Communication. See Article in End Notes: 'Documentary Exposes the Alarming Truth - TV Puts Us In Hypnotic State and Suppresses Critical Thinking'. The Mass Media can help keep People Entertained, Distracted, in Fear and when to spur-on Patriotism, for example. There have also been Articles written about how the Alphabet Agencies of the Federal Government in the USA, have infiltrated the Media since its beginning for such purposes. For example, during World War 2, the Department of War, later changed to the Department of Defense, contracted Hollywood to present War Reels at every Movie Theatre.

They used Disney Characters, etc. And in Mao's Communist China, they used Comic Books to convey the 'Glories of Communism', etc. Then after the War, the CIA, under Operation Mockingbird, was an effort, that is in place to this day, of planting CIA Operatives in every Major Newspaper Outlet. This was to influence Public Opinion when the Watergate Scandal broke, for example. And such efforts have not gone abated, but instead, thanks to orchestrated Government False Flags, like Waco, Oklahoma City and 9-11, the Iraq Invasion, etc., the Power-That-Be have consolidated the Mass Media to rally the People behind their Evil Plans.

It is no Big Secret that the CIA and other Federal Agencies in the USA, have also infiltrated Hollywood and use their Skills and Services to 'Program' Messages to the Masses. For example, the Movie about the release of the Americans taken Hostage at the Iranian Embassy clearly exposed how they enlist Hollywood Producers. The Movie was called Argo, where Ben Affleck, playing CIA Agent Tony Mendez utilized a fake Hollywood Production Company to fool the Iranians and rescue 6 American Diplomats, etc. Same thing with Stanley Kubrick and the issue of the Moon Landing Scenes.

Now, it is the Age of the Smart-Phones, with such Social Media Platforms, like Facebook, Twitter, Tik-Tok, Instagram, that Meta-Information started to be collected on its users. How many? Billions of Users. The CIA, FBI and other Federal Agencies would only dream of achieving this scope of Intel. Essentially, one's Smart-Phone is a live Spying Device for the Globalist Corporations in league with Federal Governments. Evidence?

Consider when Pokemon Go came out. It was actually a CIA-Backed, NSA-Approved Spying Device that had Users give away all Privacy Rights. When one showed such Articles to University Colleagues and Students, their reactions were, 'This cannot be true'. 'It is a Conspiracy Theory'. 'I do not care, I am not doing anything wrong', etc. So, the X-Files? One thinks that a person then, not having seen the Series, might provide a unique Perspective.

But in order for one to do that, one had to Binge-Watch many of the online Summary Videos that broke down the Timeline. The following is one's Assessment, to corroborate that the X-Files did in fact use Predictive Programming in conditioning the Masses for a coming Universal Virus and Vaccine tied to 'Aliens' and Disclosure. One had flippantly mentioned about the X-Files, 'Did I Miss Anything'. Oh my Goodness. So, this topic had one go into the Rabbit Hole, retro-actively into the X-Files Genre.

As one saw and listened to the Plot and Prevailing Narrative of the Show, one is now convinced that it is beyond Predictive Programming. It was like 'In your Face' about what the Luciferians posing as 'Aliens' and Globalists were doing and are. Before analyzing the Key Dialogs of the Characters that promulgate the Virus-Vaccine-Alien Narrative, a brief background of the X-Files will be presented, in case anyone else is also not aware of the Plot. The X-Files had a little bit of every Genre for People.

It had Aliens, Abductions, Ghosts, Demon Possession, Luciferians, Globalists, New World Order Elites, Satanists, Crazy Evangelicals, (Always in a Negative Light), Zombies, Reptilians, Secret Government Bases and Human Experiments, Secret Alien Treaties, Antarctica, Serial Killers, the Occult, etc. And it is all true in one's Research. The following is taken from the Wikipedia Page for the X-Files that best explains its Narratives and Plot. Emphases added and edited for formatting.

———————————

The X-Files is an American Science Fiction Drama Television Series created by Chris Carter. The Series revolves around Federal Bureau of Investigation (FBI) Special Agents Fox Mulder (David Duchovny), and Dana Scully (Gillian Anderson) who investigate X-Files: Marginalized, Unsolved Cases involving Paranormal Phenomena.

The Original Television Series aired from September 1993 to May 2002, on Fox. The Program spanned 9 Seasons, with 202 Episodes. A short 10th Season consisting of 6 Episodes, ran from January to February 2016. Following the Ratings Success of this Revival, The X-Files returned for an 11th Season of 10 Episodes, which ran from January to March 2018.

In addition to the Television Series, 2 Feature Films have been released: The 1998 Film, The X-Files ,which took place as part of the TV Series continuity, and the Stand-Alone Film, The X-Files: I Want to Believe, released in 2008, 6 Years after the Original Television Run had ended. At the start of their Investigations, Mulder believes in the existence of Aliens and the Paranormal while Scully, a Medical Doctor and a Skeptic, is assigned to Scientifically Analyze Mulder's Discoveries, offer Alternate Rational Theories to his Work, and thus return him to Mainstream Cases.

Early in the Series, both Agents become Pawns in a larger Conflict and come to trust only each other and a Few Select People. The Agents also discover an Agenda of the Government to keep Secret the Existence of Extra-Terrestrial Life. They develop a Close Relationship which begins as a Platonic Friendship but becomes a Romance by the end of the Series.

The following are some of the main 'Conspiracy' Theories pertaining to a Virus, Vaccine and Alien Involvement, bent on destroying Humanity. As there are too many Episodes, one cannot possibly address and consider every one of them. But these ones that are highlighted capture the Prevailing Narrative that the Satanic, Luciferian Elites are controlling and manipulating World Governments.

World Leaders are in League with 'Aliens' in Genetically Altering the Human Genome through a Virus and 'Vaccines', etc. The 'Syndicate' are basically the Luciferian Elites of the World, those of the Secret Societies and the 13 Bloodlines of the Illuminati, etc. They are the ones that sold-out the Human Race by buying into the notion that through Trans-Humanism, they would be spared and rule what would be left on Earth as a Slave Race.

Ironically, they were double-crossed and killed-off by the Aliens. For the purposes of the Biblical Perspective and Interpretation, wherever there is the Word, 'Alien', substitute that for 'Fallen Angels'. For the Word, Virus, substitute Corona Virus and/or Monkey Pox. For the 'Syndicate', substituted that for the Illuminati. The various portions of the Dialogs will be presented 1st and then at the end, one's Assessment and Interpretation will be presented.

...'To unearth a Grand Conspiracy that points to World Governments collaborating with Aliens in a Hybrid Program. That would see Mankind eradicated. Inhabitant of this Planet, Bio-Engineered by the Grey Aliens. The Contagion is a combination of a Parasitic Virus mixed with an Aggressive Form of their DNA.

Possessing a Form of Sapience, it was able to choose its Host at will, shared a Symbiotic Bond with the Alien Colonizers and transform People into Greys. A Secret, that Life came to Earth Millions of Years ago from a Meteor or a Rock from Mars.

I believe that Virus infected Early Man and transformed his Physiology, changed him into something else. Into an Alien Life Form himself of this Virus. In 1947, when a UFO crashed in Roswell, New Mexico, the UFO Crash revealed the Virus. The Virus thrived underground'.

_____

...'They learned of the Alien Plan to Re-Colonize the Earth. Is this all leading anywhere? Yeah, the Destruction of Mankind'.

_____

'Abduction by whom? By the Military working with the Government Conspirators to develop a Breed of Human Alien Hybrids that the Aliens would use as a Slave Race'.

_____

'Classified Studies were done to Military Installations. S4, Groom Lake Wright-Patterson and Dulce. Extracting Alien Tissue the Tests were done on Unsuspecting Living Subjects. And elaborately Staged Abductions in Crafts using Alien Technology recovered from the Down Saucers. Hybridization through Gene-Editing and Forced Implantation of Alien Embryos.

90

Why do such a thing? Lie about it. All in Governments you own. Government lies, as a Matter of Course, as a matter of Policy. The Tuskegee Experiments on Black Men in the 30s. Henrietta Lacks. What are they trying to do? That is the Missing Piece. But it is not hard to imagine a Government hiding, hoarding Alien Technology for 70 Years, at the expense of Human Life.

And the Future of the Planet, driven not only by Corporate Greed but a Darker Objective, the Takeover of America. And then the World itself by any means necessary. However, Violent or Cruel or Efficient by Severe Drought, brought-on by Weather Wars.

Conducted secretly, using Aerial Contaminants and High-Altitude Electromagnetic Waves in a State of Perpetual War to create Problem-Reaction-Solution Scenarios to Distract, Enrage and Enslave American Citizens at Homes, with Tools like the Patriot Act and the National Defense Authorization Act. Which abridged the Constitution in the Name of National Security.

The Militarization of Police Forces in Cities across the U.S. The building of Prison Camps by the Federal Emergency Management Agency with no Stated Purpose. The Corporate Takeover of Food and Agriculture, Pharmaceuticals and Health Care. Even the Military in Clandestine Agendas, to Fatten, Dull, Sicken and Control a Populace already consumed by Consumerism.

And I encourage you all to go shopping more. A Government that taps your Phone. Collects your Data and Monitors your Whereabouts with Impunity. A Government preparing to use that Data against you when it strikes. And the Final Takeover begins. The Takeover of America by a Well-Oiled and Well-Armed Multinational Group of Elites that will Cull, Kill and Subjugate… Happening as we sit here.

It is happening all around us. The other Shoe waiting to drop. It will probably start on a Friday. The Banks will announce a Security Action, necessitating their Computers to go Off-Line, all Weekend. Digital Money will disappear. They can just steal your Money, followed by the Detonation of Strategic Electromagnetic Pulse Bombs to knock out Major Grids. Well. Will seem like an Attack on America by Terrorists or Russia.

Or a Simulated Alien Invasion using Alien Replica Vehicles that exist and are already in use. An Alien Invasion of the U.S. The Russians tried in '47. You cannot say these things. I am going say them. To many, it is Fear-Mongering, Clap-Trap Isolationist Techno-Paranoia. So bogus and dangerous and stupid, that it borders on Treason. Saying these things would be incredibly Irresponsible. It is Irresponsible not to say it, especially if it is the Truth'.

———————————

'In 1988 there was an Out-Break of Hemorrhagic Fever in Sacramento California. The Truth would have caused Panic. Panic would have caused Lives. We controlled the Disease by controlling the Information. You cannot protect the Public by Lying to them. It is done every day'.

———————————

…'Are you Dr. Osborne? Are you the Prison Doctor? No. Who do you work for? The CDC. You work for the Centers for Disease Control. What are you doing here? Sir, I am a Medical Doctor. I want to know what is going on here. Sir? If you do not let me. in a lot of People in Washington are going to find out that you are conducting a Secret Experiment'.

———————————

…'Seems to be some kind of Deadly Contagion sweeping the Lock-Down Population, well from what I have seen'.

———————————

…'See, the Alien Fetus would give us the Alien Genome, the DNA with which we could make a Human Hybrid ,a New Race Agent Mulder. An Alien Human Hybrid who could survive the Holocaust, so you could survive and live to see your Sister'.

…'The Plan is to Stall, to Resist, to work Secretly on a Vaccine. That was your Father's Idea. To use the Alien DNA to make a Vaccine to save everyone, the World was the reason I came along. But it is too late now. Colonization is going to begin. There will be a Sequence of Events. A State of Emergency will be declared because of a Massive Outbreak of the Alien Virus by Bees and the Takeover will begin'.

…'They Police us and Spy on us. Tell us that makes us Safer. We have never been in more Danger'.

…'I am a Representative to the Secretary General of the UN the United Nations. A Position giving you Unrestricted Access to countries and Leaders around the World is not that right? Yes. How did you use this Power? Basically to further the Interests of a Secretive Group of Men who called themselves the Syndicate? What were their Interests developing an Alien Virus Vaccine? Before the Russians developed one. Now they go about that by Testing Innocent Civilians all over the World.

Test Subjects were tracked through DNA Identifiers in their Smallpox Vaccination Scars without the Subject's knowledge. Mostly, some develop suspicions. I saw Russians who cut off their Arms to prevent being Tracked as they did to an American Man you worked quite intimately with? Yes. That looks tragic. Did you believe in the Syndicate and their International Conspiracy?

No. I was paid for my expertise. In fact, you came to hate them. Yes. It is why I helped Agent Mulder when he approached me. But you were found-out and the Syndicate punished you for this? They turned me into a Test Subject…were pretending to work with the Aliens to Infect the Entire Population with an Alien Virus.

But the Conspirators were trying to save themselves by secretly and selfishly developing a Vaccine. The Conspirators believed all Life in the Universe had been Infected with a Virus including a Race of Shape-Shifting Alien Bounty Hunters, who policed the Conspiracy for the Aliens.

But they were wrong and it led to the destruction of the Conspiracy who destroyed it. A Group of Renegade Aliens who had avoided Infection with the Virus through Self-Disfigurement. And the Conspirators themselves, what happened to them? They are all Dead now, killed by the same Faceless Aliens.

Then what are you afraid of now? Why resist testifying here today? Because the Conspiracy continues, just in another Form by other Men. Objection. Mr. Skinner cannot ask Questions and give the Answers. Sustained. Fox Mulder is on Trial for Murder here. The Man he is accused of killing is one of these New Conspirators, an Alien Replacement for a Human Being. What they are calling a Super Soldier.

You can prove this can't you? You know who these Men are. Do you not Mrs. Covarrubias? Now Mrs. Covarrubias, I asked you a question. I need an Answer. No, it is okay. Let her go. What the hell are you doing Holder? She is the last best Witness that we have. Does not matter. Thank you Mrs. Covarrubias. I got nothing else for you Mrs. Covarrubias'.

———————————————

…'Your Flight is going to make an Unscheduled Stop, in exactly 22 Minutes. Corner of Liberty in Washington. Lower Manhattan…They are going to crash the Plane into a World Trade Center'.

…'What is Scenario 12D? We know it is a War Game Scenario. That it has to do with Airline Counter-Terrorism. Why is it important enough to kill for? Because it is no longer a Game. If some Terrorist Group wants to act-out this Scenario, why target you for Assassination? Depends on who your Terrorists are. A Man who conceived of it in the first place? You are saying our Government plans to commit a Terrorist Act against a Domestic Airliner?

There you go, blaming the entire Government as usual. A Faction. A small faction. For what possible gain? The Cold War is over John. But with no Clear Enemy to Stockpile against the Arms Markets is flat. But bring down a fully loaded 727 into the middle of New York City, and you will find a dozen Tin-Pot Dictator, over the World, just clamoring to take responsibility and begging to be Smart-Bombed.

I cannot believe it. This is about increasing Arms Sales. When? Tonight. How are you going to stop them? Why did you not tell the World this? Go to the Press? You think I would still be drawing Breath, 30 minutes after I made that call? The Press? Who is going to run this Story? We would. This? This is birdcage liner, Wild-Eyed Crap, right up there with Elvis is an Alien and 2-Headed Babies… Obviously they will read it. Do not be so damn Naïve'.

50 X-Files Matrix of Conspiracy 'Facts' – The X-Files Prophecies

The following is a Matrix of X-Files stated 'Conspiracy Theories' or 'Facts'. Based on the explicit details of the above Narratives that specifically mentions each of the following Factors, the various Episodes of the X-Files do read like the Agenda of Lucifer. From a Biblical Narrative, they echo the Protocols of the Learned Elders of Zion, or the Secret Covenant, etc. See Articles in the End Notes. Based on the List, the X-Files Predictive Programming has been On-Point, intentional and now a Reality in many cases.

According to the Narrative, it was the Purity Virus from the Grey Aliens that was used as the method of attacking the Human Species, at the Genetic Level. It was a Bio-Engineered Parasite in the form of 'Black Goo' (Graphene Oxide) which would take over the Body and create a Symbiotic Bond between the Aliens and the Hosts that they occupied. The Syndicate worked hand-in-hand with the Grey Aliens to develop a means of Infecting as many People and as quickly as possible. The Syndicate developed a Vaccine in secret for themselves. There was a Character, dubbed, 'The Cigarette Smoking Man'. He was one of the few faces associated with the Conspiracy.

He would block Mulder's efforts to reveal the Truth using their Men-In-Black. The Syndicate were just as bad as the Aliens in that they also performed many Human Genetic Experiments with the aim of achieving Genetic Hybridization. They controlled World Governments and more importantly, placed their World Leaders in Key World Leadership Positions to sign-away Citizen's Rights and make Secret Scientific Studies of Alien Technology. But they keep the Advanced Alien Technology to themselves.

X-File Stated 'Prophecies'	Conspiracy?	Probable?
1. Have a Grand Conspiracy by World Governments	x	x
2. Collaborate with an Alien Hybrid Program	x	x
3. Eradicated Mankind with Bio-Engineered Viruses	x	x
4. Combine Contagion with Alien (Recombinant) DNAx	x	x
5. Allow Aliens to Re-Colonizing Earth	x	x
6. Develop a Breed of Human Alien Hybrids	x	x
7. Have Humans become a Slave Race	x	x
8. Classify Secret Studies on Military Installations	x	x
9. Test Unsuspecting Living Subjects	x	x
10. Allow Abduction for Human Hybridization	x	x
11. Only have Governments use Alien Technology	x	x
12. Hybridize Humanity through Gene-Editing	x	x
13. Force Implantation of Alien Embryos	x	x
14. Conduct Tuskegee Experiments on Black Men	x	x
15. Government is to hoard Alien Technology only	x	x
16. Takeover of America and World through Violence	x	x
17. Induce Severe Drought brought-on by Weather Wars	x	x
18. Conduct Aerial Contaminants, i.e., Chem-Trails	x	x
19. Use High-Altitude Electromagnetic Waves	x	x
20. Have a State of Perpetual War	x	x
21. Create Problem-Reaction-Solution Scenarios	x	x
22. Distract, Enrage and Enslave American Citizens	x	x
23. Control America through Patriot Act and NDAA	x	x
24. Abridge Constitution in Name of National Security	x	x
25. Militarization of Police Forces	x	x
26. Build Prison FEMA Camps for no Reason	x	x
27. Have Corporate Takeover of Food and Agriculture	x	x
28. Have Pharmaceuticals taking over Health Care	x	x
29. Fatten, Dull, Sicken and Control a Populace	x	x
30. Promote Super Soldier Programs	x	x
31. Have Government taps Phones	x	x
32. Collects Data and Monitor People's Whereabouts	x	x
33. Cull, Kill and Subjugate Humanity	x	x
34. Have Banks announce a Security Action for Collapse	x	x
35. Computers to go offline to initiate Digital Money	x	x
36. Detonate Strategic Electromagnetic Pulse Bombs	x	x
37. Attack America by Terrorists and blame Russia	x	x
38. Control the Disease and Media Information	x	x
39. Have CDC conduct Secret Experiments	x	x
40. Release contagion on the Lock-Down Population	x	x
41. Have Sequence of Events	x	x
42. Declare a State of Emergency	x	x
43. Police and Spy on the People	x	x
44. Represent the Secretary General of the UN	x	x
45. Further the Interests of the Secretive Groups	x	x
46. Conduct Testing on Innocent Civilians	x	x
47. Track People through DNA Identifiers	x	x
48. Place Chips in Smallpox Vaccinations	x	x
49. Infect the Entire Population with an Alien Virus	x	x
50. Have Government commit Terrorist Act against People	x	x

Purity Virus

It is estimated that if Humanity had the true Advancements of all the Alien Technology it has been granted, it would be 100s of Years ahead of what the Average Human has now. Consider that at the present time, Probes are going to Mars, and reaching the Outer Limit of the Solar System, etc. Yet, most Driving Vehicles still are designed and operate on 1930's Combustion Engine Technology. It is the X-Files FBI Agents Mulder and Scully that unearthed this 'Grand Conspiracy' in how the World Governments were collaborating with Aliens in a Hybrid Program that would see Mankind eradicated.

There was a passionate quest to find the Truth, as 'There is a Lie out There'. The Series opens with a scene of the Icy Tundra of North Texas in 35,000 BC. There were 2 Cave-Men who stumbled into a Grey Alien Layer. The Alien kills 1 of the Caveman and Infects the other with the Extra-Terrestrial Purity Virus. The Aliens are actually the Original Inhabitants of Planet Earth. The Aliens Bio-Engineer a Virus to Infect all of Humanity with. The Parasitic Virus is a mix with an Aggressive Form of their Alien DNA. Why? It possessed a Form of Sapience that is able to choose a Human Body as a Host. In doing so, it will share a Genetic Symbiotic Bond with the Aliens.

Or in other words, it makes the Human Body, more receptive, Genetically to the Genome of the 'Aliens' or Fallen Angels, that well possess the Human Bodies. The Alien's Plan is to Re-Colonize Earth and transform Humans into Hybrids. Or in other words, the Fallen Angels and Lucifer seek to re-conquer the Earth and take sole possession of it, as they once had. In the Series, the Aliens have Secret Underground Alien or Fallen Angel Bases in Antarctica. There are Massive Facilities run by the Syndicate or the Illuminati Secret Societies, etc. The X-Files also had a Character Nick-Named 'Deep Throat'. He was an FBI Agent. It is in reference to the Watergate.

Predictive Programming

Later on, the real 'Deep Throat' reveals himself as Mark Felt who was in the FBI, and not in the Nixon Administration. Deep Throat was the Pseudonym given to this Secret Informant, who provided Information in 1972 to the Reporters Bob Woodward, who shared it with Carl Bernstein. As to Predictive Programming? What is that? At its core, it is a Tactic to reduce Resistance by introducing Concepts that seem far-fetched.

They are continuously reintroduced to make the Concepts appear more likely and thus, acceptable. People are more likely to accept Ideas based on Repeated Exposure. To detractors, they mock the notion as being devised by Conspiracy Theorists, who claim that Nefarious Governments and/or Secret Groups of Elites use Movies or Books as a Mass Mind Control Tool to make a Population more accepting of Planned Future Events.

Consider the following close approximation when one alliterates the Name of 'Marita Covarrubias of one of the Interview Scenes. The Name is clearly Spanish, but the Woman was very Nordic looking. Not that there are no Nordic-Looking Spaniards or Latin Americans but the Name is odd. Is it really, 'March Corona-Virus'? Mari, is a derivation of Mars as in the Month of March, dedicated to the God of War. Are all these 'Conspiracy Correlations' Coincidences? This is an example of Predictive Programming.

Thus, was the Corona Virus Outbreak, Predictively Programed in the X-Files? One would conclude, Yes. It was intentionally over-blown in its scope as they led People to believe the Repeated Concept, etc. Did the WHO and World Governments overplay the COVID Plandemic? Yes. Like the Federal Agent Doctor who confronted Scully as they were performing illegal Scientific Virus Experimentations.

He told Scully, 'I will let you see what I want you to see'. This says it all. It is exactly what transpired. And in one's Assessment, the Virus, Vaccine, 'Alien' Conspiracy has come to pass, a Reality. The X-Files also spurned a Spin-Off TV Series, called the Lone Gunman. But it only lasted 1 Episode, the Pilot. In seeing what they had to say, pertaining to all things Conspiratorial, one can see why. It was another Predictive Programming about 9-11.

Here is the Back-Story. The Lone Gunman aired for 1 Season with 13 Episodes from March 4 - June 1, 2001. The Episode was written by Chris Carter, Vince Gilligan, John Shiban, and Frank Spotnitz. It was Directed by Rob Bowman for 21st Century FOX. The Plot is about Rogue Agents from America's Back Ops Programs who tried to Hijack a U.S. Commercial Airliner. As it was scheduled to go to Boston's Logan Airport, it was to be taken over, remotely controlled to fly into the Twin Towers.

The blame would be put on Terrorists to secure more funding for the National Security Agency NSA. This is the stuff of Tom Clancy who wrote about the same idea in his book 'Debt of Honor' which outlines a Terrorist Attack with an Airplane. It was written in 1994. Nonetheless, the following will be one's Assessment of the Series as it pertains to the Biblical Narrative that was woven through the many Episodes.

One strongly suggests that Predictive Programming was at its finest. Many argue that the Episode did not 'Predict' anything. It does not name Names or Dates. Events portrayed in Movies and TV that end-up happening in Real Life may not be 'Predictions', but Coincidences. Perhaps. But consider that most of the 50 Points listed above are Themes found in the Bible as Prophecy for the Last Days. And it would be Circumstances that Humanity would be facing, is facing presently as forwarded by Jesus, as 'In the Days of Noah'.

100

Assessment

What were the Days of Noah like? It was about a Human Genetic Hybridization Program, Genesis 6. It was about Fallen Angels invading Earth in an attempt to take it over, as the Book of Enoch teaches. It was about the Episode of the Contingency of 200 Fallen Angels infiltrated Earth at Mount Hermon, etc. One will argue that it is not all of the over, just yet. This Genesis 6 was even incorporated in the X-Files Motif or Logo, in what it portrays. It is a Red Circle encompassing an 'X' or rather an encrypted Double DNA Helix. It is about altering the Human Genome. That is what one has argued the COVID Injections are all about with their mRNA Nano-Technology, etc.

The Motto or Mantra of the Show was, 'The Truth is out There'. It should be more like, 'The Lie is out There'. Some may criticize this Write-Up in stating correctly that there are numerous other Moves and books that suggest the same Narrative. Why the X-Files? To even suggest 'Prophecies'? As noted, one has never seen the Series, so it is an honest Objective Perspective. The other is the degree of Detail and Consistency. But do note that one is intentionally interjecting Biblical Filters here to prove the 50 Points of the X-Files Predictive Programming. And? To provide Evidence and or Proof that Predictive Programming is real and being used. And?

That what is presently being perpetrated against Humanity with COVID, Monkey Pox, is basically off the Script of the various X-Files Episodes, dealing with Viruses-Vaccines-Aliens. One major difference between other TV Series and Movies is that Movies came and went. They were a 'Single Shot' and Broadcast. The X-Files had over a Decade-Long Running Narrative that, incrementally 'Let the Cat out of the Bag', as they say. It pertained to disclose further Details that are amazingly accurate. Or they have become a Reality, no longer Science Fiction or 'Conspiracy, etc.

When compared to what is happening now, it makes sense. This is in terms of the Soft Disclosure of Alien Life, Technology, the Hybridization of Humanity, Super-Soldier Secret Projects, the Pharmaceuticals and the WHO taking over the Health of the World, an attempt to Inject all of Humanity with their Kill Shots, etc. These are all Facts and not Fiction. It is not about Viruses, although it does come from those Powers-That-Be or the 'Syndicate' Secret Societies and Not-So-Secret, that are seeking to subjugate the entire Human Race through them.

The Injections are for the purpose of altering the Human Genome and enslave Humanity through Digital Wallets and Track-in-Tracing, Bio-Metric Vaccine Passports, etc. The following is one's Biblical Assessment, taking the 50 Points of the X-File Predictive Programming Points or 'Prophecies', as one would surmise and breaking them down. It starts in the Book of Genesis for Humanity. Based on one's Interpretation of the Biblical Narrative, 'Aliens' or if one substitutes this word for Lucifer and his Fallen Angels, existed before Humanity was Created on Earth.

They ruled on Earth but due to their Rebellion against YHVH, the Creator, they were castigated and lost their Positions of Power in Heaven and on Earth, but not entirely. There is a Global Conspiracy in that Lucifer is the 'God of this World', the Bible teaches. At least for now. It took Jesus, the Son of GOD to come as a Human, a Pure Genetic Human, to save Adam's Fallen Race.

The Payment had to be Genetically Equivalent, as in a Substitutionary Payment to Buy Back Humanity and restore it, Genetically. It was Lucifer in the Garden of Eden, of whom it says in Ezekiel and Isaiah that he had apparently some sort of Dominion over it, that he introduced 'The Lie' to Humanity. And Humanity bought it. According to the Bible, it was Lucifer who Deceived Eve and with Adam, joined the Rebellion against YHVH on Earth.

Biblical Narrative

Lucifer and His Fallen Angels, or 'Aliens' use willing People and Governments to push their Luciferian Agenda. And that is? To Re-Colonize or essentially take back Earth from the Race of Humans that they see as a Threat. They seek to Deface the 'Image and Likeness' of YHVH in Humanity at the Genetic Level. Thus, the quest to Hybridize Humanity, as that will spell the Doom of all Humans. Why?

Jesus, as a Human, died for only Humans. Once the Mark of the Beast is taken, which is what COVID, Monkey Pox is designed to accomplish, it will alter the Genes of Humans. It will be enough so that it will be beyond the line of maintaining the Human Genome, exclusively. And thus, a Human Being becomes unable to be Saved by the Blood of Jesus. As the Luciferian 'Alien' New World Order will eventually come, the reality is that the Engineered Plandemics have started their X-Files Extermination Protocols against Humanity.

And sadly, Humans have sold-out the Human Race. The WHO, CDC, World Economic Forum, like the Syndicate believe their Bloodline will be allowed to live on and be incorporated in some sort of A.I. to also 'Rule the World'. Not realizing that they are but Pawns in the Evil Fallen Angel Agenda to only leave enough Humans alive as a Slave Race to serve the 'Aliens' or Fallen Angels, etc.

The Transition or Trans-Humanization of Mankind is being presently done through the mRNA Injections that are now believed to have been Bio-Engineered. What some Scientists have discovered is that, for example, the COVID-19 Injections, at least some of them, essentially are acting, in a Human like a Venom of a Serpent. And here is one of the many Correlations to the Episodes in how the 'Aliens', being Reptilians are wanting to Infect as many Humans on the Plant to Contaminate, Cull and Control them by such means.

It is well documented that many Investigators have uncovered that the U.S. Government, for example, is conducting Secret Medical Experiments in Military Basis, some Underground like in S4, Groom Lake, Dulce, etc. It is rather interesting that the X-Files Series specifically noted how the Hybridization Program of Humans would be done through Gene-Editing. And that is what mRNA is all about. Then as all this is being done, the 'Conspiracy' is also to take down the USA, in particular. Why the USA? It still has enough Bible Believers and Followers of Jesus.

But the Spiritual Threshold is fast approaching a diminishing amount. The 'Restrainer' that currently holds back the full Effects and Outcome of the Luciferians in this present Church Age is about to be lifted. It will be initiated by Jesus' own 'Out of this World' Escape or Rescue Operation, i.e., the Rapture event. But according to the X-Files Series, the way that the USA will be taken down will be done and is being done, through fomenting Violence, Hate, Division and Distraction.

All this is Reality now. This is exactly what has been going on, especially in the past few Years. Not only that but it is a Full Spectrum Dominance Attack in that these 'Mad Scientists', like Fauci and People like Gates and the like are inducing a Virus Wars against Humanity. There is to be also, a Constant State of War or Conflicts. Then there is to be Geo-Engineering of the Weather to bring about Severe Drought through Weather Weapons.

They plainly state that the way America will be taken down will be through disrupting the Supply Chains, the Food and Fuel. Also through Chem-Trails, and even an Electromagnetic Pulse Attack. This last one is yet to occur. It will probably be the Tour-de-Force when it all does go down after the Rapture event. The various X-Files Episodes appear to, as a 'matter of fact', just plainly state what is going to happen in the Luciferian Globalist Plan.

They even call it by its Name, 'Problem-Reaction-Solution'. As one who had not seen the X-Files Series, after hearing how they knew about how they were planning to 'Take over the World', it was clearly Predictive Programming at its best. It would be about the Militarization of the Police. Abridging the U.S. Constitution through 'Patriot' Acts. Creating False Flag Mass Shootings is to Disarm the Populace. It was to have the USA be Defenseless as it was the case in Australia. And every Nation who has relinquished their Inalienable Right to Bear Arms, having a Dictator ruling the Nation, have always been Slaughtered and Enslaved.

It is no 'Conspiracy' that the X-Files Series called for the World Government to have Corporations take over the Media and Medicine to control the People with. They have taken over Health, Food, Fuel, and Agriculture. This has happened now and is Real, no longer a 'Conspiracy Theory. What is next? According to the X-Files, it is the coming Collapse of the U.S. Petro Dollar as a World Reserve Currency. At some Point in Time, a World Currency Reset will convert all Money into Digital Currently. It is really, all in preparation for the Luciferian Mark of the Beast. All this COVID, Monkey Pox is a Mass Psychosis, a Mass Spell of Sorcery.

It is the Biblical notion of Pharmakeía spoken of that would be the Prevailing Circumstance in the Last Days according to the Book of Revelation. Such X-Files Predictive Programming has ensnared Humanity into the clutches of Lucifer and his 'Aliens'. Realize that in the Bible, Genesis 6 and in the Book of Enoch, these 'Aliens' came to Earth to specially Hybridize Humanity and in so doing, ensure Humanity's Eternal Doom. The Bible said that these Abductions of Humans, Genetic Experimentations occurred, 'In the Days of Noah'. And it was 1 Prime Reason why YHVH pronounced Divine Judgment. But, such Fallen Angels continued 'After', and up to this Present Day.

With COVID, they have intensified their Agenda through World Organizations like the WHO and the CDC, FDA, and the NIH in the USA, for example. They plainly state that their World Agencies like the World Economic Forum plant their Globalist Leaders in Key Positions, like Justin Trudeau that acts on their behalf, not that of Canadian Citizens, but his Luciferian Masters. They are the ones who orchestrate Wars like in the Ukraine, the Middle East, and Africa.

They have taken control of the Disease and Social Media to avert 'Misinformation'. They are the ones who still insist on a State of Emergency. This is despite now being 3 Years from when they released their COVID Virus and then their Bio-Engineered Gene Altering mRNA Injections. They Spy on the World and promote the UN and the WHO. Case in point is the New Powers the WHO will have to override any National Sovereignty.

They will have total discretion as to who gets to Lock-Down, war Masks, Have Exemption, if any, who can Travel and/or Work, etc. The Lock-Downs are to destroy the Economy of Nations and Impoverish the Masses, so as to Depend on the State. And their main Requirement will be a Bio-Metric Passport that will allow the Globalist to Track and Trace any Human on Earth. The Series predicted that this Tracking would be based on 'Internal DNA Identifiers'. The X-Files were obviously ahead of its Time.

How did they know? Now, this is not to implicate the Writers, Producers and Directors, as such may not have known of what they were actually accomplishing. In many cases, the CIA and other Intelligence Agencies Compartmentalize Information and Contacts, etc. But in a lot of cases, they are on the Scam and Agenda. Or else, their Work would not be supported or allowed to be viewed. The X-Files Predictively Programmed that the Alien Virus Vaccines would be requiring for People to take.

It would have the ability to Assemble into a 'Chip' or Transponder once inside the Human Body, etc. And that is exactly what the CEO of Pfizer stated in a World Economic Forum Panel. That 1 of their Pills, once swallowed would dissolve in the Stomach and would be a 'Chip' in itself. It would Transmit back, through Radio Frequency) to the Corporation and Insurance Companies, that a person was 'Compliant' in taking the State's Mandate Medication. But to reiterate, other Movies have suggested the same Narrative and with same Circumstances or Outcomes. True.

However, the Detail and Breadth of such a Conspiratorial Narrative is beyond impressive. But in closing, as one is coming from a Biblical Point of View as the Motto of the X-Files states, the 'Truth is Out There'. It is. His Name is Jesus the Christ. He will put a total stop to this Luciferian Agenda and Angelic 'Alien' Conspiracy. Their Luciferian Plans will fail. But until Jesus returns to Earth with the Resurrected and Raptures Believers that constituted the present Church Age, at the end of the Last Sabbath Cycle, the Luciferian Powers will have, to a degree, a Measure of Success.

However, it is Christ Jesus that will send the World the Strong Delusion, so that the World will believe 'The Lie', and in so doing, will not escape their Doom. Why? The Bible teaches that Humanity, knowing the Truth', rather chose to reject it for 'The Lie' because their Deeds are Evil and they Love it that way. The end of the X-File Conspiracy or 'Prophecies will occur when Jesus will return. At that Time, the Luciferian AntiChrist and False Prophet will be cast into the Lake of Fire. It will be later that Lucifer himself along with his Legions of Fallen Angels or 'Aliens' will suffer the same Doom for all Eternity. No longer well the 'Dragon', be able to Introduce, Deceive, and Influence Evil and Sin or Rebellion against all that is Holy, Just and Good. It will just be an 'X-File' that will never be opened again.

Main Sources

X-Files Wikipedia
https://en.wikipedia.org/wiki/The_X-Files

X Files Conspiracy scene
https://www.youtube.com/watch?v=qJjVS61HNU0

The X-Files - Marita Covarrubias explains colonization process
https://www.youtube.com/watch?v=VYcVgUxtTrY

The X-Files
https://www.youtube.com/watch?v=rlZ205ccX8M

The Lone Gunmen - Pilot 9/11 Exposed, Aired on March 4 2001
https://www.youtube.com/watch?v=SYKRXPI-KhM

Articles

#554 THE SECRET COVENANT
https://www.postscripts.org/ps-news-554.html

#37 ELDER'S PROTOCOLS
https://www.postscripts.org/ps-news-37.html

#48 CROP CIRCLES DECEPTIONS
https://www.postscripts.org/ps-news-48.html

#67 AVEBURY CYDONIA STAR MAP
https://www.postscripts.org/ps-news-67.html

Related to Topic

Operation Mockingbird
https://en.wikipedia.org/wiki/Operation_Mockingbird

CIA-backed, NSA-approved Pokemon GO users give away all privacy rights
https://sociable.co/technology/cia-backed-pokemon-go-privacy/

The CIA, NSA and Pokémon Go
https://www.networkworld.com/article/3099092/the-cia-nsa-and-pokmon-go.html

Alarming Truth — TV Puts Us In Hypnotic State and Suppresses Critical Thinking
https://drleonardcoldwell.com/2021/05/04/documentary-exposes-the-alarming-truth-tv-puts-us-in-hypnotic-state-and-suppresses-critical-thinking/

Space aliens are breeding with humans, university instructor says. Scientists say otherwise
https://www.nbcnews.com/mach/science/space-aliens-are-breeding-humans-university-instructor-says-scientists-say-ncna1008971

Argo – CIA Using Hollywood
https://en.wikipedia.org/wiki/Argo_(2012_film)

X-FILES
DNA ALTERING VIRUS
PLAN TO DE-POPULATE
THE PLANET
A Predictive Programming Excerpt

The purpose of this chapter is to provide an Addendum to the original Article, entitled, the #631: X-FILES PROPHECIES? That is about the Luciferian Globalist Plans to De-Populate the World by using Bio-Engineered Virus. In the TV Series of the 1990's and its reiterations in recent Year, the case is made that the Agenda is being Predictably Programmed. The following Excerpt will demonstrate this Agenda with chilling accuracy.

The Episode in which his portion of the Eugenicist Plant to Contaminate, Cull and Control the World Population was aired in 2016, Season 10. As it is now, the Adverse Event or Effects have had Millions of People now become damaged as a direct result of the Mandated COVID Injections. There are now New Medical Terms that are being used to cover-up the Death of Millions.

One such 'Sudden Adult Death Syndrome' or SADS. It really is more like 'Sad' in that the World Health Establishments are preventing any Doctor or Medical/Scientific Authority from correlating the Deaths of Millions to the COVID Shots. Grown Adult Men and Women are dropping Dead from Heart Attacks in the Prime of their Lives. Yet, no correlation is even allowed to question a possible link to the COVID Shots. This is even though no Factors in such a person's lives had changed, except that they took the COVID Shots. Then, the other New Medical notion is how, now Babies are subsepta to Heart Attacks.

There have been Billboards in the London Metro or in New York that state the hollowing. 'Babies can have Heart Attacks too'. But what the Dialog brings-out in the X-Files episode is a Soft Disclosure to ready the Masses in Acclimatizing them to not think twice of such a Conspiracy. And yet, it is exactly what has been Planned and now Executed. Now, Medical Experimentation has been happening for Centuries if not Millenia. What is different now?

The difference now is that for the 1sts Time in Human History, the whole world has been a Lab Rat for this COVID Experimental mRNA type of Technologies. At no other time has nearly every Nation on the Planet been in Lock-Step to such a Medical Endeavor. There is, for example, a Rockefeller Document that proves the Theory of how the Corona Virus pandemic was planned back in 2010. The "Lock Step"-Scenario 2010 stipulated a Pandemic influenza would lead to a Global Panic. China would become the Role Model of Totalitarianism. Masks would be required everywhere.

_____

X-Files: Season 10 - Aired 2016

…Tad O'Malley has been making claims…

Claims about what?

You and everyone you know has a Piece of DNA in your Genome. Put there without you knowing it.

By whom?

Well that is the Question of Today.

This is an Internet Lunatic. You are not saying you believe him?

Hold on Agent Einstein. You are talking to a Scientist.

Uh ,forgive me, Assistant Director. It may sound insensitive but the suggestion is pure Science Fiction.

What I am saying, Agent Einstein, is that the facts, as I understand them, cannot be discounted out of hand.

No one has the right or the ability to tamper with your DNA.

Unless we gave them that ability….

You say they are tampering with our DNA, that they are able to shut-down our Immune Systems by the addition of something to our DNA?

Yes. But I do not know how exactly…

How it is being triggered.

I do not know that either.

So, why is it happening now? What can we possibly do?

We need to act quickly. You were right about that.

Well, I was wrong about the Science. I was wrong about what is causing it. Dead wrong in fact.

But it is clearly a Widespread Failure of our Immune System.

Through Gene Tempering, a Virus within a Virus that was put there through the Smallpox Vaccine. It is what these Men are calling the Spartan Virus.

We have to figure this out... What is wrong with the Science.

Okay. The Spartan Virus removes the Adenosine Deaminase Gene from your DNA; remove the ADA Gene and your Immune System will simply Die.

Yeah, but I am not getting sick.

It is only a Matter of Time.

Okay, so how does it work? How does the Virus remove the Ada Gene?

A Process called Crispr...

Crispr-Cas9. RNA and a Protein cutting Genes at exact Locations.

Exactly. But in this instance, used as a weapon...

The Ultimate Weapon. The ability to De-Populate the Planet to kill everyone but the 'Chosen'.

By tampering with their DNA...

There would be Authoritarian Controls even after the 'End' of the Plandemic. Citizens would willingly give-up their Freedom. Any Resistance would be dealt with. This all came from, Scenarios for the Future of Technology and International Development, Rockefeller Foundation, Mai 2010. S.6. 18ff. It all confirmed the so-called Conspiracy. This type of Predictive Programming is exactly what is described in the Lock-Step Plan would have to occur in order to control the Narrative.

Main Sources
X-Files: Season 10 - Aired 2016
Υπομονή YouTube Channel
https://www.youtube.com/watch?v=y2rL1zNEjiI

Article

#631: X-FILES PROPHECIES?
https://www.postscripts.org/ps-news-631.html

#423: Operation Lock-Step - Rockefeller Report 2010
https://www.postscripts.org/ps-news-423.html

Free COVID Related Resource Page -Dander of the COVID Injections
https://www.postscripts.org/covid.html

YHVH-ATCG DNA CODE
SIGNATURE OF GOD
Image Bearers of the Creator

'Then Elohim said, Let Us make Man in Our Image, after Our Likeness, to Rule over the Fish of the Sea and the Birds of the Air, over the Livestock, and over all the Earth itself and every Creature that crawls upon it. So Elohim created Man in His own Image; in the Image of Elohim He created him; Male and Female He created them'. -Genesis 1:26-27

The following is a long reply but taken from the write-up one has posted online about it YHVH's Sacred Name being encoded in one's DNA, the Truth about one's Origins and Purpose. The concept is not one's Original Idea or Theory, as there are numerous Articles and Videos about how the 4-Letter Hebrew Letter Name of the Creator, Y-H-V-H is synonymous with the Human 4-Letter DNA Sequence of A-T-C-G and/or Chemical Equation.

But to have configured the Graphics, that has been totally one's Original Idea. Allow me to give a Background for Context of the Posters and Graphic Configurations. One's first exposure to 'Codes', hidden in Text, started when the Book came out by Drosnin, entitled, The Bible Code in 1997. Then since around 2009, one started Researching and Configuring Bible Codes Charts.

This was only possible as Jewish Rabbis who studied 'Hidden' Codes in the Torah provided an Open-Source Free Download of their Torah Code Software. This Software was later pulled from the Internet. One does not have, like a specific Source that one used or came across the YHVH Name linked to Human DNA. It has been due to a Comprehensive Journey of Research, that has had its Premise correlated to such a Prophetic Number-to-Letter Sequencing.

Code Correlations

The issue for one, was that as a Graphic Artist, on the side, none of the prior Researcher expounding on the Theory had adequately portrayed the Depiction in its simplified form. How it all started was that back in early 2020 when the COVID-19 Plandemic Hit, one suspected something was not 'Right' about the Virus and its origins.

One is a Researcher and works at a State University. One is a Statistician who was in charge of the Testing Office and dealt with Tests, Numbers and Statistics before the Office was permanently closed with the 'Excuse' of the COVID-19 Mandated Lock-Downs, etc. With such Research Skills, one started Researching the Topic of COVID-19, but in so doing, realized just how much of it was and is based on Basic Biology and Chemistry. With only limited Course-Work of such Subject Matter taken in College, at least one had a Primary Understanding when especially certain Doctors, Scientists and other Researchers started to contradict the Official Scientific Narrative.

What were those Contradictions? It was that the COVID-19 was Made-Made, Bio-Engineered. That the Injection would not be a 'Vaccine'. And that it was a New Technology and Experimental. And that it would change the DNA of Humans, among many other Dangerous Effects, etc. In fact, the Chief Medical Officer of Pfizer bragged about it a few Years prior. He stated in a TED Talk of how their New mRNA 'Vaccine' would essentially be Designed to exactly do that, change the DNA in Humans.

They called it the 'Software of Life'. With such New mRNA Technology, now that the Human DNA is Numerically Sequenced, it is Digitized and can be Encoded, to be 'Re-Engineered', as simple as a Computer Program, etc. The following are a few Research Papers, including the Swedish Study that prove, Scientifically, that mRNA does 'Transcribe' into the DNA of Human Cells.

Intracellular Reverse Transcription of Pfizer BioNTech COVID-19 mRNA Vaccine BNT162b2 In Vitro in Human Liver Cell Line
https://www.mdpi.com/1467-3045/44/3/73/htm?s=09

Pfizer mRNA vaccine goes into liver and changes into DNA, Swedish study finds
https://en.protothema.gr/pfizer-mrna-vaccine-goes-into-liver-and-changes-into-dna-swedish-study-finds/

Translation: DNA to mRNA to Protein
https://www.nature.com/scitable/topicpage/translation-dna-to-mrna-to-protein-393/

Development of mRNA Vaccines: Scientific and Regulatory Issues
https://pubmed.ncbi.nlm.nih.gov/33498787/

Messenger RNA (mRNA)
https://www.genome.gov/genetics-glossary/messenger-rna

Of course, the Paid Fact Checkers deny the Science. But back to the Name YHVH to DNA and Chemical Compound correlations. My Research Journey has gone on since 2020 and in that time, one has published 6 Books on COVID-19 and how it is not what is being Broadcasted. What is at the core of the issue is the New mRNA type of Injections.

They have never been Tested on Humans in a Formal Setting. The present ones have stopped for the Pfizer Shots. Their Preliminary 3-Year Study Trials are supposed to be released soon. The Release Time is scheduled for some time in late 2022 and/or early 2023, as to the Effects.

But as it has come to light, from Pfizer Leaked Documents, there is a Cover-Up of how disastrous the mRNA Injections are Wreaking Havoc on Humans. And the Media, Politicians, the WHO, CDC, NIH in the USA and other Nations have been and are being Complacent in this 'COVID' Catastrophe. This is where it does cross over into the 'Conspiratorial' Territory to some even now, but only because what was warned about by the Scientists and Doctors has all come True.

DNA

Deoxyribo Nucleic Acid is a Polymer composed of 2 Polynucleotide Chains that coil around each other to form a Double Helix carrying Genetic Instructions for the Development, Functioning, Growth and Reproduction of all known Organisms and many Viruses. DNA and Ribonucleic Acid are Nucleic Acids

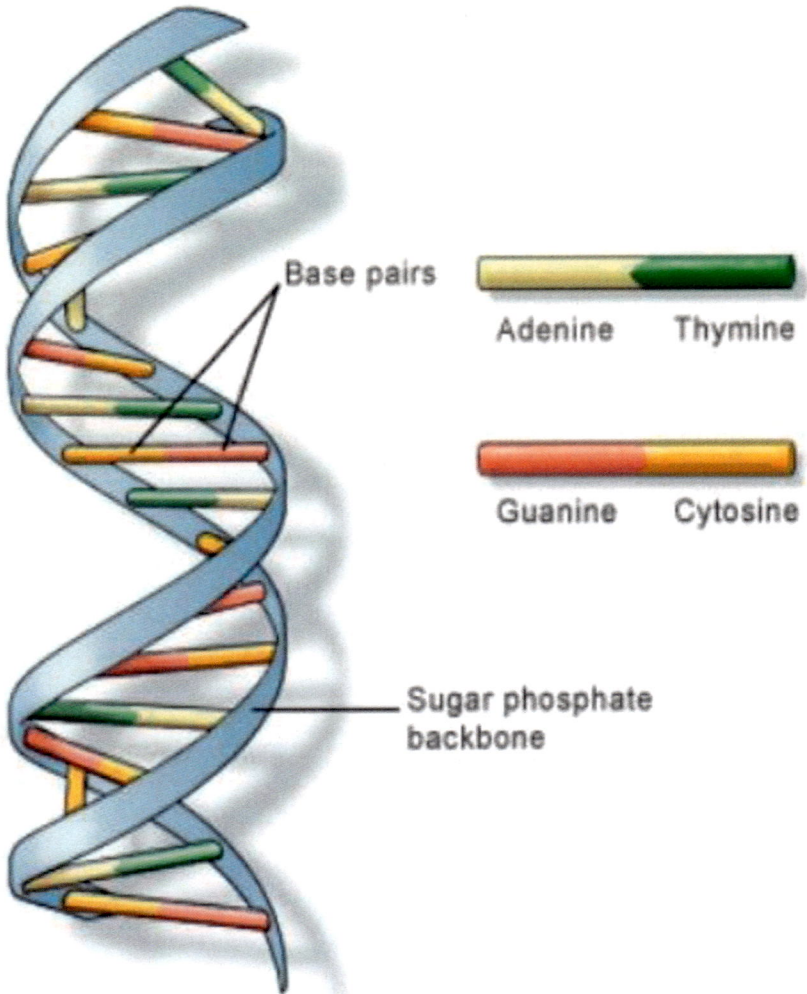

Base pairs

Adenine   Thymine

Guanine   Cytosine

Sugar phosphate backbone

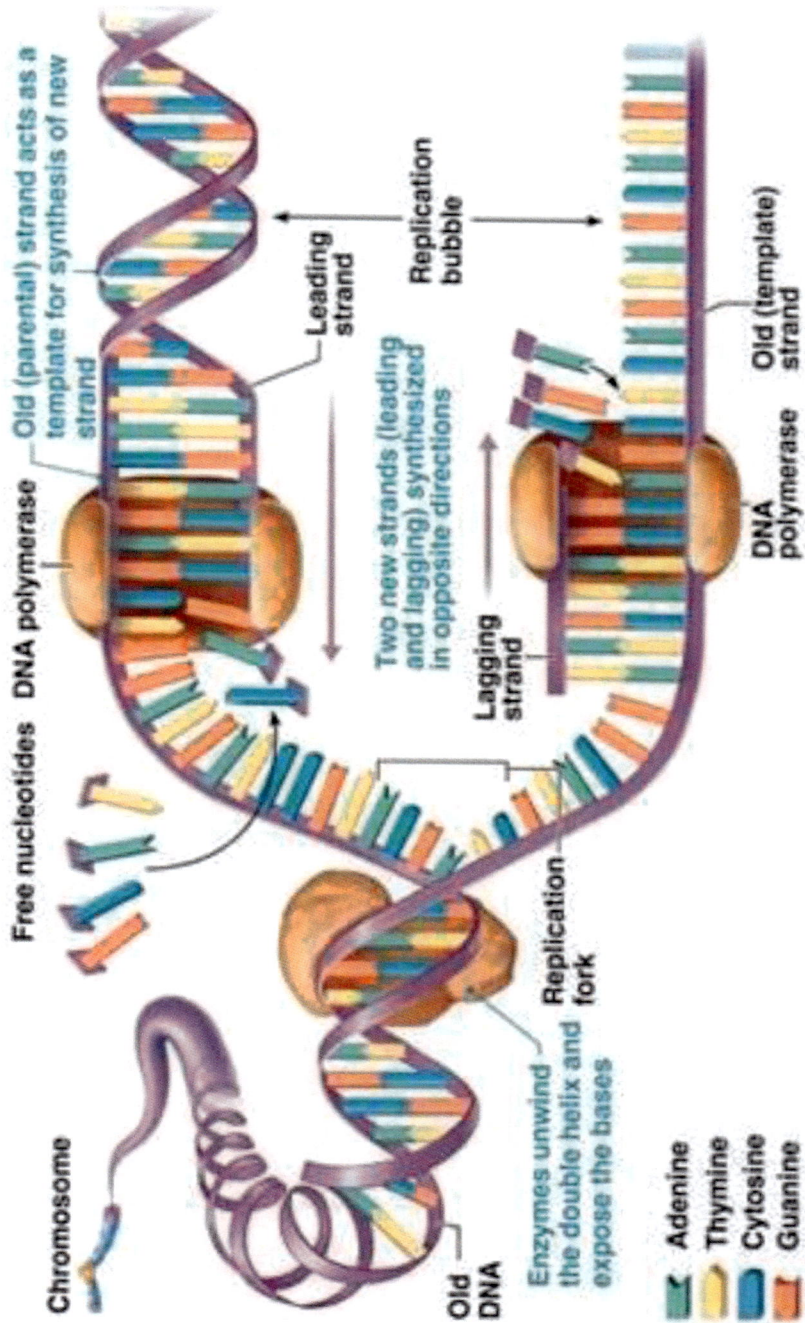

Chromosome

Old DNA

Enzymes unwind the double helix and expose the bases

Free nucleotides   DNA polymerase

Old (parental) strand acts as a template for synthesis of new strand

Leading strand

Replication bubble

Two new strands (leading and lagging) synthesized in opposite directions

Lagging strand

Replication fork

DNA polymerase

Old (template) strand

Adenine
Thymine
Cytosine
Guanine

© 2012 Pearson Education, Inc.

mage Bearers

So, in the course of doing the Research on COVID-19, one has had to read a lot of the Scientific Papers. One has had to re-learn the Basics of Biology and Chemistry, which is easy to do with either Books or online Video Teachings. Some are very good. Back to the mRNA type of New Technology. What became central to the Issue and Topic of mRNA when it does change the Human DNA.

Why is this such a Concern. It is because the Human DNA Code is what makes Humans distinct from other Beings created on Earth. And that according to the Bible, Human Beings are the 'Image Bearers' of the Creator. No other Being in the Created Universe of all that exists has been fashioned this way. And the Point? Humanity has Enemies. And the Aim is to 'Deface' and Change this 'Image and Likeness that is fashioned after the very Signature of the Creator that is infused in every Living Cell of the Human Body.

This is what is at stake. And? If the Image and Likeness is changed at the Molecular Level, with the DNA and there is enough Change to 'Erase' or Reprogram the DNA, then Humans will cease to be Humans. And? Linking the Topic to a Theological Construct, people that will have their DNA changed so much that they are no longer Humans will cease to be Redeemable. Why?

It was Jesus, GOD the Son, who took on a Body of Flesh, Genetically a Human, 100% but still being 100% GOD for the sole purpose of Redeeming the Fallen Race of Adam and Eve. It was they, that 'Sinned' by being Disobedient to the Commands of YHVH and in so doing, Death entered the Spiritual State of Being. And that also had a Physical Manifestation called 'Aging' or Dying. This is when the DNA changed, as before the Fall, the Human Body was not designed to 'Die', etc.

Cracking the Code

Thus, the need to have a 100% Human Substitution to pay or cover for the Sin and Redeem back Humanity to YHVH. That is why the Teachings of Paul reveal that in the last Part of the Entire Redemptive Work of Jesus on Cross, a New Body will be given at the point of the Resurrection and Rapture event. For those that Believe and are Followers of Jesus, one will eventually have a 'Glorified' Body like Jesus has now after His Resurrecting.

It is a Promise. So, these New mRNA Shot Types do or will change the DNA in Humans. At first, the claim that the mRNA would or could Reverse 'Transcribe' from the RNA to the DNA of a Human Cell was dismissed adamantly as 'Conspiracy' and Ludacris. Doctors and Scientists who spoke-up, based on prior Peer Reviewed Papers were laughed at and discredited.

Their YouTube, Twitter and other Social Media Platforms were banned. Such has been the case with 1 of the Inventors of the mRNA type of New Technology, Dr. Robert Malone. He has gone Public in warning not to take the mRNA Shots, especially for Children, etc. Then there is Dr. Zelenko, Dr. Tenpenny, Dr. Madej, who have come to the same Conclusions independently of each other, etc.

Thus, in one's case, the Evidence for the DNA correspondence of the 4 Letter Sequence of A-T-C-G to Y-H-V-H came from the Cumulative Research done in how, at the core of the Issue is the DNA. And thus, one had to re-learn the Basics about DNA. With that in mind, the various Biology Basic Text Book Explanations of DNA was simple enough to understand. This was also based on how the Human Genome Project, was led by NIH Scientist and Doctor, Dr. Francis Collins. He 'Cracked the Code' in Sequencing the entire DNA of not only Humans, but of a few Animals as well.

GOD'S SIGNATURE

The Project essentially 'Digitized' the Human DNA Sequence of the A-T-C-G that are the basic 'Building Blocks' of what constitutes the 'Code' of Human DNA.

IN EVERY CELL OF THE HUMAN BODY
DNA: Deoxyribo Nucleic Acid

4 Nuclide Acids bind the DNA Helices together by Sulfuric Bridges in the sequence of

A-T-C-G
EVERY 10, 5, 6, 5 ACIDS

10   5   6   5   10

HEBRAIC NUMERIC MEANING

10 5 6 5

Y-H-V-H

The Bridge, Bond, Glue that keeps the Human DNA Sequence together.

COLOSSIANS 1:16-17

For in Him [JESUS] all things were created, things in Heaven and on Earth, visible and invisible, whether Thrones or Dominions or Rulers or Authorities.

All things were created through Him and for Him.

He is before all things, and in Him

ALL THINGS HOLD TOGETHER.

GOD'S SIGNATURE

IN EVERY CELL OF THE HUMAN BODY

DNA

DEOXYRIBO NUCLEIC ACID

4 Nuclide Acids bind the Helixes together
by Sulfuric Bridges in the sequence of

A - T - C - G

EVERY 10, 5, 6, 5 ACIDS

10   5   6   5   10

HEBRAIC NUMERIC MEANING

10   5   6   5

Y-H-V-H

The Bridge, Bond, Glue that keeps the Human DNA Sequence together.

COLOSSIANS 1:16-17

For in Him [JESUS] all things were created, things in Heaven and on Earth, visible and invisible, whether Thrones or Dominions or Rulers or Authorities. All things were created through Him and for Him. He is before all things, and in Him

ESCHATOLOGY STUDIES   WWW.POSTSCRIPTS.ORG

For example, the following is a video of a Lecture Presentation of the subject of DNA and how it relates and Conflagrates Science with Faith, according to Collins. Around the 9 Minute Marker, he goes into how the DNA is now 'Digitized' based on the 4-Letter Sequence of A-T-C-G. Here is an Excerpt from the Lecture. According to Collins, DNA can be described as the following with emphasis added.

The Veritas Forum: The Language of God (Francis Collins)
UC Berkeley Events
https://www.youtube.com/watch?v=DjJAWuzno9Y

'DNA is a marvelous Information Molecule of all Living Things. You can think of DNA as an Instruction Book and you would be pretty close to right. It is a pretty Good Metaphor. It is a Book that is written in a 'Funny Language'. It has only 4-Letters in its Alphabet: A C G and T. Which are actually Chemical Bases that reside in this Double Helix. And that is the Order of those Letters that determine the Instructions that a particular DNA Molecule carries.

And all of the DNA of an Organism is called the Genome of that Organism. And we have 1 of those. Our Genome is about 3.1 Billion Letters in length. And we now have all of that Information. And you can go back to a place where you usually live and see what you can learn by pulling it up, on the web and beginning to sift through it.

Because that is the Process we are in right now. 3.1 Billion Letters is a lot of Information but it is a Bounded Set of Information. And that is actually kind of an interesting concept. That the Information necessary to take all of us from what we once were, a single cell and form this amazingly complicated Organism is a Bounded Set of 3.1 Billion Letters of DNA Code. Now that is still a lot of Information If we decided tonight, we were going to read the Human Genome.

Because it is such an exciting thing to do, I could maybe ask People to take turns. So that nobody got too tired. And we would sort of keep going. At the pace: A-C-G-T-T-G-C-A-C-A-T…about like that. And we all agreed we would stay here until we were done right?

Well, it would be a bit of a long read. Because 7 Days a Week, 24 Hours a Day, we would be here for 31 Years. That is, and that Information you have inside each Cell of your Body. Is that not an amazing thing to contemplate. And every time the Cell Divides, you got to Copy the whole thing…'

What Dr. Collins and his Team of Researchers did was to assign a Number to the Letters of the entire Human Genome and thus have a 'Code'. Now, thanks to Computer and New Bio-Engineering Technologies, Humans can now input into a Computer this entire Code. And? One can essentially become 'GOD' now as the Sequence can be changed, altered, re-arranged, etc. And some portions of the Human DNA can be taken out or a 'Code' or Gene can be put in.

The Theory or Thesis behind this work is that with such Knowledge and Understanding, Human Diseases like Breast Cancer, Diabetes or Birth Defects and the like could be eliminated, even before a Human is to be Born. The Dark Side of this mRNA type to Science is that now, Humans have become 'God'. How so?

It is in that they can Custom-Tailor a Super Race, a Soldier Race that could make a Human, Faster, Stronger, Heal Rapidly, See Farther or at Night, etc. Then, the possibilities would be endless as Non-Human DNA could be interjected into the Human Genome to make Chimeras or Human Hybrids. The Chinese, Russian and Americans have Secret Super Soldier Programs that are 'Black Budget' for this very Reason.

Defacing the DNA

It is rather intriguing that in one's Research into this New mRNA Type of Technology, the various Big-Pharma Corporation have been in Close Association with DARPA, and to this end, they seek to Transform Humanity or to Reset it to go along with the New Globalist Reset Agenda. A New Humanity for a New World Order, etc. The aim? It is to Digitize the Human Body. It is to interface 'Machine with Mankind'.

It is through the mRNA that the Body is Magnetized with Nano-Bot Technology for such a purpose to ultimately Control from within the Body. This is why there are countless People dying from this rejection of the Body. But ultimately, according to the Bible, the end result will be to funnel all of Humanity to take the Mark of the Beast.

Now as to the YHVH Codes. If one reads one's Research, Articles and Books, one will realize that one is into Biblical Eschatology. And this topic deals with Prophetic Patterns, Sacred Numbers, Bible Codes as mentioned, etc. Thus, in studying Numerology, one is well versed in the Association of how DNA, that is now Numerically Sequenced can be associated with Numbers and/or Chemical Compounds.

And Numbers have Meaning in Biblical Terms. In studying Bible Codes for example, there is what is called a Letter Distance Sequence. One source that one wrote-up about Numerical Associates to Words found in the Bible can be read from an Excerpt of one's Book on 'Hidden Codes found in the Bible. The Reader is welcomed to download it for free and explore the Topic of YHVH's Hidden Language within a Language, etc.

Bible Codexes Revelations: *Page 27*
https://onedrive.live.com/?cid=F18D5BF95B5644F2&id=F18D5B F95B5644F2%21267&parId=F18D5BF95B5644F2%216153&o= OneUp

To reiterate, the above Information has been one's own Research, independent of what has been or had already been discovered by others. There does appear to be a Correlation between the Sacred Hebrew Name of the Creator, Y-H-V-H to the DNA Numerical Sequence of A-C-T-G and Chemical Compounds.

Upon an Internet Search, the following Sites are good sources that confirm, basically the same Outcome. The earliest Article one could find is from 2014. What one has done, is just to Visualize and Depict the Correlation in a Diagram Format, that most, if not all prior Researcher had not done.

Main Sources
https://www.fivedoves.com/letters/apr2021/luisv44-2.htm
Wikipedia.com

Articles

YHVH in our DNA
https://ministermartyr.wordpress.com/2021/04/20/yhvh-in-our-dna

Hidden Name of The Creator in Your DNA
https://www.greatgenius.com/hidden-name-of-creator-in-your-dna

Videos

Name of יהוה (YHWH) in YOUR DNA! Proof of CREATION for the END TIMES!
https://www.youtube.com/watch?v=grvrTvFTfQw

YHVH name of God found encoded in our DNA
https://www.youtube.com/watch?v=Dyv-hTHUc3w
Code of Life Openly Hidden between the Lines of Ancient Text - Gregg Braden
https://www.youtube.com/watch?v=jMtt8Wvm1NM

Hidden Name of The Creator in Your DNA
https://www.delightfulknowledge.com/hidden-name-of-creator-in-your-dna

Books

Bible Codexes Revelations
https://www.amazon.com/dp/1716351502?tag=nice04f-20&linkCode=ogi&th=1&psc=1

COVID Catastrophe
https://www.amazon.com/dp/1667196723?tag=nice04f-20&linkCode=osi&th=1&psc=1

Posters

YHVH DNA - GOD'S Signature
https://nebula.wsimg.com/da1e08f706b8c1f65a8b2ac99af7ecbe?AccessKeyId=D40106E1331C24ABD7C3&disposition=0&alloworigin=1

Name of Creator - DNA
https://nebula.wsimg.com/fb5f412e075bc387746f73182c414246?AccessKeyId=D40106E1331C24ABD7C3&disposition=0&alloworigin=1

Merchandise

t-Shirt: YHVH DNA - GOD'S Signature
https://www.zazzle.com/gods_signature_dna_2_t_shirt-235046151017494537

t-Shirt: YHVH DNA - GOD'S Signature
https://www.zazzle.com/signature_of_god_dna_t_shirt-235337659352545205

t-Shirt: YHVH Name of Creator- Chemical Compound
https://www.zazzle.com/yhvh_name_of_god_dna_t_shirt-235506689439686379

CONSPIRACIES
UNIVERSITY COURSE
Sociology of Conspiracies

But as to 'Conspiracies', one forgot to mention that in the X-Files, one of the Characters was 'Deep Throat'. He was portrayed as the Former FBI Agent, Mark Felt. If one remembers a few Years back, how he came forward, publicly to 'Confess' that it was him with all that Watergate Event. Well, his Daughter, Joan, was a Professor at Sonoma State where one works at.

The 1st Year that one was there, around 2007 she was leading the International Office which was down the Hall from my Office and one crossed paths a few times as she was fluent in Spanish. On 1 occasion, one's Program joined-up to introduce our Students to the International Students. It was great, but one never really talked to her, one-on-one or knew her background or Dad. She later moved on from Sonoma and one thinks, last is that she is still teaching at the Community College Level.

one does have, here in the Santa Rosa area, some 'Notable People'. There was a former Professor that wrote an Article about the Face on Mars, having analyzed NASA Photos to say, with confidence that it was not natural occurring. There is a Sociology Professor, Peter Phillips that got his PhD in the Bohemian Grove and Conspiracy. He actually teaches a Class on Conspiracies.

SOCI 371 - Sociology of Conspiracies (4 Units)
A critical analysis of conspiracies in society using Power Elite and State Crimes Against Society theories applied to modern historical events using cultural, social psychological, public propaganda, and power perspectives: topics include political assassinations, election fraud, threats of terrorism, 9/11, and permanent war.

One had always meant to Team-Up or see if one could have taken a Section teach on Conspiracies. But never got around to it. When one had a Personal Staff Website and started to post one's 'Conspiracy' Research, 1 Parent called in that he would never allow his Daughter to be near me. And as other Staff and/or Professors would put a picture of Mao, Mohammad, Krishna, or Buddha, on their Personal Info section of their Staff Profiles, that was fine.

As soon as one put one up on mine of Jesus. One got called in by Human Resources HR and they banned one's Staff Site. True story. One thinks that is what you call 'Conspiracy', no? Speaking of Conspiracies, here, this video is about the Deep State.

Congressman Larry McDonald Exposes New World Order Agenda
https://www.brighteon.com/ed3868f1-3b62-416d-aea3-e96596b08b54

For example, there is that Question of whether Obama is the coming AntiChrist reminded one of the Painting that came out awhile back about him. See Article and Painting in link down in End-Notes. If one remembers, how on Obama's Left Hand, Sinistra in Italian/Spanish/Latin, had 6 Fingers. This is a Tell-Tale Sign of Gigantism, or Remnant Bloodline of the Nephilim. The Word, Sinistra is from where 'Sinister' comes from.

Not to say that all of you that are Left-Handed are Evil. Maybe. Most all of the Giants that have been unearthed have had 6 Fingers and Toes. The Condition is even recorded in the Bible, King of Og, etc. But as many believe Obama is or will be the AntiChrist, it makes one wonder. The only reason such a person, like Obama specifically, could be 'Him', in one's research is the connection to Nimrod. How so?

1. Nimrod was or became a Hybrid. Obama is a 'Hybrid', half White, half Black, etc.

2. The Bible states that Nimrod came from Ham. The Hamites eventually migrated to Africa and became the African Races, OK.

3. Nimrod 'became a Gibborim'. Meaning that he somehow Cracked the Code for transforming his Genome into a Giant. This is the stuff of the Super Hero Story Lines, like 'Captain America' with that Super Soldier Serum. It goes back to Nimrod.

4. Then, to the Secret Mystery Religions, Luciferians, the Masons, Kabbalists, Nimrod was and is considered the '1st Mason'. Go figure.

5. Nimrod attempted to unite the World under 1 Tower and Order, as one knows. Obama signed the Last Beam of the One World Center 'Hybrid Tower in New York. That Tower is 1776 Feet high and the 'Hyriid ' of the 2 Twin towers coming together, etc.

The Tower, one has calculated, was approximately 3 times as tall as the Burg Khalifa. It was Star Gate constructed to pierce the Dimensions and invade Heaven with. CERN anyone? So, this coming AntiChrist will be Nimrod 2.0 and finish what YHVH had 'interrupted'. This is why the Truncated, Unfinished Pyramid is their Motif of the Mason and the Official Reverse Seal of the USA.

So, for those that say the USA is not in Bible Prophecy? It is. It will be the 'instrument' to bring about the Capstone', aka, Lucifer, the AntiChrist by Proxy finish the New Tower and New Order and New Humanity, thanks to mRNA Technology. When? 2022-2023. This is based on one's Theory that the USA has a Shelf Life of 33 Sabbath Cycles of 7 Years since 1792. This is when the USA became USA, Inc and its money was Minted.

1792 Coin Act + *(33 Cycles of 7-Year Sabbaths) = 232 Years + 1792 = 2023.*

It will be when the All Seeing Eye, Lucifer comes down and completes the Pyramidion or Capstone. So what will be the Tower of Power? The 3rd Temple. Thus, the Abrahamic Family Houses, etc. It is all coming together .This is why the Globalists want to 'Gibborim' Humanity. It will serve to deface YHVH's Image and Likeness that only Human Beings Have. And to fil-in Lucifer's Army Rank with in anticipation for the coming Angelic Wars to be fought Revelation 12, etc. Lucifer is outnumbered 2 to 1. But my 'favorite' Candidate is Jared Kushner....who has his Business Office at 666 5th Avenue on the 13th Floor next to Lucent Tech, major makers of the RFID Bio-Devices.

Another Conspiracy is how Secret Societies run the World. Such Occult Organizations are Luciferians and communicated through Numbers. Take for example, the Number 555 that a lot of People see often. One would ask, what does the Number 555 mean? It is coming from a Dichotomy of Definitions, Good and Bad and how it is used. First, a Preface. Numbers and Mathematics are called the 'Universal Language'. Symbols and Numbers communicate Meaning. Every known created shape can be broken down to Numbers and a Mathematical Equation, etc. One realizes that, for example Numbers define a Concept also.

1 = Singleness/Oneness.
2 = Division.
3 = Unity.
4 = Equilibrium,
5 = Grace,
6 = Man.
7 = Perfection.
8 = Newness,
9 = Less than.
10 = Law.
11 = Chaos.
12 = Authority.
13 = Rebellion.

Christians know that YHVH is the 'Grand Mathematician' and also communicates with Numbers in the Bible. In fact, several Mathematicians have proven that with the Numbers 1 to 9, the Creation was formed. Numbers in themselves are not Evil, like the famous 666. But just as YHVH created and uses Numbers to communicate Truth, so has Lucifer.

So, with this backdrop, here is one' understanding of the Number 555. It is based on the Number 5, which means Grace, as we know. And when it is in a Triplet, it is extenuating that Characteristic and/or Principle to the Greatest Extent.

But one actually sees or realizes that there is more when the Enemy uses this Number, 555 also to communicate their 'Hidden' Knowledge to their Initiates. Case in point is that Number 555 is used of the Luciferian Freemasons. They place it in their Motifs, especially in this case on their Coffins. Why? 555 means 'Death and Resurrection'. It is insinuating that a Transition that is about to occur.

Although the Mason Motif is morbid looking, it does convey a Truth found in the Bible, in that for a Christian, Death is not the End but a Transition to Glory. This will be especially true for the Dead in Christ that will Rise-Up 1st in the Resurrection-Rapture event. And perhaps People increasingly seeing 555 could be a Serendipity occurring because the 'Great Transformation' or Rapture is about to take place.

Here is a picture of the Masonic Coffin for Illustration.
https://netstorage-legit.akamaized.net/images/vllkyt3fd5qpph129g.jpg

This too, by the way is what the New Agers are also believing and expecting. They use the Term 'Consciousness' that Humans have to be 'Transformed' for them to reach their next Level of Evolution.

Freemasonic Coffin with a 5-5-5 denoting 'Resurrection'.

This is of course a Humanist Interpretation of Truth, not realizing or rejecting that Jesus is the Resurrection and the Life. The implication then of 555 is that of a coming Change and Transformation. The last interpretation of the Number 555 has to do with Sacred Geometry. How so? Consider that in the Universe, from Humanity's Mortal and Weaker Perspective, there is the Greater or Bigger Variable.

In comparison to what? To the Earth and the Worldly Realm that is the Lesser Variable. For example, if one studies Ancient Wisdom of Sages Past, there is an overall-arching notion of Duality in relation to each other and that needs to be in Balance and Harmony, etc. It is the Concept of the Micro-to-Macro correspondences of Creation.

The Universe to Earth, the Ying to the Yang, Black-White, Good and Evil, Male-Female, etc. The 555 corresponds to the Lesser or Earthly Bound Realm. This 555 is seen in the Pentagram or Star. Its corresponding Geometry is that of 6, the Hexagram, which has in its Mathematical Make-up, 666 Geometrically. So, for us Followers of Jesus, no fear, because 1 Day, our Earthly 'Jars' or Bodies of Clay will be Transformed.

It will occur in the 'Twinkling of an Eye' from the Lesser Dimension to the Greater Dimension where Jesus is, in Heaven. That was His Promise, no? He told that to the Disciples, that He was going away to prepare a Place so that we, as His Disciples, His Bride metaphorically could be where He is, Forever, hopefully this Year. The Number 555 is about Death and Resurrection, about a coming Transformation.

Resources

Article: Everyone Is Noticing One Very Creepy Thing About The Obama Portrait
https://dailycaller.com/2018/02/13/obama-portrait-six-fingers-left-hand

Chart: Star Gate at the Burj Khalifa – Modern Type of the Tower of Babel
https://onedrive.live.com/?cid=F18D5BF95B5644F2&id=F18D5BF95B5644F2%2114655&parId=F18D5BF95B5644F2%216864&o=OneUp

666 FIFTH AVENUE
666 Fifth Avenue, New York, NY 10103
Acquisition date: 2007
Kushner owns the fee interest in a long term ground lease for the 1.45 million square foot commercial tower, which is home to Kushner headquarters. Built in 1957, the landmark building is often noted for its signature aluminum façade, prominent crown signage, and lobby designed by Isamu Noguchi. The tower sits atop several floors of retail facing Fifth Avenue, the world's most prominent retail corridor.

666 Fifth Avenue - Kushner
666 5th Avenue Is Waiting In The Background - RFID Chip Mark Is Coming
(((666))) 5th Avenue Is Waiting In The Background - RFID Chip Mark Is Coming (linkedin.com)

Lucent Technologies Logo
Lucent Technologies Logo – Absolute Truth from the Word of God (grandmageri422.me)

Chart: The Great Metamorphoses
https://nebula.wsimg.com/05003e950edaa9d5517ee6412de2a8f5?AccessKeyId=D40106E1331C24ABD7C3&disposition=0&alloworigin=1

GREAT PYRAMID PATTERNS
END OF THE AGE? 2022
Countdown to the New World Order

The purpose of this chapter is to examine the Great Pyramid of Giza Patterns. It is an Enigma for sure and an amazing Piece of Work. So much of it is beyond Comprehension as to what needed to be known to Geometrically position the Structure to True North and have it assigned to certain Stars like Orion and ones in Draco. It was Robert Bauval, from Belgium who was the 1st Westerner to detect the Celestial Star Alignments of Orion with the Pyramids.

In fact, the whole River Nile is construed to correspond to the Entire Milky Way Pattern. It is Astro-Archeology at its best. But here is the deal. Here is a Deep Dive into the Great Pyramid Patterns. Why? One postulates that the Great Pyramid Pattern could suggest when the End of the Church Age is to occur, down to the Year. And with that, it would stipulate the Rapture event being before that time, assuming a Pre-Tribulation Rapture Timing and Scenario. Below are 3 Postulates that calculate the year, presently being 2022 that suggest will be the End of the Church Age. Evidence?

The Factors have to do with the Measurement of the Height of the Great Pyramid itself. Then having that Pattern transported into other Locales around the World, mainly the USA. Specifically the Washington Mall. Then there is the Theory of the USA having a Great Pyramid Type of History corresponding to the Chambers. But more pronounced is the stipulation that the USA has but 33 Sabbath Cycles of 'Life' All these 3 Suppositions and Hypothesis point to the Year 2022.

Back before 2015-16, one thought that that year was to be the Concluding Epoch, Rapture, End of the USA and World War 3. After all, it was the Time of Obama and the similar circumstances existed then or began but nothing compared to what is now and will be. One suspects that The-Powers-That-Be attempted the Transition then but it was not Time. What Time?

Great Pyramid Time. All this to say that in Hind-Sight, there was still that Last Sabbath Cycle of 7-Year. One remembers in the Research how it could have been a possibility but and People were saying, 'How can it get any worse?', etc. But with a recurring Theme and more information understood, perhaps the 7-Year Countdown was to have occurred and has since 2015. This then means that 2022 'has to be then the Year of the Transition of Ages. Believers in Jesus and well as those in the World sense something is up, 'Something Wicked Comes this Way'.

So, these are just Number Calculations, it does not prove anything. One can only present the Evidence and then declare a certain Confidence of the Patterns. The Patterns are then undeniable. The issue is that one can never say that one is 100% Confident that it will be the case, 2022. What one can say, with more Confidence is that the Pyramidion or the Capstone is what constitutes the last 7-Year, from 2015 - 2022. Perhaps.

---

1. GREAT PYRAMID CAPSTONE PATTERN – Mason Motif
From base of Great Pyramid to include Cap Stone
= 5776 inches or 481 feet

481 Feet Radius x 2 = 962 ft. Diameter or 962 ft. Diameter x Pi (3.14…)

From 1776 Base Year = 19-year average X 13 Steps = 247 Years
247 Years + 1776 = 2023rd year

---

2. MALL PYRAMID PATTERN
If the map layout is a Time/Space 'Clock' and there are 14 Total Steps from 1776 to the truncated top, then the last 14th Piece Capstone would be 2015-2022.

Using Latitude = Year Count
> 38.96° DC Latitude / 2 = 19.48°
> 19.5°(rounded) x 13 steps = 253 Years
> 1776 + 246 years = 2029

SPEED OF LIGHT ENCODED

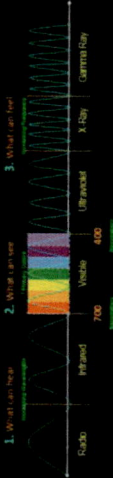

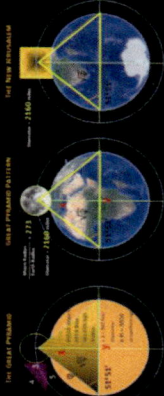

LIGHT

I AM THE LIGHT OF THE WORLD.
Whoever follows Me will not walk in
darkness, but will have the Light of Life.
JESUS CHRIST
John 8:12

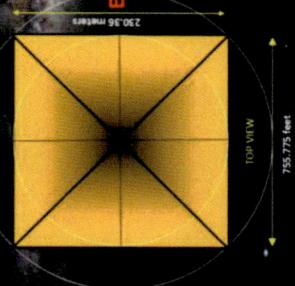

THE GREAT PYRAMID
is actually an Octagon with 8 sides.

Capstone is @ =
29°58'45.28588"N

230.36 meters
755.775 feet
TOP VIEW

"29.9792458" meters per seconds or Speed of Light

Circumference of Outer Circle = 1024.463491 meters
Circumference of Inner Circle = 723.697975 meters

Difference in measurement = 299.78556 meters
= "million meters per second = 299.79245

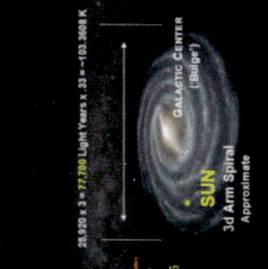

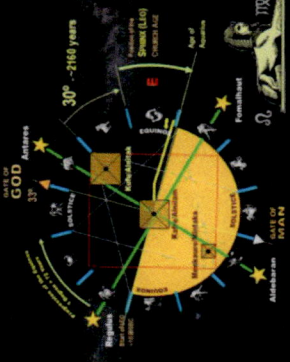

INCIDENT LIGHT 60°
45°

1. What can here.   2. What can we   3. What can feel

Radio   Infrared   Visible   Ultraviolet   X Ray   Gamma Ray
700   400

GALACTIC CENTER
(Bulge)

SUN
3d Arm Spiral
Approximate

25,920 x 3 = 77,700 Light Years x 33 = ~103.3608 K

2160 Years x 12 =
Stars at 41.2 (4:32) = Precessional
A 'GREAT YEAR'
= 25,920 YEARS
1 Age = 2160 YEARS

2025
23.5°
Earth

GATE OF
GOD Antares
33°

GATE OF
MAN

30° ~2160 years

Age of
Pisces

The Pyramid Clock illustrated on the chart is depicted in
'reverse' order or format not illustrated on most drawings
online. It mirrors the coordinates from a cosmic perspective,
not an Earth perspective.

THE GREAT PYRAMID
THE NEW JERUSALEM

GREAT PYRAMID OF COLUMBIA

From base of Great Pyramid to include Cap-Stone

= **5776** Inches

481 ft.
481 Full Foot Radius X
2.90 Ø Diameter
867.4 Diameter x Pi=5.58 ÷

2016=154 +/-Year 2022-23

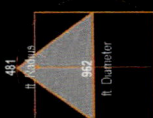

The Oval Office
is the Eye of Horus
Left Eye of Lucifer
stuck down.

The Owl, Oval-Cranial speaks to the Skull Eye of the Pieris Mons.

GREAT PYRAMID
5776 INCHES

481
ft. Radius

952
ft. Diameter

3022
ft. Circumference

YEAR = INCHES THEORY?
CAPSTONE YEAR?

Google Earth

38°53'51.63"N 77°02'01.56"W elev 0 ft. eye at 27569 ft.

CAPITOL HILL
Alien Skull Motif

KOEHAB

Historical Society

ALPHA DRACONIS

ASCENDING PASSAGE
Devil's Arm

KING'S CHAMBER
WHITE HOUSE

OBELISK

QUEEN'S CHAMBER

Jefferson Memorial

THE PIT

ORION

SIRIUS

FACE OF MARS

Lincoln Memorial

BLESS OUR ENTERPRISE 2022
2015
5776
MDCCLXXVI
1776
NEW WORLD ORDER

SYNAGOGUES OF SATAN

7 YEAR Pattern
From V776 Base Year
19 Years Average X 13 Steps
= **247** Years
247 Years + 1776 =
2023th Year

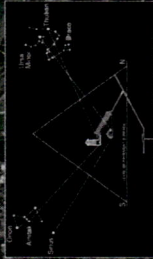

LUCIFERIAN ATLANTIAN CAPITAL PYRAMID

COUNTDOWN TO THE IMPLOSION OF OLD WORLD ORDER AMERICAN PHOENIX

143

AMERICAN EXPERATION DATE

33RD SABBATICAL CYCLE COUNTDOWN TO END OF THE AMERICAN WORLD ORDER

NEW WORLD ORDER
SYNAGOGUES OF SATAN

BLESS OUR ENTERPRISE
JH-B
EYE OF LUCIFER
The Great Work
A 'Nimrod' will
finish it.
YHVH
TOWER OF BABEL
Interrupted by

5776
13
STEPS
MDCCLXXVI
1776

Light
SABBATIC CYCLE?
7 YEARS?
2022-2029

The 'Expiration Date'?

2-0-2-2   The 'Capstone'

33rd cycle is from 2015-2021

2021 was 'Zero'

33rd cycle

239 years (9-23-15)

1792 + 7 years (Sabbatical Cycle) x 33 = 230 years = 2022

*excluding end year

1776

Bless Our Work
Lucifer's Eye-Stone
72 Blocks | 13 Levels
MAY 1, 1776
'5776'

From
Base of Great Pyramid
to include Capstone
= 5776 inches
481 feet

New World Order
'MASONS'

I.R.S.
5776
1776

COINAGE ACT
From Apr 2, 1792 to Sep 13, 2015
- 223 years
- Skull & Bones (322)

JUBILEE COUNTDOWN

1966   1973   1980   1987   1994   2001   2008   2015   2022

TABLE OBSERVATION

482
Feet Radius
5776
inches high

962
Feet Diameter
3022
Feet Circumference

MAIN SOURCES

© Compositor and some graphics by
Luis B. Vega
vegapost@hotmail.com
www.PostScripts.org

144

GIZA TIME CLOCK OF EPOCHS

MYSTERIES OF THE PYRAMID CLOCK ANNOUNCING A NEW TIME

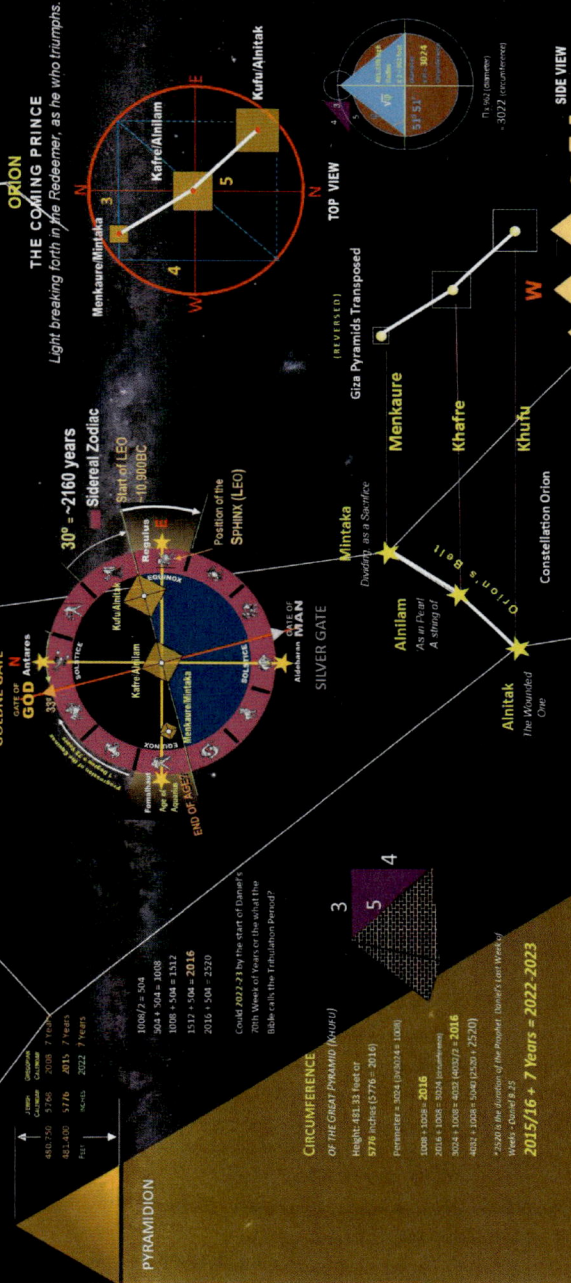

ORION
THE COMING PRINCE
Light breaking forth in the Redeemer, as he who triumphs.

Menkaure/Mintaka

Kafre/Alnilam

Kufu/Alnitak

3

4

5

E

N

W

TOP VIEW

SF 51

3024

π x ½61 (diameter)
= 3022 (circumference)

SIDE VIEW

[REVERSED]
Giza Pyramids Transposed

Menkaure

Khafre

Khufu

W

Constellation Orion

Orion's Belt

Mintaka
Dividing, as a Sacrifice

Alnilam
*As a Pearl
A string of*

Alnitak
*The Wounded
One*

30° = ~2160 years

Sidereal Zodiac

Start of LEO
~10,900BC

Position of the
SPHINX (LEO)

GOLDNE GATE
GATE OF
GOD Antares
N

33°

EQUINOX

SOLSTICE

Kufu/Alnitak

Kafre/Alnilam

EQUINOX

Menkaure/Mintaka

Regulus

E

ECLIPTIC

GATE OF
MAN

Aldebaran
SILVER GATE

END OF AGES

Could *2022-23* by the start of Daniel's
70th Week of Years or the what the
Bible calls the Tribulation Period?

1006/2 = 504
504 + 504 = 1008
1008 + 504 = 1512
1512 + 504 = **2016**
2016 + 504 = 2520

3

5

4

PYRAMIDION

JEWISH Calendar	GREGORIAN Calendar		
450.750	576s	2008	7 Years
442.1400	577s	2015	7 Years
Past		2022	7 Years

CIRCUMFERENCE
OF THE GREAT PYRAMID (KHUFU)

Height: 481.33 feet or
5776 inches (5,776 = 2016)

Perimeter = 3024 (3x3024 = 1008)

1008 + 1008 = **2016**
2016 + 1008 = 3024 (circumference)
3024 + 1008 = 4033 (4033/2 = **2016**
4032 + 1008 = 5040 (2520 + 2520)

*2520 is the duration of the Prophet Daniel's Last Week of
Weeks - Daniel 9:25*

2015/16 + 7 Years = 2022-2023

LAS VEGAS GREAT PYRAMID

146

LONDON BANK GREAT PYRAMID
LUCIFERIAN MASTERS OF MAMMON COUNTDOWN

Latitude-Year Theory
0°05′ 20.22″ W
0°05′ 20.15″ W
0°05′ 20.08″ W
0°05′ 20.01″ W
0°05′ 19.94″ W
0°05′ 19.87″ W
0°05′ 19.80″ W
0°05′ 19.73″ W
0°05′ 19.66″ W
0°05′ 19.59″ W
0°05′ 17.76″ W

Eye of Horus
(7 Heavenly Bodies)

New World Order

2022
2015

LUCIFER'S
Right eye blinded in
Angelic Conflict

2008
2001

'MASONS'

1994
1987
1980

New World Order

1973
1966
1959

'Bless Our Work'

1776

Temple of Mammon

45°

90°

7 1 2
6 5 3
   4

(Work Done)
NORTH-WEST ANGLE
90°
2015 to 2022

1948
1936

1911

1805

BANK · OF · ENGLAND ·

Bank of England
It's NOT a Bank
and it's NOT
of England

'Domine Nos Dirige'
'Master Direct Us'

CITY
OF
LONDON
DOMINE DIRIGE NOS

PATRON GOD OF FINANCIAL GAIN
MERCURY

LUCIFER:

GoogleEarth

Imagery Date: 4/10/2020   51°30′48.16″N   0°05′20.22″W elev 0 ft   eye alt 1552 ft

13 CRYSTAL SKULLS USA PYRAMID
SERPENT ACROSS THE 'DIVIDED' UNITED STATES

THE ASTRONOMICAL TRINITY

A COMPARATIVE STUDY OF THE 'UNIVERSAL TEMPLATE'

TEMPLE MOUNT GREAT PYRAMID
120 PENTECOSTAL PATTERN HISTORY OF THE HUMAN RACE

SUN
Holy of Holies
ARK OF COVENANT

Ezekiel's Temple
Herod's Temple
Solomon's Temple
Tabernacle of Mo

KING'S Chamber

HOLY OF HOLIES
Dome of Tablets

QUEEN'S Chamber

MOON

Star Shaft pointing to Polaris
Shaft pointing to Christ chalf/dub sky

Ground Level—Bedrock

STARS

Church of All Nations

SUBTERRANEAN Chamber

3rd TEMPLE POSSIBLE LAYOUT

GOLDEN GATE

Google Earth

(Looking West
Toward Past and
Return to Heaven)

Descending Passage

Ascending Passage

Escape Shaft

THE LOCATION OF TEMPLE

150

CELESTIAL CITY OF THE BRIDE

The New Jerusalem
on New Earth and Heaven

360 miles = 360°

300 mile walk from Ephesus to Laodicea.

EARTH
THE 7 CHURCHES OF ASIA
JESUS CHRIST - BODY OF

180
225
135
Laodicea
Philadelphia
270
Pergamon
Thyatira
Sardis
Equator
0/360°
315
90
Smyrna
Ephesus
45

APOSTLE JOHN

'John'
Moon

Patmos

300 miles / 6
segments of mile distances = **50**
'Pentecost Signature'

Google Earth

29°52'32.60" N   32°22'48.54" E   eye alt 16728.53 mi

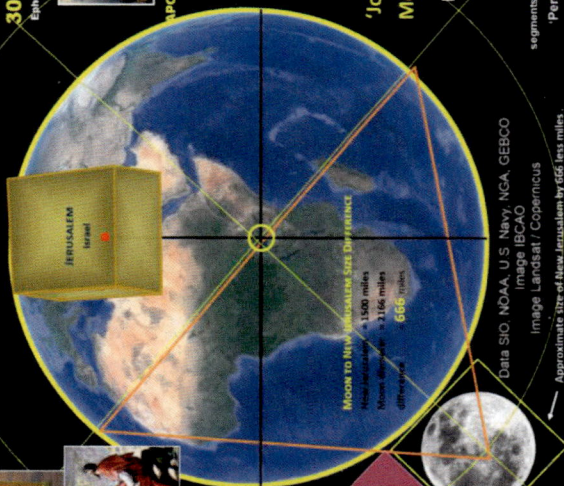

JERUSALEM
Israel

RIVER OF LIFE

MOON TO NEW JERUSALEM SIZE DIFFERENCE
New Jerusalem   **1500** miles
Moon diameter   **2,116** miles
difference   **666** miles

Data SIO, NOAA, U.S. Navy, NGA, GEBCO
Image IBCAO
Image Landsat / Copernicus

Approximate size of New Jerusalem by 666 less miles.

$a^2 + b^2 = c^2$

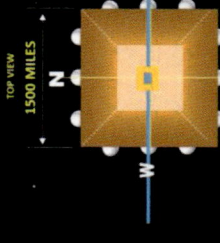

TOP VIEW
1500 MILES

N
E
W
S

1500 MILES

NEW HEAVENS

SIDE VIEW

Holy
of
Holies

NEW EARTH
(No Oceans)

12 GATES OF THE TRIBES OF ISRAEL
12 FOUNDATIONS OF APOSTLES

151

If 2029 is the Maximum Limiest of the Calculation, it could allude to being the End of the 7-Year Tribulation Period. If one then Subtracts 7-Years, it will be 2022.

*2029 - 7 Year Tribulation Period = **2022***

---

3. USA EXPIRATION DATE - 33RD SABBATH GREAT PYRAMID PATTERN
Based on the Premise that the Coin Act of 1792 set the Sabbath Cycles.
What Year would be the Occult End of the 33rd Cycle?

33 Sabbath Cycle of 7 Years = 231 Years

*Coin Act 1792 + 231 Years = **2023***

---

4. BANK OF ENGLAND PYRAMID – COUNTDOWN TO FINANCIAL RESET
The following is the breakdown of the Year-To-Latitude Correspondence.

*0°05' **20.22**"W – Top of Ground Extension*
*0°05' **20.15**"W – Top and End of Building Corner (Southern Point)*
*0°05' **17.76**"W – Bottom and Start (Northern Face)*

It is about a 'Bank' that rules the World Economies that is tied to the Shemitah 'Law of Return'. Will the New Luciferian Monetary System commence, based on the law of 7-Year Debt Cycle? That year would then be 2022, thereabouts.

The Great Pyramid is essentially a Cosmic Clock that is keeping track of the 'Beginning and Ending' of the Ages. I concur with the Notion from Isaiah 19 that it is an 'Altar' in the Middle of Egypt, at the Border, and thus a 'Door', or Star Gate'. The following will be several Images that depict the Great Pyramid from different perspectives.

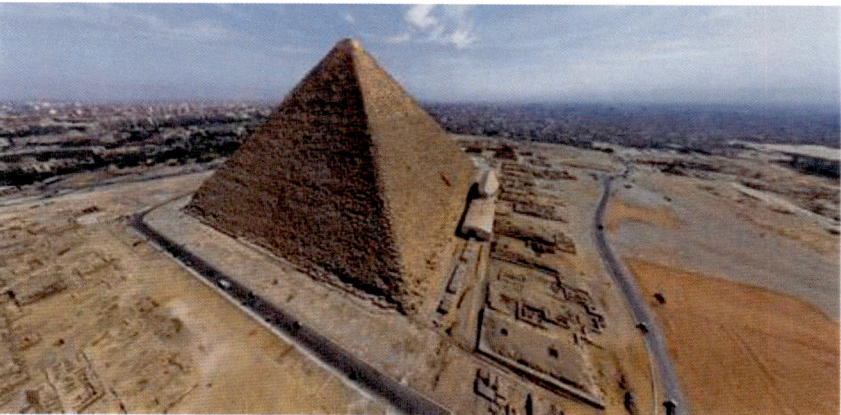

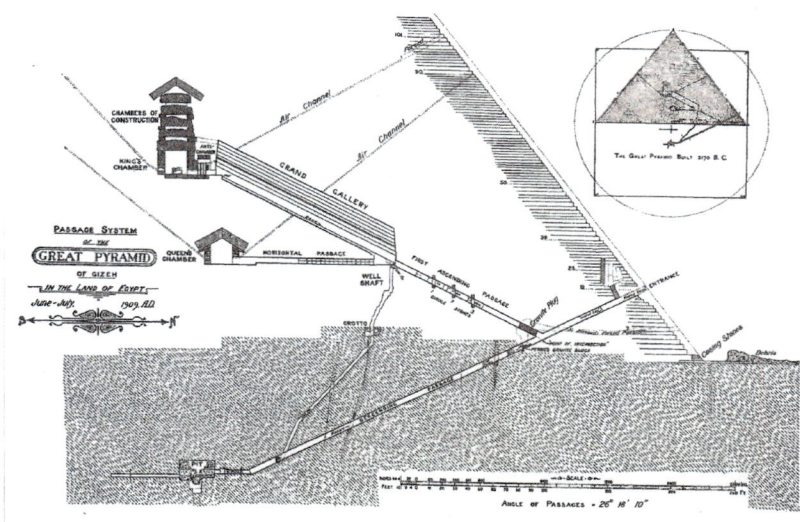

Passage System of the GREAT PYRAMID of Gizeh
—In the Land of Egypt—
June - July, 1909 A.D.

The Great Pyramid Built 2170 B.C.

ANGLE OF PASSAGES = 26° 18' 10"

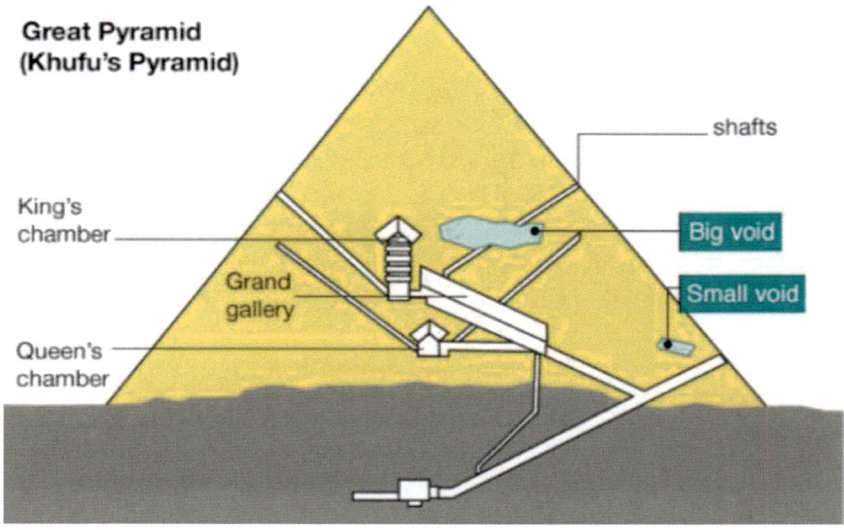

Great Pyramid (Khufu's Pyramid)

King's chamber

Grand gallery

Queen's chamber

shafts

Big void

Small void

It is believed that the Sphinx, which is older than the Great Pyramid was constructed before the Flood. It was Dr. Schoch from Boston College who in the 1990s theorized that the weathering of the Sphinx was due to massive overflow of Water. Or in other words, it survived the Flood of Noah. The Great Pyramid is really an Octagon, having 8 Sides as the 4 Faces are bent at the middle. And again, one comes across the Connection to Mars. How so? For example, the Name of Cairo, in one Ancient Interpretation that means 'Mars'.

And using Google Earth, Cairo and the Pyramids also have that Cydonia, Mars Triangulation. The Great Pyramid also incorporates the Phi Ratio and Pi Factors. It also entombs the Speed of Light. See Charts below for a Visual. In one's Research on this Topic, if you superimpose the Great Pyramid with its 3 Main Chambers, that of the King's Chamber, the Queen's Chamber and the 'Pit', over the Temple Mount where YHVH's Temple once stood and will again, they match precisely.

The King's Chamber corresponds to the Holy of Holies where the Ark of the Covenant was placed for the King of Israel, the Creator, etc. Also, interesting is that the Sarcophagus in the King's Chamber match exactly the Dimensions of the Ark of the Covenant with Poles. Then the Queen's Chamber matches the area of the Temple called the Court of the Women. And then the 'Pit' corresponds to the Church of All Nations at the Foot of the Mount of Olives.

If one has ever visited that Church, if one looks to the Ceiling, it is all covered with Stars. Why? One's other hypothesis is that the Great Pyramid's Chambers and the Temple of YHVH correspond to the Creator's Notion of a Universal Correspondence or Axion of sorts, of the 'Sun, Moon and the Stars'. It is a Phrase often used in the Bible and for Prophecy. But consider the King's Chamber and Holy of Holies is the Sun.

156

The Queen's Chamber and the Holies is the Moon. And the Pit or Church of All Nations is the Stars, etc. And…there are Corresponding Colors that accompany the actual Chambers of the Great Pyramid. The King's Chamber has a Gold tint to it. The Queen's Chamber has a Grey tint to it. And the Pit has a White tint to it. So, next time one sees those Chambers, have that in mind.

The other Hypothesis is that the Domes on the Temple Mount also follow the same Color Scheme and Size Ratio to the Sun, Moon and the Stars. These are just glimpses of the amazing Hidden Knowledge that YHVH has shown the World through the Great Pyramid Patterns. It is also believed that the New Jerusalem will have both a Pyramid and Square Dimension to it. Such are the Mysteries of YHVH.

Articles: Great Pyramid Pattern Related

#296: SPEED OF LIGHT - GREAT PYRAMID PATTERN
https://www.postscripts.org/ps-news-296.html

#50: GIZA PYRAMID CLOCK
https://www.postscripts.org/ps-news-50.html

#9: WASHINGTON MALL PYRAMID
https://www.postscripts.org/ps-news-9.html

#283: LAS VEGAS FALSE FLAG - GREAT PYRAMID PATTERN
https://www.postscripts.org/ps-news-283.html

#155: COLUMBIAN CAPITAL - GREAT PYRAMID PATTERN
https://www.postscripts.org/ps-news-155.html

#50: GIZA PYRAMID CLOCK
https://www.postscripts.org/ps-news-50.html

#398: 13 CRYSTAL SKULL ACROSS AMERICA
https://www.postscripts.org/ps-news-398.html

#416: TEMPLE MOUNT - GREAT PYRAMID PATTERN
https://www.postscripts.org/ps-news-416.html

#349: THE CELESTIAL TRINITY
https://www.postscripts.org/ps-news-349.html

Charts

GREAT PYRAMID PATTERNS
https://nebula.wsimg.com/db371b355078f3d4eac28edb7629b1a9?AccessKeyId=D40106E1331C24ABD7C3&disposition=0&alloworigin=1

Videos

Ancient Aliens: Great Pyramid's Shocking Precision (Season 12) | History
https://www.youtube.com/watch?v=dDgr4uvet-g

Speed of Light is the same NUMBER as The Great Pyramid Coordinates
https://www.youtube.com/watch?v=aU_nLVcchFg

LONDON
CYDONIA STAR MAP
GODS OF MAMMON
Countdown to the New Financial World Order

The purpose of this chapter is to consider the City of London and its surroundings in how it is configured to the Cydonia, Mars Triangulation of Structures. Before those 3 Locales are identified, a foundation of what the Cydonia, Mars Triangulation will be presented for context and Prophetic Meaning, in a Biblical sense. The Bible depicts, to some degree, if at least Metaphorically that in Heaven, there are Buildings, a City, a Throne, Gates etc., Such is the obvious case on Earth. Who is to say that in-between Heaven and Earth there are no such things either in the cosmos, in Dimension and Star Gates are used to travers amongst these 3 Heavens? By whom? The Argons of old?

Good and the Fallen Angels that the Bible speaks about? The Bible does speak of 'Rulers' and Princes of the Air'. Then with the latest Rovers to Mars, for example, there is mounting evidence through Images taken that infer possible layouts and unexplainable Objects. Could Celestial Cities be found and inhabited by either 'Good' or 'Fallen Angels' in other Planets, or Star Clusters, like in the Pleiades? This study will specifically be in reference to the now famous Cydonia, Mars Pyramid Complex is also apparently, as a World Capital patterned with its Triangulation.

This Cydonia Triangulation Pattern has been discovered on Mars among the most Prominent Mars Researchers who have authored many Books on the Controversial Topic. But what is unique and novel is that this Researcher has catalogued over 500 Cydonia Triangulation Patterns, all over Earth's Sacred Sites and Modern Capitals. Perhaps this Cydonia Pattern was and/or is a very Prominent Location of Heaven itself or something to that effect. Many have asked since Recorded History if 'Extra-Terrestrials' have visited Earth. The answer is yes, technically based on the definition of the word.

In the Greek, Extra means Outside and Terra means Earth. Thus, the question remains, has anyone come from outside of Earth to Earth? The answer is yes according to the Bible. The Bible emphatically claims that GOD Himself, YHVH, the Angels, Lucifer and the Son of GOD, Jesus have come to Earth from Heaven. Jesus Christ Himself confirmed this to Israel that this was the case in John 1:51.

For example, the Fallen Angels of Genesis 6 were called the Anunnaki. They came to Earth from such places or that were stationed on Star Clusters like the Pleiades. Perhaps the Triangulation is a 'Celestial Signature' from where the Angelic Rebellion of the Fallen Angels that are in a current State of War against YHVH took place. Then there is the account of the Book of Enoch in which the Watchers came down to Mount Hermon, 200 of them led by the Mighty Angel, Azazel. They made a Pack to go into Women for the purpose of Genetically altering the Human Genome of Humanity.

The issue is that these Fallen Beings, perhaps that came from Cydonia, Mars, were and still are in direct connections with certain Human Family Bloodlines. To them, the Forbidden Knowledge and Sacred Dimensions are disclosed. Such specific Pleiadian Patterns on Earth are replicated by those that seek and worship the Fallen Ones. But it is not of YHVH's doing. As an example of those that create such Cydonia, Mars Patterns on Earth, Greater London's Geographic Area will be shown to be patterned after the Pleiadian Cydonia, Mars Pyramid Complex, as well as the entire City.

This Cydonia, Mars Pattern directly reflects and correlates to those that control the Real Power behind such Cities as London and the World's Economy. These are the 'Master of Mammon', the self-proclaimed 'Gods' of London who rule over the Financial Global Power that sits within the City of London, ruled by the Bank of England. It is NOT a Bank and it is NOT of England. To this end, there is a degree of Conspiracy playing-out. The Bible declares that in the Book of Job, the Angels of YHVH assemble before the Throne of Heaven. And so does Lucifer. Thus, Fallen Angels and Lucifer know the Dimensions of Heaven and its layout. Is it like one finds on Mars or Earth's Sacred Sites?

160

LONDON CITY CYDONIA STAR MAP
MARTIAN MOTIF TRIANGULATION PATTERN

Eye of Lucifer

'Spirit of ZION' 'MAMON'

MARTIAN MOTIF CHANNEL

Google Earth

Imagery Date: 5/5/2018   51°30'45.33" N   0°05'53.52" W   elev   0 ft   eye alt 12.59 m

Olympic Stadium
FACE OF ALA-LU
'Allah'

D&M PENTAGON
Royal Observatory

19.47°
Minutes of Arc

333

3.33 Nautical Miles

6.66 Moments

Heron Tower
The Sherkin
The Monument
Cannon Station
Bankof London
Cannon Street
Southwark Cathedral
Hop Exchange

PLEIADES CITY
City of London

Atlas
Pleione
ALCYONE
Merope
Maia
Electra
Celaene
Taygete
Asterope

N MARTIAN MOTIF
CYDONIA, MARS
40°44'33.60N 09°27'40.29W

FACE OF ALA-LU

2.34 km
1.5 miles

11 miles face to face

60° heading

19.47°
Minutes of Arc

333°
heading

D&M
PENTAGON

9.906

11 nautical mile
1260 arc seconds

PLEIADES CITY

161

The Cydonia Pyramid Pattern could very well be one that is mirrored after Heaven itself. Perhaps such Fallen Angels have constructed such Triangulations based on Heavenly one. Then there is an alternate but similar Creation Account from Genesis 1. Before the Creation of Mankind by YHVH. In the Lost Book of Enki, states that Ala-Lu was the King of Nibiru, the Planet of the Crossing. He was banished and ends-up on Earth. He is later exiled to Mars where he builds the Giant Cydonia Pyramid Complex and is commemorated by a Face Mausoleum of his likeness.

This is one ancient explanation for the Mars Cydonia Pyramid Complex Phenomena. This Cydonia Pyramid Complex is Mathematically Sound with Angles and Degrees that match those found all over the Earth, as in Greater London. The Key Clue is the 333° Heading from the Royal Observatory in London that matches that of the same Heading of the Pyramid Complex on Mars. How could it have possibly been known for those Buildings of the Royal Observatory to match those on Mars? Here is the Triangulation.

1) Royal Observatory
This site matches with the D&M Pyramid on Mars. Interestingly, it is from this precise location that the point of longitude is determined for the entire Earth.

2) Olympic Stadium
This site corresponds to the Face of Ala-Lu on Mars. Coincidentally, there is a 'Eye' Pavilion next to the stadium. In essence, the 2012 Olympics paid Homage to the return of the banished Lucifer as the Rising Phoenix or Mercury, the Monas Hieroglyphica that was the Mascot also

3) City of London
Astonishingly, the 'Spirit of Zionism' was the Theme of the Olympics and Motto of all things thus confirming to some degree that it is these Luciferian 'Zionists' who have deliberately designed such Bench-Marks all over London and the world to depict their Cydonia Pattern on Earth, As Above, So Below. And it is through the Financial Markets of the World that they Rule.

God of Mammon

Their God Mercury, is the God of Mammon, Medicine, Media and Thievery gives them all Power to do so. This is a clear example of such Information being funneled to and from 'Secret Societies' by Luciferian Entities that the Bible exposes as Fallen Angels teaching Humanity their Crafts and Satanic Dark Magic Secrets, forbidden by YHVH as divulged in the Book of Enoch.

The Bible in Genesis records the effects of such an increase of Specific Knowledge but does not attribute that directly to the Fallen Ones as the book of Enoch does. Nonetheless, with this Cydonia, Mars Bench-Mark 333° Degree Heading correspondence, there follows an easy line-up to the Triangulation. Then consider the City of London's Coat Of Arms. It is the Boxing Dragon.

It is a Homage to the Beast that is the 'God' of this World', Lucifer that the Bible describes as the Dragon, the Shining Serpent and has given Power, Authority and 'Mammon' to his Minions, to do his will on Earth. It is a Plan against YHVH's purpose. That is to Redeem a Lost Humanity.

The Game Plan of these False 'Zionist' Worshipers of Mercury, logistically is to establish a Central Bank 'Temple' in every Nation so as to control the Money Supply, Charge Interest, Destroy The Middle Class, Bankrupt the Nation on the backs of Working People that are extorted by Unlawful Taxes and Regulations.

As noted, the City of London is an Independent Sovereign City-State. It is not even Subject to the United Kingdom Crown. IT is ruled by the Lord Mayor, not the Queen, etc. The City of London is one of the Financial Capitals of the World, if not the Premier.

Lords of Mammon

All the World Markets are regulated from the Bank of England. In actuality, this 'Bank' is a 'Temple or Pyramid of Mammon' given by the Dragon. The reason why such are called False Zionists is because Jesus Christ exposes them as such. In Revelation 2: 9 it states, 'I know your Afflictions and your Poverty--yet you are Rich! I know about the Slander of those who say they are Jews and are not but are a Synagogue of Satan.' The Bible states that when Lucifer completes his 'Pyramid' or Temple, he will then establish his New World Order.

Lucifer will then install his Anti-Messiah as the Savior of the World. They will set the World on itself Financially as the 7-Year Sabbath Cycles constitute Financial Resets. During the 7-Year Tribulation Period, that of the Last Sabbath Cycle per the Prophet Daniel, the Beasts will command all People on Earth to take their Mark on and in their Bodies. It will be the New Financial Mode Of Currency. Without this Mandatory Opting-In, like a nationalized Medicine, there will be no means of Buying or Selling. Christ Jesus warns and forbids this taking of the Mark because it will condemn People's Souls to Eternal Damnation. Why?

Perhaps the Mark will also be tied into some sort of DNA Transhumanism Manipulation that will render Humans as Non-Humans and thus, Unredeemable by the Blood of the Lamb, Jesus Christ. It is interesting again, that Lucifer, as Mercury the 'God of Mammon' or Money is also the possessor of the Caduceus, the Double Helix Serpent staff that denotes the 'Physician' God Of Medicine. Far from it. The truth is that Lucifer is not the 'Good Physician' in this case.

He seeks to Kill as many Humans as possible. History has proved that through such Institutions as the Banking Systems and Nationalized Medicine, they have caused the Death of Millions and the Slaughter of Innocent People. The following is how a Sovereign Nation is taken over by the Protocols of the Elders of Zion, if one believes they are not a 'Conspiracy'. The Game Plan is the same as one Modern Scholar, Saul Alinsky has simplified it.

166

LONDON CITY PLEIADES STAR MAP

MARTIAN MOTIF TRIANGULATION PATTERN

BANK OF LONDON
FINANCIAL CENTER

PLEIADES STAR CLUSTER
7 DAUGHTERS OF ATLAS

MARTIAN MOTIF
CYDONIA, MARS
40°44'33.60N 09°27'40.29W

FACE OF ALA-LU

D&M PENTAGON

PLEIADES CITY

MARTIAN MOTIF
YOUTUBE CHANNEL

OLYMPIC STADIUM

OBSERVATORY

APPROXIMATE
London Cydonia Motif
PATTERN

THE CITY

Aviva Tower

Lloyds/Willis

(ALCYONE)

THE MONUMENT
Commemorator of
THE GREAT FIRE OF
1-666

Cannon Station

Southwark Cathedral

Hop Exchange

The Shard

Atlas   Pleione

ALCYONE

Merope   Maia

Elextra   Celaene   Taygete

Astelope

Electra

Google Earth

These methods have been used by the Cadre behind the Dictators of the Fascist and Socialist types of AntiChrists that have Ruled throughout Human History.

1. Have the State control the Masses through a Mandated Nationalized Healthcare System.

2. Increase those living in Poverty so such are Powerless but to Depend on the State.

3. Increase Taxes to the point that the National and Personal Debt is Un-Payable and subject to Foreign Oversight as National Sovereign Constitutions and Laws are Superseded.

4. Confiscate all forms of Private Firearms and Militarize the Police to enforce the State's Laws.

5. Have the State control all Means of Production and Distribution as it Pertains to Food, Housing And Labor.

6. Have the State control the Content of Education and Outlaw any Alternative Forms of Education, such as Private, Religious or Home-Schooling.

7. Have the State ban Christianity from Public and Private Observances, i.e., Prayer, Freedom Of Assembly and Worship.

8) Create a Diversion from the Real Issues by using such means as Racism and Classism to Divide and Conquer the Masses.

The Money Changers that Rule the World with their Temples of Mammon or Ill-Gotten 'Gain' of Stolen Monetary Wealth has been obtained by Greed. They Perpetrate Wars, Murder, Slavery, Extortion and Sorcery in the guise of 'illumination' but are steeped in their Allegiance to Lucifer who is the God of this World, the Ala-Lu of Mars, etc. It is Lucifer that bestows these Temporal Kingdoms on Earth, to those we wills, while he can. This 'Pyramid Scheme' will cease once Jesus returns to establish His Kingdom. The Bible declares Jesus' victory of Lucifer as Lucifer is now in a Banished State But he is still in Strife against Jesus Christ and His Church on Earth.

Some Observations

The Bible states that Jesus defeated Lucifer on the Cross and by Jesus' Resurrection, has sealed Satan's Doom. Until Christ's return, Lucifer has built his kingdom on such 'Pyramid' Sacred Geometry and as with the Cydonia, Mars Triangulation. The Luciferian Globalists think they will Rule alongside Lucifer in their Restored 'Golden Age'. To this end, they await their coming 'Anointed One' also. They are waiting for their false Messiah or AntiChrist. To this end and 'Great Work, a Temple in Jerusalem will be built for him. That 3rd Temple is really the epitome of the Great Pyramid and Masonic Seal Motif. And to that end, these Cydonia, Mars Patterns are found in all the major Luciferian World Capitals like Astana, Canberra, Washington DC, the Vatican, etc.

This Triangulation in Sacred Gematria forms a Star Gate, 3-Dimensionally. These World Capitals are but Entry Points in the Fabric of Piercing Dimensions. They are the Centers of Total Power, even Cosmic Power that is harnessed and activated by such a Triangulation. In the bigger Scope of things, such Sites are then divided-up between Political, Religious and Monetary oversight of all the Nations and Peoples on Earth, for the time being. The following is a direct comparison between the Cydonia Mars Pyramid complexes with that of the Bank of England-Observatory-Olympic Stadium Cydonia, Mars layout. Both have the following attributes.

1) Pleiades City = 7 City Bank Skyscraper Financial District.
2) Face of Ala-Lu = Olympic Stadium 'Allah' or Eye of Lucifer.
3) Royal Observatory = D&M Pyramid.

***333°** Heading*

19.47°*Minutes of Arc The Pyramid atop building at 1 Canada Square is at a 333° heading and at 51 degrees 30 m **17.76"**N*

From D&M Pyramid to the Face of Mars is 12 Miles at a 188 Degree Heading. The Face of Mars is 1.24 Km wide and 1.5 Miles in length. From the D&M Pyramid to the Pyramid Pleiadian City is 11 Nautical Miles 1ith 1260 Arc-Seconds.

Bank Count-Down Pyramid

The D&M Pyramid itself is 6,606 Yards or (6-6-6). And it is 6 Kilometers in approximate length. The length of the Pyramid City is .66 Nautical Miles or 7.67 Miles Ground Length or 12.34 Kilometers. From the Pyramid City to the Face is 13 Miles at a 60 Degree Heading.

The Money Changers, Masters of the Mammon have encoded their Great Plan of when their Pleiadian Fallen Angel Lucifer will initiate his New Age or World Order. Their Mammon Temple, the Bank of England is situated in such a way that through Sacred Geometry, it configures the Luciferian Masonic Temple. The Chart following this study will show the City of London's Financial Center, rotated 188 Degrees from North for a 'Pyramid' Perspective.

This 'Bank' Temple is at the Heart of the 'Molech' Owl-Bat Configuration in the City that is Private and not part of England. The All-Seeing Eye of Ra, or Horus, Orion is at the apex of the Bank building with a 7 Street Intersection. This Intersection 'Star' corresponds to the 7 Heavenly Bodies the Esoteric and Secret Societies use for their 'Great Work' Sorcery. Based on an encoded Latitude-Coordinate To-Year Theory, there is a direct association to the Bank Building being a 'Pyramid Countdown Clock' to the New World Economic Reset.

This theory came about originally from the inspiration of the Late Researcher David Flynn who discovered, through Google Earth, that certain Distances correlate to Dates from the Equator and Paris-London Meridians. This Researcher took it a step further to assert that the very Degrees of Longitude also could correspond to years, given a fixed location, etc. If thus an assertion is valid, then the Financial Collapse will occur sometime in late 2022 that will usher in their New 'Phoenix' 7-Year Economic Cycle. Biblically Speaking, this next coming 7-Year Financial Cycle will be none other than Daniel's 7th Week of Year.

170

LONDON BANK GREAT PYRAMID
LUCIFERIAN MASTERS OF MAMMON COUNTDOWN

Latitude-Year Theory
0°05' 20.22'W
0°05' 20.15'W
0°05' 20.08'W
0°05' 20.01'W
0°05' 19.94'W
0°05' 19.87'W
0°05' 19.80'W
0°05' 19.73'W
0°05' 19.66'W
0°05' 19.59'W
0°05' 17.76'W

New World Order

2022
2015

2008
2001

1994
1987
1980

1973
1966
1959

LUCIFER'S
Right eye blinded in
Angelic Conflict

'MASONS'

New World Order

Eye of Horus
(7 Heavenly Bodies)

GoogleEarth

7 1
6 2
5 3
4

90°

1948
1936

1911

1805

Temple of Mammon

1776

'Bless Our Work'

45°

Imagery Date: 4/0/2020   51°30'48.6''N   0°05'20.22''W elev   0 ft   eye alt 1552 ft

(Work Done)
NORTH-WEST ANGLE
90°
2015 to 2022

BANK OF ENGLAND

Bank of England
It's NOT a Bank
and it's NOT
of England

CITY OF LONDON

'Domine Nos-Dirige'
'Master Direct Us'

PATRON GOD OF FINANCIAL GAIN
MERCURY
LUCIFER

The corner of the Bank of England is called the North-West Angle. This study suggests that this particular building is acting as the Fulcrum of the City Financial Layout and corresponds to the Apex of the Pyramid Temple and termination of the Count-Down Time of the year 2015. What this means is that the remaining distance from that point at the Bank of England's southern point equates to 2022, a 7-Year Interval, etc.

It is at a 90 Degree Angle, but the Biblical Question, is if that correlates to the 'End' of the Financial Endeavor of Lucifer and his False 'Zionist' Minions. The Base of the Pyramid starts at the Northern Face that nearly approximates the 17.76 Latitude of the famous and well recognized Masonic Luciferian Unfinished Pyramid. It is an 'Enterprise' or Work that is to take 13 Steps or Segments of Time, with 1776 as the base year. Note that the Crest of the City of London has a Motto. It says, *'Domine Dirige Nos'*. It is Latin for, 'Master Direct Us', as in Lucifer, in one's Assessment, etc. The following is the breakdown of the Year-To-Latitude Correspondence.

0°05' 20.22"W – Top of Ground Extension
0°05' 20.15"W – Top and End of Building Corner (Southern Point)

2) 0°05' 20.08"W
3) 0°05' 20.01"W

4) 0°05' 19.94"W
5) 0°05' 19.87"W
6) 0°05' 19.80"W

7) 0°05' 19.73"W
8) 0°05' 19.66"W
9) 0°05' 19.59"W

19) 0°05' 17.76"W – Bottom and Start (Northern Face)

What does this mean? If 2015 is a milestone in its countdown, it could be the case that then, a last Sabbatical Cycle remains until their 'God of Mammon', a.k.a., the AntiChrist as the proxy of Lucifer comes calling. It would be a 7-Year Period that many
172

Bible scholars suggest could be Daniel's 70th Week of Years, etc. Time will tell. Is this a Temple and patterned after a Pyramid. It is about a 'Bank' that rules the World Economies that is tied to the Shemitah 'Law of Return'. Will the New Luciferian Monetary System commence, based on the law of 7-Year Debt Cycle? That year would then be 2022, thereabouts.

*2015 + 7 = **2022***

The Encrypted Pattern of the City of London Pyramid came to light in part, after the Fall Feast of Rosh HaShanah-Sukkot 2015 that sent shockwaves across the Financial World. Will this time be the Concluding Stage in the Worldwide Economic Reset to come?

Does this Bank Building in the Heart of the City of London encrypt this Sacred Geometry based on Latitudes that signify when the Luciferians will usher in the beginning of the Financial and Medical Mark of the Beast System? Even so, 'YHVH Dirige Nos', as those that have patterned the City of London after the Cydonia, Mars Pyramid Complex are one in the same in terms of who is behind the Power of the Invisible Hands, the Gods of Mammon.

Main Sources
CityofLondon.gov.uk
Earth.Google.com
Wekipedia.com

ISRAEL'S STRIKE ON IRAN
INEVITABLE NUCLEAR CONFRONTATION
And the Middle East Arms-Race

'Peace for us means the Destruction of Israel. We are preparing for an All-Out War, a War which will last for Generations.' -Yasser Arafat

The purpose of this chapter is to show that certain Times related to the particular Phases of the Moon have influenced Israeli and Muslim Military Strikes in the Middle East. In particular, precise Moon Phases have correlated to a Direct Timing as to when Israel struck her Muslim Enemy's Nuclear Facilities in the past. If the Pattern is Reliable, then one can approximate when Israel is likewise to have some sort of Strike on Iran's Nuclear Facilities. The Premise is that it could take place in like manner, given the Pattern of the Moon Phases in which Israel has stuck in the past. There will be several points and examples from prior Military Campaigns presented that can lend Clues, as to the possible Timing of the next strike by Israel, which could be based on the Phi Ratio Theory. Nonetheless, this study strongly suggests that Israel's Strike on Iran's Nuclear Sites will most likely lead to the coming Jewish-Muslim War of Psalm 83. In fact, it has already started.

This War will be 1) Regional 2) Religious and 3) Nuclear by some estimates and evidence presented in this segment of the study. The information presented will only emphasize patterns and probabilities. According to the Bible, the Israeli-Arab, Age-Old Conflict will come to a Head at Armageddon. The Stages have now been set for an all-out Regional War that will inevitably involve the exchange and/or a detonation of a Nuclear Device as described in the Gog-Magog War of Ezekiel. It is one thing for a Nation to aspire to have Nuclear Energy as a means of an Alternative Source but what Israel rightly fears is that the Nuclear Capability of its Muslim Enemies' Weapons of Mass Destruction will be used on Israel.

ISRAELI NUCLEAR MOON STRIKES

A NUCLEAR CONFRONTATION IN THE MIDDLE EAST NUCLEAR ARMS RACE

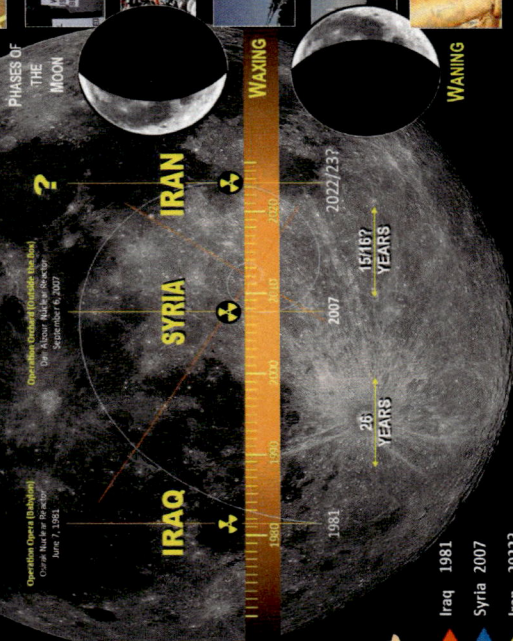

PHASES OF THE MOON

⊕ RATIO PATTERN OF TIME
Israel's Strike on Iran could possibly be based on the Approximate Mathematical Relationship Between the 1st and 2nd Israeli Strike on Iraq and Syria's Nuclear Reactors

Operation Opera (Babylon)
Osirak Nuclear Reactor
June 7, 1981

Dier Al-zour Nuclear Reactor
September 6, 2007

WAXING

WANING

IRAQ — SYRIA — IRAN — ?

1981

2007

2022/23?

26 YEARS

15/16? YEARS

Iraq 1981
Syria 2007
Iran 2022?

MOON PHASES DURING ISRAELI NUCLEAR REACTOR STRIKES

IRAQ — JUN 7 — Waxing — STRIKE

SYRIA — SEP 6 — Waning — STRIKE

IRAN — MONTH? — Waxing / Waning ? — STRIKE ?

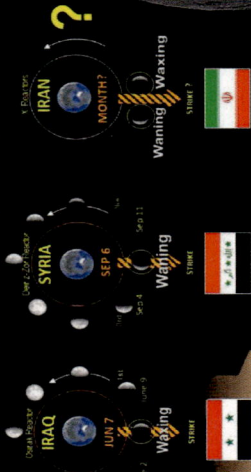

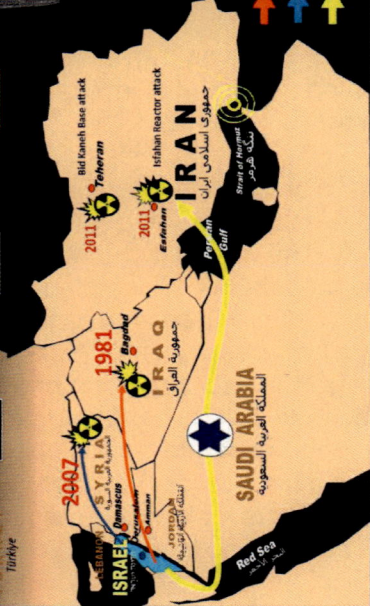

A Religious War

Moreover, having a supposed Civilized Nation such as Iran, boasts that once it will have such a Nuclear Capability, it will not hesitate to Eradicate Israel 'Off the Map' is concerning. It is no Secret that the aim of the Muslims is to Destroy Israel. What raises the Stakes is that the Nuclear Persian Army has put Israel on notice that they will use them to Destroy Israel. Why? It is because of the mere Existence of Israel as their worldview is fused into their religion, Islam. As Iran races to complete enough uranium to arm one of their Missiles with a Nuclear Warhead, their clear Aim has not been to produce Nuclear Energy to power their Nation. The Israeli-Arab Conflict can better be Assessed and Explained as a 'Religious' War. At the core of the Israeli-Arab Conflict is the Religious Question and Theological Interpretation of who has the 'Birthright?'

Jacob or Esau? Isaac or Ishmael? Who is viewed as the Agents of evil and good on Earth. This Jewish-Muslim Conflict between these is only a means to an end in the bigger scheme of things to come Prophetically. This struggle for the Birthright has occurred since the Twins were in the Womb of Rebecca. One has gone the way of Cain and the other, the way of Abel. For Israel, it is the Struggle is for the very Heart and Soul of the Jew. It is for which 'Christ' or Messiah will be accepted, Jesus or someone else? These 2 camps within Judaism have struggled against each other for dominance and the Birthright. Jesus scolded and admonished the Religious Leaders of His. They had total control of the 'Religion and Traditions of Men'. Jesus told them that they had to choose between 2 'Fathers', and 2 Christs.

It was either Abba Father, or Lucifer. They had to choose between Jesus, as the Anointed Christ or Lucifer as the 'Anointed Cherub Christ'. This battle is still raging on. Those that controlled the Jewish Religion then, control the Religion now. In fact, Jesus foretold a Day when Israel would rather accept 'Him who comes in his own Name', but not the SON of GOD that was sent to Redeem them. According to the Bible, it was Esau who despised his Birthright and Sold it to Jacob. Out of Spite, Esau then married Canaanite Wives and has opposed Jacob's Descendants ever since.

Esau's Descendants became the Edomite, Moabites, the Palestinians, etc. Such came to oppose the Hebrews from having access through the Wilderness when Moses was leading them to the Promised Land. They stood to Curse the Israelites by hiring Balaam. Another Descendant of Esau, was Haman would later conspired to Eradicate all of the Jews of the Persian Empire during the time of Esther and Mordecai in Susa. Such has been the case also with the Nazi Regime as the highest offices of the Party were Jewish, descendants of Esau that perpetrated the 'Final Solution' against the Jews; to murder every one of them off the Face of not only Europe, but the World if they had their Satanic Way.

This coming War between the Jews and the Muslims will only be a process to yet another Stage. There is another Level of Consolidation of Power for the Luciferian Agents that are in Control of this present Evil World. The ultimate Showdown will be between the 2 Christs, technically that of Jesus Christ and the Anointed Cherub, Lucifer at the Battle of Armageddon.

According to the Bible, it is really a no Contest. Jesus Christ, is the True and Only Christ. Jesus, the Anointed One will destroy the Armies of the AntiChrist at Armageddon by His mere Presence and Splendor of this Word that formed Creation out of Nothing. Since 1948, the Modern and Sovereign State of Israel has had to fight for its Survival. It has also been a Victim of a Surprise Strike on the Jewish Holiest Day –Yom Kippur in 1973. To have Israel 'Exist' or even Co-Exist is Anathema to the Radical Islamist. Why?

Because to have Israel 're-birthed' after the so called 'Last Revelation Of God' from a False Prophet Mohammed invalidates the Quran and Islamic Religion. Why? It is because YHWH is not done with Israel and in fact thus YHVH will honor His Word to preserve the Birthright given to Jacob and his Descendants, not to Esau's whom now most are Muslim by Religion and Arab by Race. As to the End Game Plan of the Luciferians against Israel? The Radical Muslims have been allowed to take over country by country to insure an Encirclement of Israel and go in for the Kill - at some Appropriate Time with Subsequent Invasions of Israel by the Muslims.

178

1) The Inner-Ring of Muslim countries
Speculated to by the Psalm 83 War.

2) The Outer-Ring of Muslim Nations
Led by Russia speculated to be the Gog-Magog War.

3) The Battle of Armageddon
As the Nations of the World encircle Jerusalem.

It has been estimated that Israel has anywhere between 200-400 Thermonuclear Weapons in its Nuclear Arsenal. These can be launched from Land, Sea and Air. This gives Israel a 2nd Strike Option with its Submarines in Deep Water, even if much of the country is destroyed. This is called the Samson Option. This Samson Option is a Term used to describe Israel's alleged Deterrence Strategy and Capability.

It is a Doctrine of Massive Retaliation with Nuclear Weapons as a 'Last Resort' against Nations who Military attacks or threatens Israel's Existence. Much like Mutual Assured Destruction (MAD) with the US vs. USSR during the Cold War, Israel would exercise this Option, if Israel would be seen as about to be destroyed by its Muslim Enemies. The Samson Option is taken from the Biblical Story of Judges 13. Samson brings down the Enemy Philistine Temple by pushing the supporting 2 Pillars apart so that he was tied to them to be shown as a Spectacle. He not only killed all the Philistines in it, but also himself by this act. He 'Brought the House Down'.

It should be noted that Israel is not part of the international Body of Nations that are accountable to the UN's Nuclear Watch-Dog Group. Nor is Israel part of the Non-Proliferation Treaty that promises Peaceful Purposes of its Nuclear Energy Program; mind you neither is Pakistan for that matter. At the core of this Religious Conflict between the Descendants of Jacob and Esau, Isaac and Ishmael is whether Israel has the Biblical Legal Claim and Right to the Land. There are numerous Biblical Covenants made to Jacob and Isaac by YHVH regarding the Abrahamic Covenant. There are other Prophecies that state that Israel in the Last Days would be re-gathered to their former Borders.

Samson Option.
One can also observe that the Nations that also existed then in Ancient Times surrounding Israel, also now exist as well. It was not until World War 2 that all these Arab-Persian nations came out of 'Mandates' as did Israel....Syria; Lebanon from the French, Egypt, Iraq and Jordan from the British, etc. Israel thereafter was to be sanctioned a State by a UN Partition Plan that coincidentally the Palestinians rejected and declared War on Israel instead.

The entire Nation of Jordan was to have been the Palestinian Portion of the Partition Plan but the British double-crossed the UN and the Jews by establishing a Hashemite Kingdom instead. How the Nations and the UN are once again seeking to Divide the Portion set aside for the Jews that included Judah and Samaria, the ancient Kingdoms of Israel to carve out a State for the Arabs called Palestine.

'The Palestinian People does not exist. The creation of a Palestinian State is only a means for continuing our Struggle against the State of Israel. For our Arab Unity. In reality, today there is no difference between Jordanians, Palestinians, Syrians and Lebanese. Only for Political and Tactical Reasons do we speak today about the existence of Palestinian People, since Arab National Interest demand that we posit the existence of a distinct 'Palestinian People' to oppose Zionism'. -Zahir Muhse'in

In the Eschatological View of Islam, Israel has to be Subjected and eventually Destroyed to give Islam sustained Credibility and Legitimacy. The mere fact that the Hebrew Nation was reborn in 1948 and survived a 7-Arab Army Onslaught is a direct Assault and Affront to the Tenets of Islam.

If Israel is to be the 'Head of the Nations' once more, in the not too distant Future, then it is to say that Islam is not the true Successor of YHVH's Revelation but an Imposter and Usurper Religion that denies the Person and Redemptive Work of the true Messiah, Jesus Christ. But so do the Ruling Religious Jews of Israel presently. According to Mohammed and the Quran, Christianity but more urgently, Judaism has to be Destroyed.

Right to the Land

This is according to its Teachings because it is tied to YHVH's Promise of the Land and its 'Title Deed'. In Shi'ite Theology, Israel cannot be allowed to Exist indefinitely because it would mean the following if the Nation of Israel is to exist.

1) It validates the Hebrew Bible and would negate Allah.
2) It would mean that the Jews do have the Right to the Land.
3) The Palestinian Covenant pertains to Isaac, Jacob, David.
4) Islam is not the Religion of Peace and Tolerance.
5) Mohammed is not a 'Prophet' of YHVH nor the Last.
6) Mohammed, is in fact a False Prophet.
7) Islam is just another Anti-Christ False Religion.

The Notion that Islam and Judaism stem from the same 'God' is Foolish Logic and a wrong Interpretation. Allah is never mentioned in the Bible nor is Jerusalem in the Quran for that matter. No Muslim will ever Call Allah, 'YHVH'. The Islamic Belief-System only pays Lip Service to Abraham, the Prophets, King David, and even Jesus Christ etc. In essence, the Core Belief is that Islam is the successor of not only Judaism, but Christianity; the final Revelation and Authority from 'God.'

In fact, Islam is the only 'Religion' that is designed to Negate the claims of Christianity, of Jesus Christ precisely. In Islam, Jews but especially Christians are viewed as 'Heretics' and their Scriptures, the Bible as being corrupted. Currently any Convert from Islam to Judaism or Christianity is under Penalty of Death despite the claims of the Tolerant and Merciful Islamic creeds, hell-bent on Religious Dominance. Based on 1 John 4:3, Islam denies the Deity of Jesus Christ, and that He did not Physically Die on the Cross of Calvary.

This in effect, nullifies the Saving Work of the Anointed One sent by the Creator YHVH as the only means of Salvation from Humanity's Sins. In essence, Islam is a Religion that is Systematically Anti-Christ, opposing the very Gospel of the Kingdom, the Promise of the LORD and the Work of the Cross. Islam rejects Jesus Christ and awaits their own Messiah, the Mahdi. The Quran cannot accept that YHVH of the Bible is not done with Israel. No Muslim will ever say 'YHVH' is Great!'

They despise that the Promise of the Land was given to them. The Land was given by YHVH to Abraham's Descendant through Isaac and Jacob. And that one-day, 1 of their Descendants, Jesus Christ of the Tribe of Judah, will rule the World. This makes no room for Islam in the scheme of YHVH's Timetable and Millennial Kingdom that is to be set-up by Jesus Christ at the end of the Battle of Armageddon. As to the Moon Phase Theory on when Military Strikes occurred with Israel and their Enemies.

- In the Yom Kippur War of 1973, the Arabs used the Moon Phases to strategically attack Israel by Air.

- In 1981, Israel destroyed Nuclear Facilities in Iraq and Syria in 2007 during specific Moon Phases.

- Israel struck the 2 Enemy Nuclear Facilities, either on a Waxing or Waning Moon Phase.

- Thus, the Next possible 'Strike Zone' Window could be in some future Waning/Waxing Moon Phase.

Waxing Gibbous Moon Phase Strikes

1) YOM KIPPUR WAR-October 6, 1973
Occurred during a Waxing Gibbous Moon Phase.
This War is known as the 1973 Arab-Israeli War and the 4th Arab-Israeli War. It was fought between Israel and a Coalition of Arab states led by Egypt and Syria. The war Began with a joint surprise attack on Israel's Holiest Day.

2) IRAQ WAR -2 August 2, 1990:
On a Waxing Gibbous Moon Phase and Ended on Purim.
It is commonly referred to as the Gulf War I. The War was undertaken by a U.N. Authorized Coalition Force of 34 Nations led by the United States against Iraq in response to Iraq's Invasion and Annexation of Kuwait.

3) IRAQ INVASION - March 19, 2003
On a Waxing Gibbous Moon Phase and Began on Purim.
It is commonly referred to as the Gulf War II. It was also known as Operation Iraqi Freedom. A Combined Force of Nations were led by the US, who sought to rid Iraq of Weapons of Mass Destruction and execute a 'Regime Change'.
182

Waxing Crescent Moon Phase Strikes

1) IRAQ: Osirak Nuclear Reactor-June 7, 1981
Occurred during a Waxing Crescent Moon Phase.- Operation Opera or Babylon

Israeli War Planes bombed and destroyed Iraq's Osirak Nuclear Research Facility near Baghdad. At that time, Prime Minister Menachem Begin claimed the Reactor was about to go into operation and was a threat to Israel because it could produce Nuclear Weapons. There was considerable Circumstantial Evidence that Iraq was indeed developing a Nuclear Weapon. Interestingly, now the Israeli Prime Minister, like Menachem Begin then, faces the same dilemma with Iran.

2) SYRIA: Operation Orchard- September 6, 2007
Occurred during a Waning Crescent Moon Phase. – Operation Orchard or Outside the Box

Israeli War Planes bombed and destroyed a Nuclear Reactor in the Deir ez-Zor Region of Syria. The site was a Nuclear Facility with a Military Purpose. An International Atomic Energy Agency (IAEA) investigation did report evidence of Uranium and concluded that the site featured an Undeclared Nuclear Reactor. According to some Reports, a Team of elite Israeli Shaldag Special-Forces had arrived at the site the day before to aid in targeting. This Imminent War Scenario is exactly how Current Events are playing-out with the Explosions at various Iranian Nuclear Facilities and/or Military Missile Bases.

Current MOSSAD Covert Operations

1) Bid Kaneh -November 12, 2011

An Explosion hit an Iranian Military Base near the town of Bid Kaneh outside Teheran, killing 17 Members of the Iranian Revolutionary Guard Corps and Maj.-Gen. Hassan Moghaddam, Chief Architect of the Islamic Republic's Ballistic Missile Program. Israel's MOSSAD is accused of orchestrating the Blast.

An Explosion hit Isfahan, home to several Nuclear-Related Sites. It is said to be mostly a Uranium Conversion Facility. It is claimed that this Facility was severely damaged. The Incident took place 2.5 weeks after an Explosion at an Islamic Revolutionary Guard facility Bid Kaneh. It is believed that MOSSAD was involved.

The following is a Comparative Narrative of the Armed Forces of Israel and Iran. The argument or Narrative is that Iran has gotten to the point that it has Enriched the Uranium needed to Nuclearize its Weapons, it has also mastered and ICBM Intercontinental Ballistic Missile System that is able to deliver a Nuclear Warhead not only to Israel, but now to Mecca and Europe.

Army of the Guardians of the Islamic Revolution

سپاه پاسداران انقلاب اسلامی

It is often called the Revolutionary Guards. It is a Branch of Iran's Military, founded after the Iranian Revolution that ousted the U.S. backed Shah of Iran. The Revolutionary Guard is charged with protecting Iran's Shi'ite Islamic System.

Israel Defense Forces (IDF)

צְבָא הַהֲגָנָה לְיִשְׂרָאֵל

It is commonly known in Israel by the Hebrew Acronym, Tzahal (צה"ל). It comprises all the Military Forces Of the State of Israel. They consist of the Army, Air Force and Navy. It is the sole Military Wing of the Israeli Security Forces and has no Civilian Jurisdiction within Israel.

In particular, precise Moon Phases have given the direct Timing as to when Israel struck at their Enemy's Nuclear Facilities in the past. And so have its Enemies. As noted, the Yom Kippur War in 1973 began when the Muslim Coalition launched a Joint Surprise Attack against Israel. The Code-Named for the operation was called Badr (Arabic for 'Full Moon). Thus, the point is that by using Moon Phases, it can be determined, to some extent, how effective the Israeli Air Force will be in striking Targets due to Visibility, Lighting etc.

Moon Struck

If the Pattern is Reliable, then one can conclude that an imminent Air Strike by Israel is soon to take place in like manner with Iran. In fact, Covert Ground Strikes have already occurred. Israel and Iran are in fact in a De-Facto Cold War. Israel has acknowledged it had something to do with the Covert Sabotage of the Explosions at the Missile Testing Sites of the Revolutionary Guard Base, outside Teheran and the Isfahan Nuclear Reactor.

This Theory of considering the various Moon Phases to determine a 'Window or 'Strike Zone' does not mean it has to happen but that there is a High Probability that it could or in some future date it could happen. If so, such a Strike will likewise be dependent on a Waxing or Waning Moon Phase regardless of Season and/or Visibility Conditions. With the latest Technologies of Radar, like the Synthetic Aperture Radar (SAR), Targets can be identified and taken out in any Weather Condition, Day or Night. These Moon Phase Strike Patterns by Israel are also suggested to have followed a Phi Ratio pattern of Time. Meaning?

If the 1981 and 2007 Strikes are subject to the Phi Ratio Stipulation, then the Full-On Strike on Iran will occur in 2022/23. It is precisely correlated with the prior Strikes on Iraq in 1981 and with Syria in 2007. What will likely be more probable is that the next level of an Israeli Strike will be more Precise and most likely be Nuclear because the Covert Operations have not really deterred nor stopped Iran's Militarization of its Nuclear Program. If Israel is to strike Iran's Nuclear/Military Missile Sites and based on its prior Strike Phi Ratio Pattern, the Strike will occur either on a Waxing or Waning Moon Phase, as that would be the Opportune Time.

Main Sources
CIFWatch.com
Guardian.co.uk
MissingPeace.com
UPI.com
Ynetnews.com

Article

Prince of Persia
https://www.postscripts.org/ps-news-41.html

Video

Operation Opera - Israel's Raid on the Iraqi Reactor 1981
Mike Guardia
https://www.youtube.com/watch?v=MFObTJxFuWI

Iran Resource Page
https://www.postscripts.org/iran.html

CHART: Iran Nuking Israel NukeMap Scenario
https://nebula.wsimg.com/10f1ff8b0da994674fcb91e8b046c714?AccessKeyId=D40106E1331C24ABD7C3&disposition=0&alloworigin=1

CHART: USA Nuking Iran NukeMap Scenario
https://nebula.wsimg.com/e3aaeb28665a44af5ab8a9e19d1db52b?AccessKeyId=D40106E1331C24ABD7C3&disposition=0&alloworigin=1

ISRAELI STRIKE FACTORS
THIS TIME IS DIFFERENT
Factors that will Play-In the Rapture Scenario

The purpose of this chapter is to consider the Israeli Pending Strike on Iran's Nuclear Reactor Sites. With the June 7 , 2022 41st Anniversary of Israel taking out the Iraqi Nuclear Reactor, one remembers having done an Observation about it along with the subsequent Strike from Israel, again on the Syrian Nuclear Reactor in 2007. One looked at the Timing and considered what was similar and why those specific Days. The reason why this has now become pertinent is that the Iran Deal with the UN and Key Nations have allowed Iran to continue with their Enrichment Program to procure enough Uranium to make several Nuclear Weapons.

And it has come to light that the Iranian Military Higher-Ups had been caught recording in saying that their objective, all along for their Nuclear Energy Program was to obtain Nuclear Weapons to be used to Destroy Israel. As to the original Study of the Israeli Strikes on the Nuclear Reactors in Iraq and Syria? One came to see a possible Moon Phase Correlation, in how certain Days of Attack are determined by the Phases of the Moon.

That was one hypothesis to test. The Article will follow this synopsis at the end for review. Then the other Hypothesis was that if one applied the Phi Ratio Theory of Time to these 2 Dates, 1981 and 2007, one could Mathematically Triangulate the 3rd.Meaning, one could then approximate when Israel would Strike at Iran's Nuclear Sites. And the Year would be? 2022-23. See Timeline in Chart Illustration. The original Article was posted to the Five Doves website back in 2011. It was actually the Year Israel did plan to Strike Iran, but it was not allowed by Obama.

But also, logistically, Israel was not quite there yet. Now it is different. In what way? Israel procured the New F-35's and modified them to not need them to be refueled in Mid-Mission. And that has been in the News as of this write-up. This is a Game Changer and it is on…Iran knows now that the Israeli Strike is inevitable. It is probably going to happen sometime, sooner rather than later1. Any delay would just have Iran prepare all the more. It is not that Israel has not Struck Iran's Nuclear Facilities in the Past.

State of the Art, Israeli IAF F-35s is a Game Changer. PxHere.

It has to a large degree but has been unsuccessful. What is also different, in Iran's case is that it is not just 1 Nuclear Reactor, like Iraq and Syria had. Iran has several Sites. So, this time around the F-35, which are Stealth, will be able to go through, undetected and do all those Multiple Strikes from the Air. And Israel has those New Supersonic Type Missiles, like the one they used in Beirut. Or like others have investigated and believe a Missile of this type was detonated in Tonga. This could be a Scenario of the proverbial 'Calm before the Storm'. But if it be the case, then it would be another Prophetic Piece of the Puzzle in seeing the Scenario play out. How So?

One has held that what Sparks the next Major Middle East War amongst the various Muslim Factions and Israel is the Destruction of Damascus. That in turn would unleash all those Para-Military Factions, like Hezbollah, Hamas, Jihad, etc., to attack Israel on all Fronts.

That is why Israel prepared with Operation Chariots of Fire, in that it was an all-inclusive Military Branch Drill that simulated simultaneous Attacks upon Israel. But the Strike on Iran could be the Spark and then the Attack ensues against Israel, which in that case, Israel then Nukes Damascus, etc. Then this will ensue the AntiChrist come on the Scene to deliver that 7-Year Peace Accord and allow the Jews to Build the 3rd Temple.

All this to say, that intertwined with all this is the Rapture Window, as many have had Visions and Dreams of how the Rapture Event will be tied to some Catastrophic War-Type of event going on at the same Time. And it is Scriptural of how the 'Escape' is worded in such a term of a 'Sudden Destruction'.

So, it is to be determined but as the Days, Weeks and Months pass, the End Times Scenario is becoming Sharper and Clearer to discern. Israel has not spent all this Time and Energy just for a mere 'Rehearsal'. No, one suspects it is for the Real Deal that is about to occur, a Strike on Iran, based on the Moon Phases and Phi Ratio approximation of a 3rd Triangulated Point in Time, based on 2 prior Israeli Strikes on Nuclear Reactors.

#18: ISRAEL STRIKE ON IRAN
https://www.postscripts.org/ps-news-18.html

Article

Prince of Persia
https://www.postscripts.org/ps-news-41.html

Operation Opera - Israel's Raid on the Iraqi Reactor 1981
Mike Guardia
https://www.youtube.com/watch?v=MFObTJxFuWl

Iran Resource Page
https://www.postscripts.org/iran.html

CHART: Iran Nuking Israel NukeMap Scenario
https://nebula.wsimg.com/10f1ff8b0da994674fcb91e8b046c714?AccessKeyId=D40106E1331C24ABD7C3&disposition=0&alloworigin=1

CHART: USA Nuking Iran NukeMap Scenario
https://nebula.wsimg.com/e3aaeb28665a44af5ab8a9e19d1db52b?AccessKeyId=D40106E1331C24ABD7C3&disposition=0&alloworigin=1

7 REASONS WHY ISRAEL WILL GO TO WAR WITH 6 ENCIRCLED MUSLIM ENEMIES THIS SUMMER

An Astronomical Survey of the Summer Solstice Orion Circle at the Silver Gate

'When the Waters become hard as Stone and the Surface of the Deep is Frozen? Can you bind the Chains of the Pleiades or loosen the Belt of Orion? Can you bring forth the Constellations in their Seasons or lead out the Bear and her Cubs?'
-Job 38:30-32

The purpose of this chapter is to consider the Orion Circle that is Astronomically encircling the Silver Gate of the Cosmos, with Orion as its Central Character. At this 'Door' or Star Gate is the Celestial Guardian, Orion. He comprises the Celestial Motif, having 7 Stars and depicted with the Torch of Fire, of Illumination and Freedom. It is what many Statues around the world are patterned after, primarily that of Libertas having the 7 Rays of Light protruding from the Head as seen in the U.S. Statue of Liberty.

What one likes to compare is how this Orion Circle will have the 'Torch Effect', caused by the Sun as it lights-up Orion's Torch on the Summer Solstice, that being on every June 20-21.Why this is or could be Geo-Politically Significant is that it is where and when the Sun is at, at the Silver Gate, that it is where and when one should be taking note of. The event could be a Sign that is being emphasized. Thus, the Watchers of the End Times could ascertain possible Prophetic Innuendos because of the Sun's position, Astronomically in the Orion Circle.

ORION WINTER CIRCLE

PORTALS OF HEAVEN - COSMIC 'STAR GATE' PROPHETIC SIGNIFICANCE

At Silver Gate on Summer Solstice

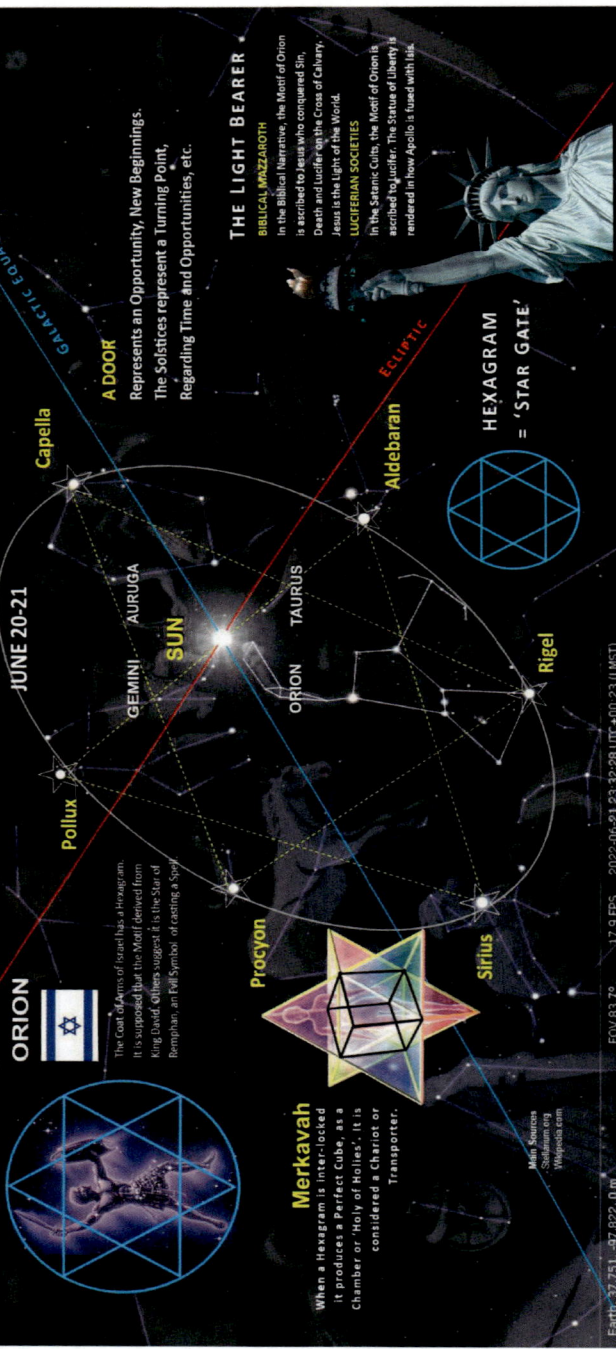

GALACTIC EQUATOR

JUNE 20-21

Capella

AURIGA

GEMINI

Pollux

SUN

ORION   TAURUS

Aldebaran

Rigel

Procyon

Sirius

ECLIPTIC

A DOOR

Represents an Opportunity, New Beginnings.
The Solstices represent a Turning Point,
Regarding Time and Opportunities, etc.

THE LIGHT BEARER

BIBLICAL MAZZAROTH

In the Biblical Narrative, the Motif of Orion
is ascribed to Jesus who conquered Sin,
Death and Lucifer on the Cross of Calvary.
Jesus is the Light of the World.

LUCIFERIAN SOCIETIES

In the Satanic Cults, the Motif of Orion is
ascribed to Lucifer. The Statue of Liberty is
rendered in how Apollo is fused with his

HEXAGRAM
= 'STAR GATE'

ORION

The Coat of Arms of Israel has a Hexagram.
It is supposed that the Motif derived from
King David. Others suggest it is the Star of
Remphan, an Evil Symbol of casting a Spell

Merkavah

When a Hexagram is inter-locked
it produces a Perfect Cube, as a
Chamber or Holy of Holies'. It is
considered a Chariot or
Transporter.

Earth: 37.751, -97.822, 0 m   FOV 83.7°   17.9 FPS   2022-06-21 23:32:28 UTC+00:23 (LMST)

Main Sources
-Stellarium.org
-Wikipedia.com

To this end, one will present 7 Reasons why Israel will go to War with the Encircled Muslim Enemies, sometime within the 3 Months of Summer. This is what one sees, as an Astronomical Survey of the Summer Solstice Orion Circle that is going to be mirrored on Earth with Israel. Why just Israel? First, a short Description of what the Orion Circle is about will be presented. The Orion Circle is a composition of 6 Major Stars that surround the Constellation of Orion, having 7 Stars.

The 6 Star form a Geometric Encirclement of a Hexagram wherein, the Silver Gate is nearly Dead-Center. Orion is the Center-Piece within the Hexagram Circle. Some call this Motif a Hexagram, the 'Star of David'. And it is the National Emblem on the State of Israel's Modern Flag. It is in the Center with 2 Flanking Blue Bars across the Tapestry of the Flag that denote the Extent of the Land Covenant that YHVH made with Abraham.

In Genesis 15, it states that Israel would be granted a Land from the River Euphrates to the River Nile. This has yet to be accomplished, but will during the Millennial Kingdom, once Jesus returns to Earth to rule from Jerusalem, Israel, etc. There are others though, as there is always an Anti or Opposing Definition, mainly coming from the Luciferians.

The Enemies of Jesus Christ have attempted to hijack the Narrative of the Mazzaroth or the Zodiac in how all the Motifs Meanings are inverted. This to suggest that the 'Star of David' is said to have never been a Family or National Emblem of King Davis or Israel. And that in fact, it is the Satanic Symbol of the Ancient God of Remphan. It is a Symbol that was brought-up by YHVH in how He condemns it as many in Israel rather Venerated it and followed after that 'God', being Lucifer, etc. And to also note that the Hexagram is used by the Occult in Casting Spells and conjuring-up Demons and Fallen Angels. How so?

Through Sorcery, Black Magic and Blood Sacrifices, the Hexagram, when 3-Dimensionalized produces a Perfect Cube. This becomes the 'Chamber', or Door or Star Gate in which Entities appear and disappear, etc. And what would these 6 'Stars' encircling Orion be? Clockwise from Northern Orientation are the following.

STAR	NAME MEANING
1- Capella	Small Female Goat
2- Aldebaran	Leader - Governor
3- Rigel	Leg - Foot
4- Sirius	Glowing – Illumination
5- Procyon	In a Position Before – Redeemer
6- Pollux	He Who Comes

And what about the Motif of Orion as Libertas and the Statue of Liberty? It is suggested by some People who study the Luciferian Occult, that the Statue is portraying a Personage that is Gender Fluid. It is a deliberate representation of the mixing of the Sexes, Powers and Purpose of the Male God, Apollo and the Female God, Isis. It is essentially Lucifer in Drags, the Original 'Transvestite of the Cosmos'. It is this Hexagram used to cast a Spell in this Last Generation. Of what? The Trans Energies that wreak havoc on the West's Young Generation, right down to Babies wherein Sexuality is being taught to Kindergarteners, etc.

How does the Orion Circle come into play with Israel, an Encirclement, the Summer and a Star Gate? Thus, to summarize, the Orion Circle, Astronomical depicting Orion at the Silver Gate as the Torch Bearer, encircled by the 6 Stars, can be seen as Israel. And that precisely when the Sun is entering the Silver Gate, that demarcates the beginning of the 3 Month Summer Season is when perhaps, Israel, as the Great Orion will have the Encircling Stars as Enemies, that being the Bordering Muslim Military Factions come and Attack Israel, all at once.

196

1. *The Summer Solstice is a time of Transition. It signifies a Turning Point as that is what the Seasons of the Year represent. In this case, June 20-21 is the Astronomical beginning of the 3 Months of Summer. Thus, one can expect that in World Events and specifically regarding Israel, a Transition and Turning Point has been reached. It will be played-out. What that will be, remains to be seen. But if what the News coming out of Israel and the Middle East is suggesting, there will be War, as the Encirclement of Israel is what the 6 Stars that surround Orion, in this case represent, an 'Encirclement'.*

2. *The Orion Motif represents the Dichotomy of the Person. What does that mean? It means that, for example, in the Biblical Narrative of the explanation of the Constellations, it is the Storyline of the Savior. It demonstrates, with each Constellation Personage and Motif a particular Segment or Chapter in the Redemptive Work of Jesus Christ, the Greater Orion. Orion is Famous in all Civilizations as the Mighty Hunger, the Conquering Warrior, etc. He is the 'Light of the World' who has overcome Sin, Death and Satan, etc.*

However, the converse is true for the Luciferians, who attribute this Celestial Guardian of the Silver Gate to Lucifer, and/or the AntiChrist. It is Lucifer that is portrayed as the Savior of Humanity in how he defied the GODs and brought down to Earth, the Forbidden Fire of Illumination and Knowledge to Humanity. It is a Promise to make Humans as 'God's, etc.

3. *The Silver Gate represents a Door of Opportunity, at the Time that the Sun traverses through it. It is at the Center of the Orion Circle and it appears to be 'Activated', Astronomically. It is when the Sun does go through this 'Door', at this Time and Place in the Cosmos, exactly on June 20-21. What the Silver Gate represents is 'Opportunity'.*

How and what that will look like on Earth, Geo-Politically, concerning Israel is to be seen. But again, if any indication of just how dire the situation is in the World at Large and for Israel, specifically, it is an Opportunity for the Encirclement of Israel's Muslim Enemies to Collectively Strike 'Orion', or Israel. It is also an Opportunity for Israel to Strike at the Encircling Enemies that seek to destroy Israel.

4. The Orion Circle is a Motif of Israel, in the sense that Orion, being Encircled by a Hexagram can be attributed to the Star of David and thus, a Euphemism for Israel.

Or in Metaphorical Terms, it is Israel's Time to Shine based on the Summer Solstice Sun 'Torching' the Lamb that Orion is holding, directly at the Celestial Gate. Israel has, miraculously risen from the Ashes and Ovens of the Concentration Camps in Nazi Germany during World War 2 to become the 8th Most Powerful Nation on the Planet.

Thus, to have this Celestial Correlation of the Sun Illuminating the Torch on the Summer Solstice is an Astronomical Indication that the 'Lights have been turned on', for Israel from this point going forward but specifically during the 3-Month Summer Season.

5. So, this to suggest that during the Summer of 2022 from June 20 to September 20, the World will be focusing on Israel and what might come of such Geo-Political outcomes, yet to be determined. One can take a Political Science Educated Guess and suggest that it will be War. Why?

The 6 Stars encircling Orion, or Israel are indicative of the 6 Major Muslim Menace that will, at some point in time, during the Summer of 2022 attack Israel. And what would these 6 Muslim 'Stars' encircling 'Orion' or Israel be?

198

1. Edom	= Peoples of Jordan	Fatah
Moab	= Peoples Central Jordan	Fatah
Ammon	= Peoples of Northern Jordan	Fatah
2. Ishmaelites	= Peoples of Saudi Arabia	Muslim Mercenaries
3. Hagrites	= Peoples of Egypt	Muslim Brotherhood
Amalek	= Peoples of Sinai Peninsula	Muslim Brotherhood
4. Byblos	= Peoples of Lebanon	Hezbollah
Tyre	= Peoples of Lebanon	Hezbollah
5. Philistia	= Peoples of Gaza	Hamas
6. Assyria	= Peoples of Syria and Iraq	ISIS, Al Shabaab

6. The Orion Circle is about an 'Encirclement'. As noted already, the Circle of Stars surrounding Orion has a Biblical Interpretation. It is based on the work of E.W. Bullinger. The Star Capella, is in the Constellation of Auriga, the Shepherd. He is Pierced at the Heel by the Horn of Taurus.

He is holding Lambs as that is the Motif for what Jesus did for the Flock as the Good Shepherd. Jesus Died on the Cross of Calvary, being Pierced through by the Enemy, Taurus. It was emblematic of the Red Star, Aldebaran, representing Lucifer and the Law. Jesus as Orion confronted Taurus to rescue and Redeem the Pleiades or the 7 Churches of Asia, etc.

One calls this the Great Celestial Bull Fight'. Then there is the Star Sirius, the Dog Star along with Procyon, considered the Syrian Sign and ending with Pollux in the Couple. In the most ancient renditions, the Constellation of Gemini was that of a Man and a Woman.

7. The Orion Circle, at this point in Time in History, concerning Israel as the 'Orion' that is Encircles could very well represent the Tension, Geo-Politically of how Israel is surrounded. And Israel does confront, presently, in its History an Existential Threat. And that is? It is coming from the Threat of Nuclear Annihilation at the Hands and Effort of a Shi'ite Muslim End Times believing Mullah Regime.

It is no accident that the Israeli Defense Force, the IDF took about a Month to Drill for an Encirclement Invasion, on all Fronts. This included, for the 1st Time in Modern Israel's History, a coordinated Military Drill that included the Army, Air Force, Navy and Intelligence Agencies, all focused on coming Muslim War, all bordering Israel, perhaps this Summer.

This could be the Geo-Political Scenario as the justification of such an Encirclement Attack by the Para-Military Muslim Factions would be because Israel attacks the various Iranian Nuclear Facilities. This would be a Game Changer as Israel has destroyed 2 Prior Nuclear Reactors in Iraq and Syria. The major difference now is that Iran has multiple Reactor Sites and a lot of them are in Deep Underground Facilities. However, what is different now and what will be to Israel's Advantage are those Israeli modified F-35s that do not need any Intermittent Refueling.

As the F-35's are Stealth, it will be a Surprise Attack that Iran will not see it coming. But Iran is prepared for an Attack, as much as Israel has been and so have all of Iran-Armed Sunni and Shi'ite Para Military Factions that are armed to the Teeth, as they say. Will the Orion Torch that is Astronomically 'Lit' by the Sun on June 20-21 be a Euphemism that it will be from that Time forward, within the 3 Months of Summer that the 'Fuse will be Lit' on this War? Most likely.

Main Sources
Stellarium.org
Wikipedia.com

Article

#622: OPERATION CHARIOTS OF FIRE - PSALM 83 WAR HAS BEGUN
https://www.postscripts.org/ps-news-622.html

#620: 888 MONTH BIRTHDAY - ISRAEL'S 74TH YEAR ANNIVERSARY
https://www.postscripts.org/ps-news-620.html

#608: GOD OF WAR IS COMING - MARCH 22, 2022 (322)
https://www.postscripts.org/ps-news-608.html

#592: 7 SHEPHERD'S PROPHECY - MICAH 5 STUDY BY KEN JOHNSON
https://www.postscripts.org/ps-news-592.html

#298: Psalm 83 War
https://www.postscripts.org/ps-news-298.html

#41: Prince of Persia
https://www.postscripts.org/ps-news-41.html

#18: ISRAEL STRIKE ON IRAN
https://www.postscripts.org/ps-news-18.html

Books

Behind IDF Military Lines: The War In-Between Wars
https://www.amazon.com/dp/1716237599?tag=nice04f-20&linkCode=ogi&th=1&psc=1

Eternal Battle for Zion: Burden of the Nations
https://www.amazon.com/dp/1300033010/ref=sr_1_1?dchild=1&keywords=the+eternal+battle+for+zion&qid=1624692054&s=books&sr=1-1

GOD DAMN AMERICA
FALL OF THE
SOVIET AMERICAN UNION
Great American Eclipses

'In my Opinion, it will not cease, until a Crisis shall have been reached, and passed - A House Divided against itself cannot Stand. I believe this Government cannot endure, permanently Half Slave and Half Free. I do not expect the Union to be Dissolved - I do not expect the House to Fall - but I do expect it will Cease to be Divided. It will become all One Thing, or All the Other'. -Abraham Lincoln, close of the Republican State Convention June 16, 1858

The purpose of this chapter is to provide a compilation of Research and Articles spanning over a Decade dealing with the 'Demise of the USA'. It will be a Political Science Commentary about it but that will incorporate a Biblical Filter as to why and what is going to happen next to the American Union. It is basically going to Fall, if one's Decade-Long Research suggests what it has suggested. The Trend is even Prophetic in some cases. One is doing so with a Heavy Heart, as they say because one is an Immigrant and owes a lot to the American Union.

It is not 'Perfect' Union and it has committed 'Sins' in the Past, and is being used for Evil with Endless Wars and the Military Industrial Complexes, etc. But what made America Great was that its People were Great. That what made People Great was that, for the most part, the Spiritual, Moral and Religious Threshold was that of a Christian Nation where Jesus was King. No longer. And one would say, that being a Follower of Jesus, is now, in a once 'Christian Nation' has made at least Half of the Population overstay one's 'Welcome'. The American Union was truly Exceptional.

What an Experiment. Not since the Garden of Eden did an Organized People form a Union 'By the People and for the People'. This has been attempted and in fact that is what the Communist Nations espouse, that they are 'People's Democratic Republic of whatever, etc. Not realizing that Christianity is what made the American Union be true to its Creed. It was true in how Thomas Jefferson surmised that only a Civilized and Informed Citizenry, that was Christian could have a Government that would be accountable. No more.

Based on one's Assessment, although there is about Half of the Nation that is not in the 'Woke' Camp, there is less than a 3rd now that would consider themselves 'Christian'. And a recent Poll asked the Z Generation, if they were Religious or Believed in GOD? The Percentage is now in the 30% Range. They rather do believe that Aliens exist and are Benevolent and soon come to Rescue them and be their 'Lords and Saviors'. But one would not rather live anywhere else. Why not?

It is due to its Constitution, Bill of Rights and commitment that all are the 'Same under the Law'. Sure that may be 'Pie in the Sky' thinking and Naiveté, but at least there are some vestiges of Hope and Idealism that one and Millions others have aspired to. So, the Millions seek to put their very Lives on the Line to enter the USA, Illegally.

The Title of this Article is crass and may be considered Vulgar to some but it is intentional, as far as it having multiple meanings. It is not intended to be thought of or taken as a Curse Phrase, although that is certainly an option to some. The intent of the Title or Phrase is to bring-out the supposition that America, the USA is poised for Divine Judgment. Why? It has to do with what at least half of the Americans have become, Un-American. To speak of defending Guns, being Pro-Life, America First, Secure the National Borders, is 'Hate Speech'.

204

To criticize spending 53 Billion rather on Americans than Ukrainians, is now 'Racism' to them. It is one thing to Disagree or be Divided even, but those on the Left, the Luciferians, the Globalists are Hell-Bound on utilizing this Great Divide to also Murder the Phoenix. It will be the required 'Sacrificial Vitim' as their Aborted Babies on the Altar of 'Progressiveness' and 'Wokeness'.

The American Union has come to the place where it is being given over to a 'Reprobate Mind'. How so? One has to basically be a University Biologist to define what a Woman is. The American Supreme Court Nominee, a Woman could not even answer or make a 'Judgment' on what a Woman was. And with the Leak of how possibly Roe vs. Wade could be overturned, the Ugly Side of Americans, both Women and Men, came out with Satanic Rage, it appeared.

So, on the issue of Abortion 'Rights' to murder one's Babies, America is Damned or needs to be Damned. No nation that has embraced this level of Immorality has survived as a Ruling Empire. The introductory Premise is that one is comparing the American Union, to that of the former Soviet Union. The Soviet Union collapsed on December 25, 1991. The Soviet Union could no longer maintain the 'Union' due to going basically 'Broke'. But it was 'Broke' in more ways than one. It was 'Broke' Morally, Socially, Religiously, or the lack thereof, and Financially.

It went Bankrupt. It had over-extended itself in its Military Endeavors and its People were reduced to 3rd World Level Impoverishment. The Stores had empty Food Shelves. Fuel and Food were Rationed. Only the very Elite had vehicles and hoarded the Food and Fuel. There was a Thriving Underground Market. The Ruble was worthless. The People were reduced to Faceless, Soulless Walking Zombies in a lot of cases. At least considering the Population compared to other Western Nations.

Fall of the Soviet Union

IMAGES OF THE COLLAPSE

1991

Images of the Collapse of the Mighty Union of Soviet Socialist Republics. The Union was set up for Republics to join the Confederation rule by the Politburo from Moscow in the Russian Soviet Republic.

What happened is that Boris Yeltsin, who ascended to the Presidency of the Russian Socialist Republic voted to Secede from the Soviet Union. The Vote was passed and this caused the Collapse of the Soviet Union.

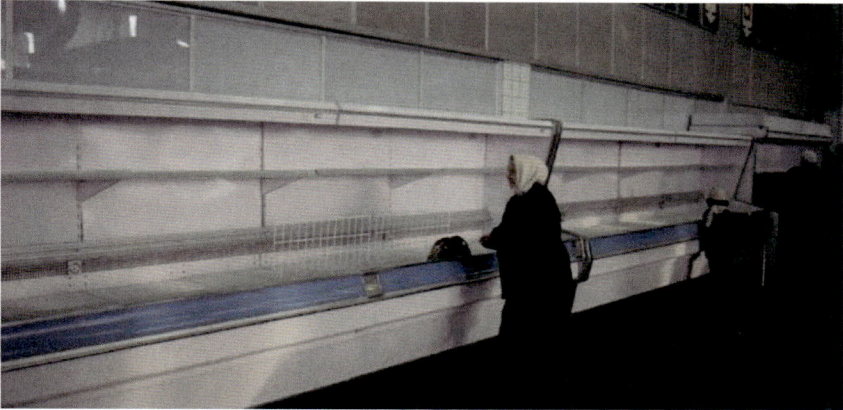

Fall of the United 'Soviet' States

IMAGES OF THE COLLAPSE 2022+

Images of the Collapse of the Mighty Union of Soviet Socialist States. The Union was set up for States to join the Federation rule by the Constitutional Congress and Presidency from Washington in the District of Columbia.

What happened is that the Left of Center, who ascended to the Presidency of the States changed the Laws that made the USA Energy Dependent, Increased the National Debt, Spurred Hikes in Fuel and Food as they became Scarce. Crime and Lawless abounded as the LGBT Agenda was Celebration, all the while Record Crop Failures and Droughts plagued the Nation. The following are Images from Free PxHere Website.

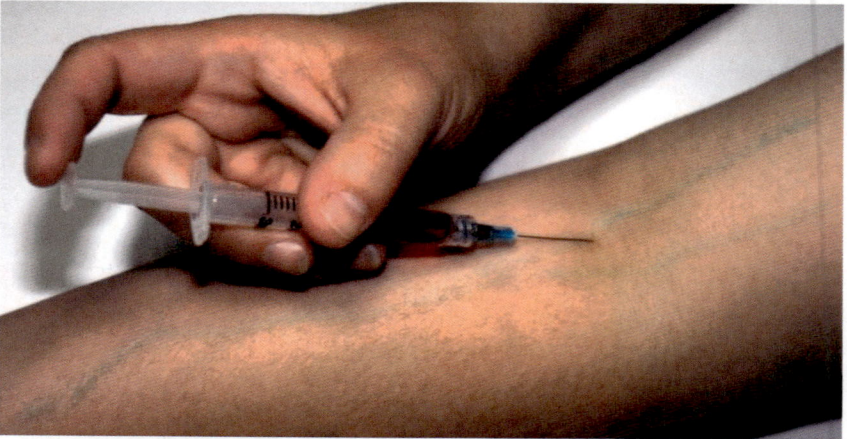

This was from one's own Personal Account during the last Year of the Mighty Soviet Union in 1990. What one saw there, has now been seen in the USA. It is not a 'temporary' Cycle or Chapter in the Economy or Morality of the USA. No, One surmises that the Powers-That-Be have now orchestrated what many are now seeing is the Orchestrated Controlled Demolition of the American Union, as was the Soviet Union. It has taken Decades for America to have come this Fall down, but it has arrived in one's Political Science Estimation.

Many People over those years, especially with the Advent of Obama being placed in the White House and now Biden, as some would rather call Obama's 3rd Term, are saying that the American Union is on the brink. There is even talk of a 2nd Civil War for a few years now. The American Union has never been so Divided in almost every issue now. This is what the former Republican President, Abraham Lincoln also surmised.

He echoed the Prophetic Utterance of Jesus Christ, that 'A House Divided Cannot Stand'. It is a Spiritual Law, a Divine Principle that not only can be applied to whole Nations but to Individual People, as that is what makes-up the Building Blocks of a Nation. Thus, the point is Divide the People, Divide the Nation. Mission Accomplished. And based on over a Decade of Observation as a Political Scientist, and Follower of Jesus, the American House is about to Fall. Why?

The various Premises are based on Biblical Prophecy, Astronomical Occurrences as Signs in the Sun, Moon and the Stars, and the Sabbath Cycles. There are Online Links to 22 Articles that will explain such a Conclusion one is making pertaining to the Fall of the American House that is Divided and why. There is also enough Research Material to compile 2 Books on the Subject of the Demise and eventual Fall of the USA.

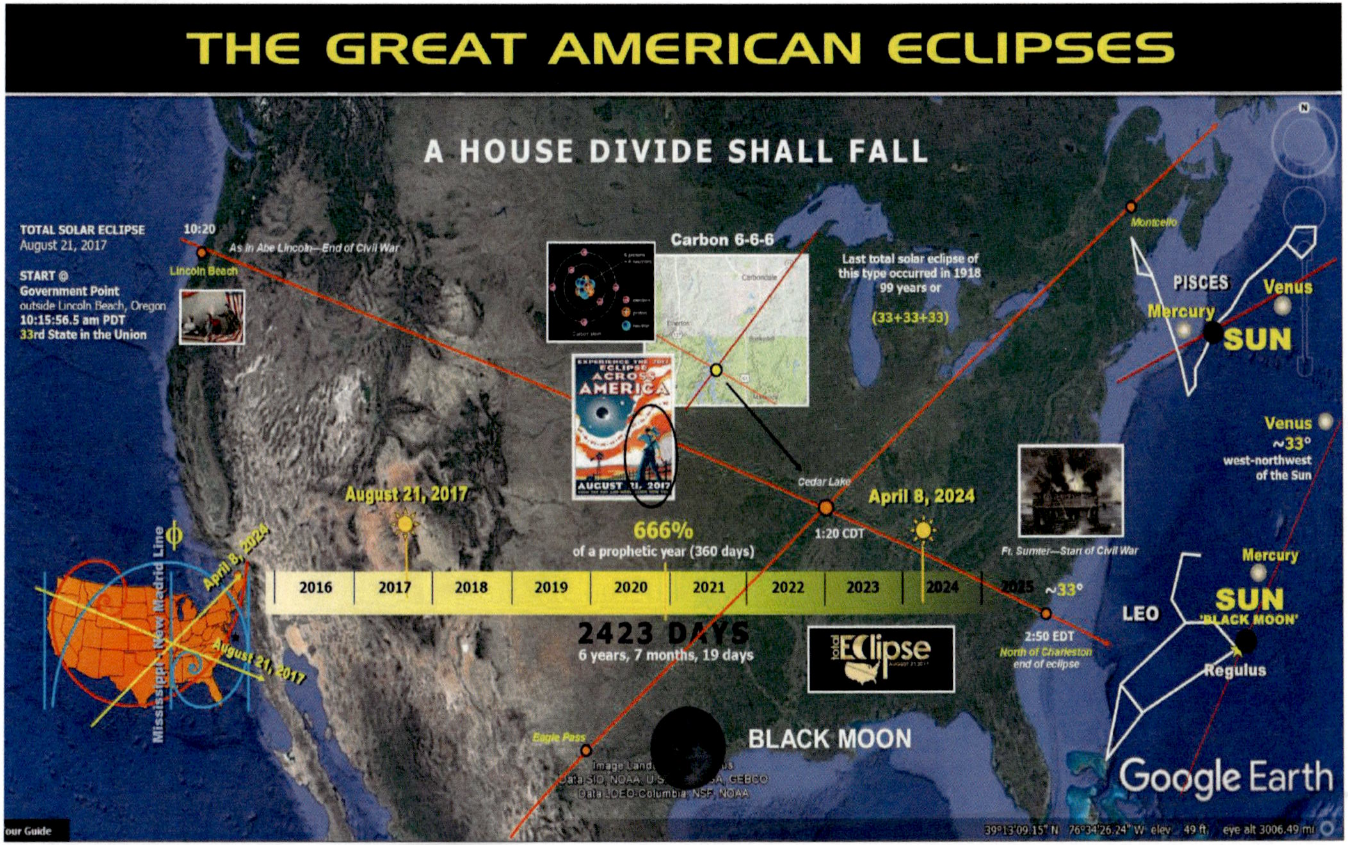

THE GREAT AMERICAN ECLIPSES
A HOUSE DIVIDE SHALL FALL
TOTAL SOLAR ECLIPSE
August 21, 2017
START @
Government Point
outside Lincoln Beach, Oregon
10:15:56.5 am PDT
33rd State in the Union
10:20
As in Abe Lincoln—End of Civil War
Lincoln Beach
Carbon 6-6-6
Last total solar eclipse of
this type occurred in 1918
99 years or
(33+33+33)
Montcello
PISCES
Venus
Mercury
SUN
Venus
~33°
west-northwest
of the Sun
Cedar Lake
April 8, 2024
1:20 CDT
August 21, 2017
666%
of a prophetic year (360 days)
Ft. Sumter—Start of Civil War
2016
2017
2018
2019
2020
2021
2022
2023
2024
2025
~33°
2423 DAYS
6 years, 7 months, 19 days
2:50 EDT
North of Charleston
end of eclipse
LEO
Mercury
SUN
'BLACK MOON'
Regulus
Mississippi - New Madrid Line
April 8, 2024
August 21, 2017
Eagle Pass
BLACK MOON
Google Earth
39°13'09.15" N 76°34'26.24" W elev 49 ft eye alt 3006.49 mi

It will show that there have been and are Evil Luciferian Forces that have taken over the USA. But what is more sad to consider is that it is because its People have been taken over. In every facet over the Decades, really since its inception, the Great Work of the Luciferians has been to commandeer the New Atlantis, as they perceive the USA to be. They see the USA as their Mythological Phoenix Bird that only has a certain amount of Sabbath Cycles to live before being transitioned into the next New Order. One has surmised that for the American Union, it has been 33 Sabbath Cycles of 7 Years, starting with the Coin Act Year of 1792.

The American People have been, now at least about half the Population, commandeered to help undo the Union. Now, many Readers from other Nations do raise the point that such Articles as this are so 'Americentric'. True. But it is because the American Union, currently, is the 'Head of the Nations'. It is the Standard and Beacon on Earth Presently. Idealistically, it is a Nation set apart, even Biblical to many degrees as many Historians do argue. The American Union is even compared to ancient Israel and or Egypt. America is the 'Tabernacle Nation' as the 4 Main divisions of the Tabernacle of Moses can amazingly be superimposed topographically.

Then how the FEMA Agency has divided the Union into 10 Regions and Anthropomorphically, even the 10 Toes appear to correspond to the Islands of Hawaii on one 'Leg' and the Aleutian Islands of Alaska on the other 'Leg', etc. There is the Mighty Mississippi, that like the River Nile of Egypt has many of its cities and places along the River specifically Named after the ones in Egypt. And this will be the argument of how the Great American Eclipse of 2017 plays the Prominent Role or Omen of the present State of a Divided Union and why. The American Union is also Prophetically compared in how it is following the Biblical Footstep of how also Israel once was the Beacon of Light.

The USA was as the City on the Hill, Mount Zion. But then Wicked Kings and their Perverted Sons took power and led the Nation to a Division and Civil War. But in that case, it was the North that Seceded and the South that wanted to preserve the Kingdom. Here were technically 13 Tribes if one counts the Sons of Joseph. The USA had 13 Colonies. The Number 13 stands for Rebellion, etc.

However, all this up to know has just been the preparatory foundation for the real point of the Write-Up. It does have to do with a Number, 33. And it has to do with the Parallel of the Demise and Fall of the former Soviet Union. Consider the following Equation. The Soviet Union 'collapsed' officially in 1991.

If one adds 33 Years from that date to when the 2nd Total Solar Eclipse crosses the American Union on April 8, 2024, it will be exactly 33 Years. Coincidence? And? One is surmising that as the Soviet Union completely and officially collapsed there and then, so too will the American Union collapse in that Year, officially and completely, just the same. The Luciferians have Flip-Flopped the Empires in how now it is the American Union that is the 'Evil Empire' and its Leaders and Sons are no better than Mafia.

*Fall of the Soviet Union: **1991***

*to **2024** Solar Eclipse = **33** Years*

Mirror to the 33 Day Countdown to the Revelation 12 Sign. It is as a Prelude of 33 Years, how now the Great American 'Soviet' Union will fall? From August 8, 2024?

_____

Definition of SOVIET
Soviet

*so·vi·et | \ ˈsō-vē-ˌet, ˈsä-, -vē-ət *

*1 : an Elected Governmental Council in a Communist
Country*

2 Soviets Plural
a : Bolsheviks
*b : The People and especially the Political and Military
Leaders of the Soviet Union*

But one must realize that this 33 Year Coefficient is a
Divine Judgment. It is a Divine Marker that is made with
Astronomical Precision as to 'X' out the American Union for
its unrepentant Stance, its Heart, its Morality, or lack ther
of, its Wickedness, Murders, Thievery, and turning its Back
on YHVH, much like Israel did. And? Israel was allowed by
YHVH to be invaded by its Enemies, being taunted and led
Captive.

If the 33 Sabbath Cycle of 7 Years since the 1792 Coin Act
is valid, then by September of 2022, soon after Rosh
HaShanah, the USA Petro Dollar will collapse. This will be
the Globalist Reset Throw-Switch that will ensure the Death
of the American Union and its Mythical Phoenix. The
American House, like Israel will not be able to Stand, and it
will be 'Led Captive'.

It will not be able to recover as Millions of Followers of
Jesus will have been Evacuated from Earth. And with the
Medical Effects of Billions of People having taken the
COVID Kills shots, the Adverse Effects will turn a large
portion of the Population into 'Zombie' Like State of Being.
Consider how the American CDC put out in 2021 an actual
'Zombie Apocalypse Preparedness Guide'. What?

Jesus is the Vaccine

That portion of the official CDC Website was pulled but it can be viewed in the Internet Archive Pages through Time Machine at the following link.

https://web.archive.org/web/20210108190727/https://www.cdc.gov/cpr/zombie/index.htm

Do the People at the CDC know something whey 'Let the Cat out of the Bag' as they say? Why was the Website Page pulled? It is because they know the Adverse Effects of the COVID Kill Shots will have such Effects on those People that will survive.

And this will give rise to the Lie that Will be Believed, in that 'Aliens' have at last come to Publicly be made Manifest and provide the Solution for the World's Reaction and Problems, the Luciferians have had orchestrated since the Garden of Eden. But it is Lucifer's House that will be Divided and will not Stand.

His Destiny is sealed by Jesus of Nazareth thanks to the Work on the Cross of Calvary. Jesus left His Father's House, and 'Divided' Himself when Sin was placed upon His Body as the Scapegoat and Sacrificial Passover Lamb. After putting Sin, Death in the Grave, Jesus reversed the Division and Demise of all of Humanity. Why?

To once again afford Humanity, those that would say 'Yes' to his Offer to share all that He is and has, to be Friends of YHVH for all Eternity in Bodies just like what Jesus has now, made of Pure Energy, indestructible. Jesus restored the Union of the Communion Humanity first had with YHVH in the Garden of Eden. It has been Restored.

Consider that in the Virus Metaphor, such as COVID, a Virus is only alive and can only live in a Host, so long as a Host is alive. It then can spread from People to People. The Virus is only spreading the Genetic Code, as that is all it is. So long as the Host is alive, so will the Virus be. Thus, if the Host is Killed, so will the Virus be also Killed and the Spread of Infection and Transmission by the Virus will stop.

This is what Jesus came to do for a Helpless 'Sin Infected' Humanity. So long as the 'Virus' of Sin attached itself to the Hosts, that being very Human Being, because they are Alive, having Physical Life in their Bodies of Flesh, the 'Virus' of Sin can prevail, becoming unstoppable with no Cure. It would take a Human Body, an Un-Contaminated Human Specimen to be willingly be Infected with the Virus of Sin, and then be put to Death.

By this act, the Virus of Sin would also be 'Put to Death'. This is what Jesus did for Humanity. Jesus, being Sinless and having to have been born without Adam's Genetic Contaminated Flesh, had to be born Immaculately. This is why half of Jesus' Chromosomes were only from His Human Maternal Parent, Mary. The reason being that Jesus then had no Natural Human Sinful Nature. Best part is that Jesus willingly chose to take upon Himself then the whole 'Virus' of Sin upon His Physical Body, on the Cross of Calvary and Die.

By doing so, Jesus put to Death the 'Virus' Sin Nature of the Flesh as Jesus Died Physically. And the 'Virus' of Sin was buried in the Earth with Jesus' Body, to never come back up. It was Jesus', the Sinless One, as a Human who was thus Resurrected because in Himself, dwelt now Sin Nature, and thus could not Die, Eternally. This is the Exchange or 'Cure' Jesus is offering to all of Humanity. Jesus has become the Remedy, the Solution, the 'Vaccine' that can now Inoculate and Give Spiritual Immunity against the Sting of Death, which is the Law and the Sin Nature.

225

They are what Condemns all Humanity to an eventual Death, not just a Physical one due to the 'Virus' of Sin, but an Eternal Death. This means an Eternal Separation from the very Life Source of the Creator. Jesus offers this Remedy, Free-of-Charge. But it is now incumbent for the 'Sin Patient' to administer this Inoculation.

It has to be applied to one's Being or else the 'Virus' of Sin will persist and will eventually lead to not only a Physical Death, but that of an Eternal Death. Jesus affords Humanity, those that would say 'Yes' to his Offer to share all that He is and has, to be Friends of YHVH for all Eternity in Bodies just like what Jesus has now, made of Pure Energy, Indestructible. Jesus restores the Union of the Communion Humanity had with YHVH in the Garden of Eden. Take this 'Vaccine'.

The only hope for a restoration of the American Union is a National Repentance, of returning to Jesus as LORD and Savior. One thinks though, that although there might be Micro-Revivals in a regional and/or Individual Level, the Die has been Cast.

The coming 'X' Marks the Spot, Astronomical Confirmation that America is Finished is going to happen, unfortunately. But as with the World prior to Noah, as the People of Sodom and Gomorrah, GOD had to Damn them. As it has been expressed by many People, if GOD does not Damn American, it has to apologize to the Pre-Flood World, Sodom and Gomorrah.

Main Sources
Wikipedia.com

Articles

#551: UNITED STATES OF BABYLON - FEMA Regions
https://www.postscripts.org/ps-news-551.html

#442: THE PURGE - *End of the American Experiment*
https://www.postscripts.org/ps-news-442.html

#431: AMERICA IN GOD WE TRUSTED - Visions Of America's Last Days
https://www.postscripts.org/ps-news-431.html

#419: AMERICA'S EXPIRATION DATE? - 33rd Sabbath
https://www.postscripts.org/ps-news-419.html

#389: GEORGE WASHINGTON PROPHECIES - Fall Of The Republic
https://www.postscripts.org/ps-news-389.html

#370: PILLARS OF THE SACRED SPACE - Plan To Demolish the USA
https://www.postscripts.org/ps-news-370.html

#331: TABERNACLE REPUBLIC - American Continental Pattern of Resources
https://www.postscripts.org/ps-news-331.html

Books

Rise of Baphomet Spirit: Prepare for End of the World
https://www.amazon.com/dp/1387400843?tag=nice04f-20&linkCode=ogi&th=1&psc=1

The Fall of the Phoenix: On the 33rd Sabbath
https://www.amazon.com/dp/1716816564?tag=nice04f-20&linkCode=ogi&th=1&psc=1

Free Great American Resource Page

Great American Eclipses
https://www.postscripts.org/great-eclipse.html

THE LAODICEANS
DOCTRINE OF WOKENESS
Mennonite Church USA affirming Perversion

'I know your Deeds—your Love, your Faith, your Service, your Perseverance—and your Latter Deeds are Greater than your First. But I have this against you: You Tolerate that Woman Jezebel, who calls herself a Prophetess. By her Teaching she misleads My Servants to be Sexually Immoral and to Eat Food sacrificed to Idols. Even though I have given her time to Repent of her Immorality, she is unwilling. -Revelation 2:10-21

The purpose of this chapter is to comment on a recent decision, in Mid-2022 about one's Christian Denomination. It has come to be known that one' Denomination, Mennonite Church USA, of which one's Home Base Church in Bakersfield, Laurelglen Bible Church belongs to, Passed a Resolution Affirming Same-Sex Marriage. And where now, Pastors are able to perform Same Sex Marriages and have committed to the LGBTQ Inclusion 'Woke Agenda'.

One calls for the Denominational Leadership to Repent of this Gross Sin. It is clear in the Bible that both the Old and New Testament Teaching that this form of Sex is a Deviation, Un-Natural and goes contrary to the 'Image and Likeness' of YHVH. And of Jesus as He intended for Marriage to be before the Fall.

The Bible clearly teaches that the LGBT+ Lifestyle is Sinful, a Perversion of the original intent of Sexuality. The Apostle Paul further characterizes it by linking the Intent back to the Garden of Eden with Adam and Eve, not Adam and Steve. The Lifestyle is an Abomination to YHVH for which the Old World was destroyed in Noah's Flood and that of Sodom and Gomorrah.

Instead of the Body of Christ Influencing and Transitioning Society and Culture, it has been the Society and Culture that has Transformed and Influenced the Church. But it is no surprise as Jesus Himself had a lot to say about such a Denomination. It is Loving, Faithful and famed for its Service to others in Need. It Perseveres. But it now Tolerates the Sin of Sexual Deviation.

It has now become part of the Laodicean Type of Iteration that the End of the Church Age would close out with. And how would that look like? A Doctrine of Wokeness. It is where Jesus has been 'Voted' out and the Leadership has been allowed to be taken over by Women 'Pastors'. A Woman can have the Office of Pastor, in so much as she is leading and caring for a Women's Ministry or Service. But not to be a Pastor over a Congregation in which Men comprise the Body and there is Teaching.

This is Scriptural, it was not Cultural. And the reason why? It tells that due to the Disposition of the Feminine Side of the Brain, Eve was more easily Seduced. Thus, the Church allowing Jezebels to Lead and Teach has led to Error and Apostasy, to a large degree. Consider the example of Deborah and Barak. In those Days, there were no Men that took the Lead, rather it took a Deborah to step in, knowing that a Man should lead.

If there are no Men who want to Lead or can, then a Deborah can come in. But even then, she was subject to Barak in his failings, etc. This is what Jesus said, not this Writer. Such a Disposition in Churches have allowed for Immorality to be Tolerated. And this is a prime Example of such a case with Same Sex Marriage and the Toleration of the LGBT+ Lifestyle. It is not that Jesus 'Hates' the People. No, He Loves them, enough to have Died for them, but to not remain in their Sin. This, after all was the Teaching of the Woman and the Well. The following are from PxHere.

230

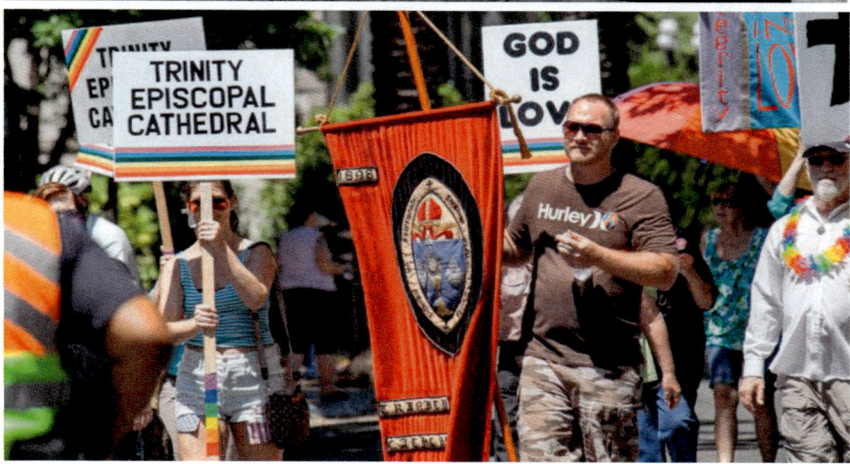

MORAL DECAY OF THE UNITED STATES AND THE WORLD

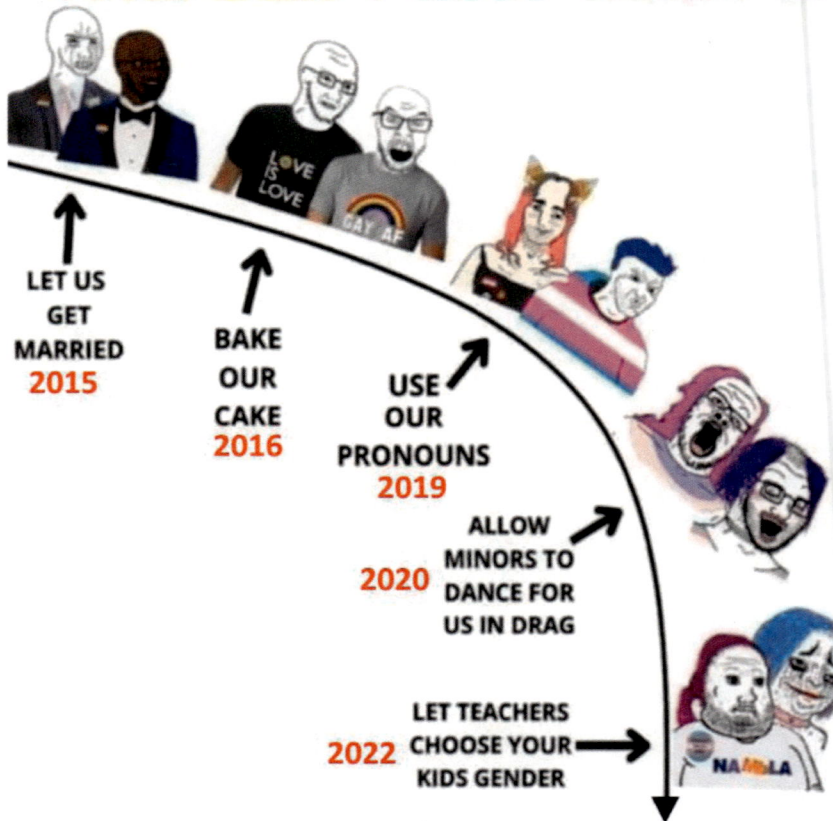

THE SLIPPERY SLOPE

LET US GET MARRIED 2015

BAKE OUR CAKE 2016

USE OUR PRONOUNS 2019

2020 ALLOW MINORS TO DANCE FOR US IN DRAG

2022 LET TEACHERS CHOOSE YOUR KIDS GENDER

NAMBLA

People were Eating and Drinking, Marrying and being Given in Marriage, up to the Day Noah entered the Ark. Then the Flood came and destroyed them all. It was the same in the Days of Lot: People were Eating and Drinking, Buying and Selling, Planting and Building. But on the Day Lot left Sodom, Fire and Sulfur rained down from Heaven and Destroyed them all.

LUKE 17:27-29

Or of that incident where the Jewish Religious Leaders brought a Woman caught in the very Act of Adultery to Jesus. They expected Jesus to Stone her, etc. But as the Apostle Paul rightly taught, once a Person genuinely comes to Jesus, and gives one's Life to Christ, there is a Change, a Transformation that occurs in the Inner-Most Part of the Human Being. This is because it is there that GOD the Holy Spirit dwells. And its Function is to Convict of Sin and Teach all Truth.

If the Church is affirming Same Sex Marriages and the LGBT+ Community, it is lying to itself and Disrespecting the Commands of Jesus. It is the Regenerating Power of the Holy Spirit that gives a True Follower and Believer of Jesus the Power to Transform and Change, From Glory to Glory. And Sin is not Tolerated but Repented of. This is what Paul admonished the Brethren in Corinth, in how they were Sexually Sinning worse than the Non-Christians at the Time. And that says something as Greece was famed for its Pagan Sexual Perversions. He rightly reminded them that 'They were formally' those types of People living those sorts of Depraved and Perverted Lifestyles. But in Jesus, there is a New Creation.

One cannot understand a so-called 'Christian' living in that sort of Sexual Sin and Lifestyle and claim to be a Follower and Believer of Jesus. In His Word, YHVH admonishes His People to be 'Holy as I am Holy'. But instead of the Church being an Agent of Separation from Sin, it has embraced it within. What a Shame and it Defiles the Testimony of who and what Jesus is and did. Thus, Jesus will remove such Laodiceans from His Presence. They rather offend Jesus than Sinners, It would rather be more fitting if such People, Jezebels and now the Mennonite Church USA would not call themselves by Jesus' Name. Please call yourself something Different other than 'Christian', because such are not. Please do not dishonor Jesus' Name.

One has yet to know of the Church's Response, if it will remain in the Denomination or leave. The mere fact that this Topic dealing with the Sin of Sex will need to be discussed? It is indicative of the Church Age Spirit of the Laodiceans. They have taken over one's Denomination now. But one saw it coming. During one's Time there, even though one was 'Mennonite', one was considered 'Liberal', East of the Mississippi, but Conservative by California 'Woke Standards'. Do not get it wrong, most if not all the People there during one's Direct Involvement there were amazing.

One is still in contact with a lot of them since moving up to Northern California, and one has kept track, by Mailing List and Online Presence, etc. But the New Generation has a different 'Vibe'. Not the same and not surprised if it will go along with the Denomination LGBT+ Mandates. No doubt, some Individuals and Families will be leaving. What is odd, is that in one's sleep a day before this Announcement, one had Flash-Backs to when one's College and Career Ministry would team-up to be involved in the Children's Ministry.

One would go to Hungary and Romania for Children's Retreats as the Parents attended Church Conferences on how to reach-out to Eastern Europe, etc. Those were Amazing Times. But then it clicked, why was one having this Flash-Back? It answered one's own Question in one's Spirit and why the Church will go along with it. When one was there in Person, the Church was Famed in Town for its Children's Ministry and Missions, and for a Loving and Accepting Disposition. Awesome. But a recurring Statement would always come-up when New Parents would want to visit and/or join the Church. It was that one's Church had 'Great Programs for Kids'. True. But that was the Answer. It was not about the Parents Feeding on the Word, dealing with Sin, becoming a Disciple and Follower of Jesus or a better Couple reflecting Jesus and the Church.

No, it was because 'My Kids could play and be entertained' as I 'Punch-In' for my Religious Obligation to appease one's Conscience, perhaps. Now the Children's Ministry did teach Sound Biblical Doctrine but 'Going to Church' is not about finding a Social Club. Why not? It is through such means that those Tares, those Laodiceans creep in and are allowed to influence the Wheat. And now to the point that in this Denomination's Leadership, the Laodiceans have taken Control and this is now what they dictate and expect. The Doctrine of Wokeness.

Truly, the Last Iteration of the Church Age Type, that of the Laodicean Disposition means the End of the Church Age is at hand. As one knows, the Name, Laodicean means, 'Rule of the People' or by Vote. And that is exactly what the Denomination Government was set to, the Vote of the Laity. Not Jesus as the Head or to get His Mind or Opinion and Commands that are Clear, found in Scripture when it comes to the Sins of Sex. It is the Teachings of Jezebel that causes the Flock to commit Sexual Fornication/Adultery, etc. It is a Denomination ruled by a Poll of the Prevailing Cultural Norms. It is like what one mentioned about Brother Chooch's Prophecy Polls.

Not to disparage his take and intention, as it is an innocent tool to use in his Teachings about Prophecy and possible Interpretations. All good. But Prophecy is not determined by Popularity Polls. No Poll Prophecy. So, just to say that this latest Denomination in the USA to go 'Woke' is a clear Signs of the Times and why Judgment begins in the House of GOD. And Must. We say, 'The World cannot go on like this another Year'...Well, one would say, the Church Age cannot go on another Year, with this Laodicean Disposition, where Jesus is Voted-Outside the Body of Believers. Sad. May the True Bride of Christ never end-up in such a Spiritual Situation. One just has to now learn what one's Home Church will do. One might be having to go over to Brandon Holthaus' Church across Town.

But one does have a 2nd Home Church in Santa Rosa. It is an Independent Bible Church, so one has a bit more time, maybe.

'Even though I have given her Time to Repent of her Immorality, she is unwilling. Behold, I will cast her onto a Bed of Sickness, and those who commit Adultery with her will suffer Great Tribulation unless they Repent of her Deeds. Then I will strike her Children Dead, and all the Churches will know that I am the One who searches Minds and Hearts, and I will Repay each of you according to your Deeds'. -Jesus Christ, Revelation 21-23

Main Sources

Mennonite Church USA Passes Resolutions Affirming Same-Sex Marriage, Committing to LGBTQ Inclusion
https://www.christianheadlines.com/contributors/milton-quintanilla/mennonite-church-usa-passes-resolutions-affirming-same-sex-marriage-committing-to-lgbtq-inclusion.html

THE GREAT APOSTASY
COMPROMISED CHURCHES OF AMERICA
A Statistical Analysis of Evangelicals in the USA

'It instructs us to renounce Ungodliness and Worldly Passions, and to live Sensible, Upright, and Godly Lives in the Present Age, as we await the Blessed Hope and Glorious Appearance of our Great God and Savior Jesus Christ. He gave Himself for us to Redeem us from all Lawlessness and to Purify for Himself a People for His own Possession, Zealous for Good Deeds'.
-Titus 2:12-14

The purpose of this chapter is to highlight the Percentages of the so-called Professing Protestant Church, that is, the specific Strata of Bible Believers that would be called the Evangelicals, Conservatives, Fundamentalist, etc., in the USA. The point will be made that the once Great Union of the USA that sent Missionaries in the Spirit of the Church of Philadelphia has succumbed to the Luciferian Agenda to destroy it from within, to Sabotage the Tenets of the Teaching of Jesus and His Apostles.

Obviously, the Body of Christ on Earth is impossible to Defeat as that is what Jesus Promised. But it has been Damaged as it has compromised with the World, as it was foretold it would. Why? Jesus explained in the Parable of the Field, that a Good Farmers sowed Good Seed, of Wheat in his Field. Then at Night, the Enemy came and sowed Tares. The Servants of the Land Owner then asked if they could 'weed-out' the Tares. The Land Owner stated that it would be too Risky and such a tender Stage that some Good Wheat could be accidentally plucked up along with the Tares. So, the solution was to allow for both Types of Grains to grow up and in the End, the Fruit would clearly distinguish them apart, and just in Time for the Harvest.

APOSTASY OF THE PROTESTANTS

CLOSING-OUT OF THE ~2000 YEAR CHURCH AGE PLAGUED BY TEACHINGS OF EITHER THE JEZEBELS OR THE NICOLAITANS

As of 2022, the Majority of Protestant Bible Believing Christians have gone Apostate ➤ 85/100

~145 Million Protestants in the USA

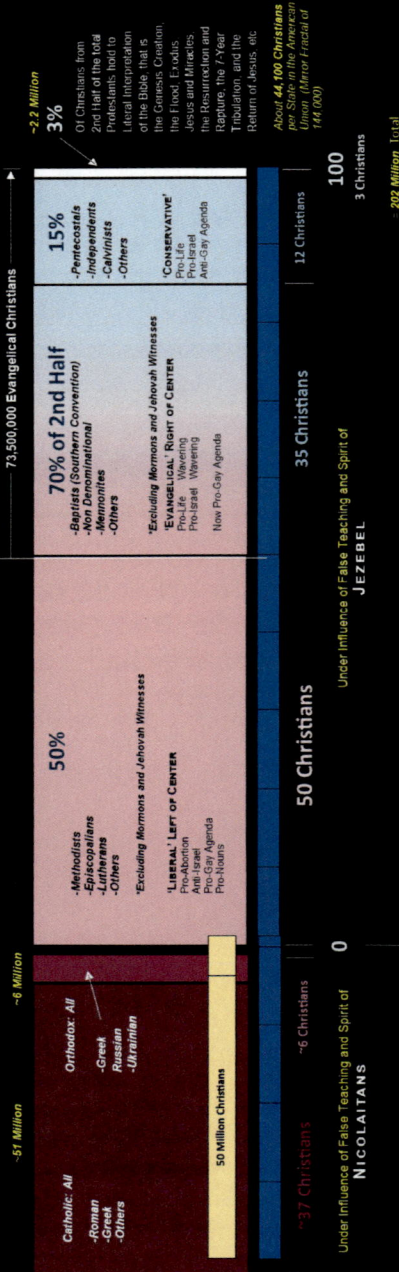

73,500,000 Evangelical Christians

Protestants in the USA

~2.2 Million
3%

Of Christians from 2nd Half of the total Protestants, hold to Literal Interpretation of the Bible, that is the Genesis Creation, the Flood, Exodus, Jesus and Miracles, the Resurrection and Rapture, the 7-Year Tribulation and the Return of Jesus, etc.

50%

-Methodists
-Episcopalians
-Lutherans
-Others

*Excluding Mormons and Jehovah Witnesses

'LIBERAL' LEFT or CENTER
Pro-Abortion
Anti-Israel
Pro-Gay Agenda
Pro-Norris

70% of 2nd Half
-Baptists (Southern Convention)
-Non Denominational
-Mennonites
-Others

*Excluding Mormons and Jehovah Witnesses

'EVANGELICAL' RIGHT or CENTER
Pro-Life   Wavering
Pro-Israel Wavering

Now Pro-Gay Agenda

15%
-Pentecostals
-Independents
-Calvinists
-Others

'CONSERVATIVE'
Pro-Life
Pro-Israel
Anti-Gay Agenda

No Pro-Gay Agenda

~51 Million   **~6 Million**

Catholic: All
-Roman
-Greek
-Others

Orthodox: All
-Greek
-Russian
-Ukrainian

50 Million Christians

~37 Christians   **~6 Christians**

Under Influence of False Teaching and Spirit of
NICOLAITANS

Scale in Population

0   50 Christians   35 Christians   12 Christians

Under Influence of False Teaching and Spirit of
JEZEBEL

100

3 Christians

= **202 Million** Total

About **44,100 Christians** per State in the American Union (Remnant Israel of 144,000)

50 Million Christians   50 Million Christians   50 Million Christians

238

And the Distinction? The Tares, although looking nearly identical to the What produce no Fruit and stand erect, as if Proud, etc. By contrast, the Wheat has lots of Kernel Fruit and due to its weight, bends downward as in a state of Humility. As to the Fruit of the American Churches? The USA was founded on sound Biblical Principles and Worldview, but secretly, many of the Founders and Cadre were and are still Luciferian Anti-Christian People. And?

They seek an Anti-Christian Agenda but masked as 'Christianity'. It is used of the Masons, for example. They are a False Correlating Vein of supposed Christianity. But through it, as the Tares are supplanting a Luciferian Agenda in the appearance or Message of Christianity, as the Wheat. Since 1776, this Parallel and False Christian Great Work has pretty much compromised the Protestant Churches, going into 2023.

The Core Protestant Christianity distinguished the USA in one's opinion. The Protestant Churches made the USA Great. Alexis de Tocqueville, in his 'Democracy in America, Summary and Belief', was impressed by much of what he saw in American Life. He admired the Stability of its Economy and wondered at the Popularity of its Churches. He concluded that it was because of the Churches that such Stability resonated from the Traditional Family that built-up America.

But there has been a Sinister Hidden Agenda, a true Conspiracy to usurp the Church and thus the Government of the USA. How? Just read, 'Rules for Radicals' by Alinsky, who dedicated the Book to Lucifer. And of whom Hillary Clinton made her Master's Thesis based on the Book. And what does this Spiritual Compromise look like in the Churches of the USA? In 2020, the Cultural Research Center Survey revealed Data compiled in January 2020, that showed that only 2% of Millennials hold a Biblical Worldview.

Returning to the Vomit

This is even though 61% of them still identify as 'Christian'. Then there were other Surveys that showed that of the Professing Protestant Evangelical Core, that being around 70 Million, approximately, only 3% reported that they believed in the Core Tenets of the Bible. Only 3% hold to the Literal Interpretation of the Bible, that is, the Genesis Creation, the Flood, Exodus, Jesus and Miracles, Resurrection and Rapture, 7-Year Tribulation, Return of Jesus, etc.

Thanks also to the Decades of TV-Movie-Book Predictive Programming, especially after World War 2, the CIA, MK-Ultra, and the like, provided the Platforms to slowly but surely change the Moral Fabric of the USA to where it is now. It has resulted in a Division down the Middle in not only the Political, Social and Financial 'Divide', but also within the Church. As evidently it has not been the Church that has influenced and changed the Moral Fabric of Society, but it has been the other way around, sadly. In his Study's Info-Graphic, the Statistics essentially follow the 2 Delineations that Jesus pointed out in the Book of Revelation concerning His 7 Churches and their Spiritual Condition.

The Book of Revelation starts out by Jesus appearing as the Resurrected Redeemer. He is shown as a High Priest, interceding on behalf of the Church as would the High Priest of Israel in the Temple Holies, etc. In this case the 7 Branch Menorah is a Euphemism for the 7 Churches of Asia and how they would be corresponding to 7 literal Historical Segments of the entire Church Age, beginning with Ephesus and ending with Laodicea. In this capacity, Jesus is also a Physician that is Evaluating the 'Fruit' of each Church and is making a Prognoses and offering a Remedy for the Condition that is seen as an Ailment preventing the Church Light or Segment in History from fulfilling its Mission and Objective for that Testimony.

It is rather interesting that the Last Testimony, that of the Laodiceans is so bad, that Jesus is 'Voted' out of the Assembly Body as that is what the Greek Name means. It is the only Assembly or Testimony where Jesus then calls, not the Whole Body to Repent and Return, but Jesus is calling the Individual People within to come out for that type of Testimony.

It is not that the Statistics provided are absolute in that every single Christian who are within such types of Churches that are also complicit with the Luciferian 'Conspiracy'. Many may be sincere and are subject to the circumstance, such as being born in that Family Denomination, Church, Culture, etc. The following will show the Break-Down of the Statistics one seeks to Highlight and bring to one's Attention.

The Point being, is that out of all the Professing Protestant Denominations in the USA, only about 3% of the 2nd Half of the Piece of the Pie still holds to the Core Traditional Teachings of the Bible, and specifically to an End Times type of Paradigm, etc. It is truly the very Few that are on the Wall Watching for the Rapture, for example.

Top Protestant Denomination in the USA (Not all inclusive.)

-Baptists
-Methodists
-Episcopalians
-Lutherans
-Pentecostals
-Calvinists
-Other/Independents

*Excluding Mormons and Jehovah Witnesses

Total Population: = *145 Million*

If include
Roman Catholics: *= ~51 Million*
Orthodox: *= ~6 Million*
                        *= **202 Million***

If one takes Half of the 145 Million Protestants from the Equation, being Left of Center, as in Laodiceans and having gone Gay, Pro Abortion and Same Sex and Marriage, you have the following Statistic. There would be 145 Million divided by 2 Halves.

*= **73.5 Million** supposed 'Conservative' Evangelical Christians.*

It was estimated by a Poll and reiterated in a Presentation by Jack Hibbs that of the Profession Evangelical Christians in the USA, only 3% hold to the Literal Interpretation of the Bible, which is the Genesis Creation, the Flood, Exodus, Jesus and Miracles, the Resurrection and Rapture, 7-Year Tribulation, Return of Jesus, etc. The 3% accounts for the overall Age Spread. For example, out of this Statistic, only 2% of Millennials, hold to the Traditional Biblical Worldview. It is the lowest % among all Adults. Truly alarming.

(3/100) of 73,500,000 Evangelical Christians.
*= **2,205,000 Core***

This means that approximately just over 2 Million Evangelicals are only truly Adherents to the core Tenants of the Bible and End Time Scenarios. If one uniformly distributed this 2,205,000 Christian Population that believes in the End Times, evenly to all the 50 States in the American Union, it would amount to 1 Medium Size Town, per State.

*Then, **2,205,000** Core Evangelical Christians / **50** States.*
*= About **44,100 Christians** per State in the American Union.*
(Mirror Fractal of 144,000).

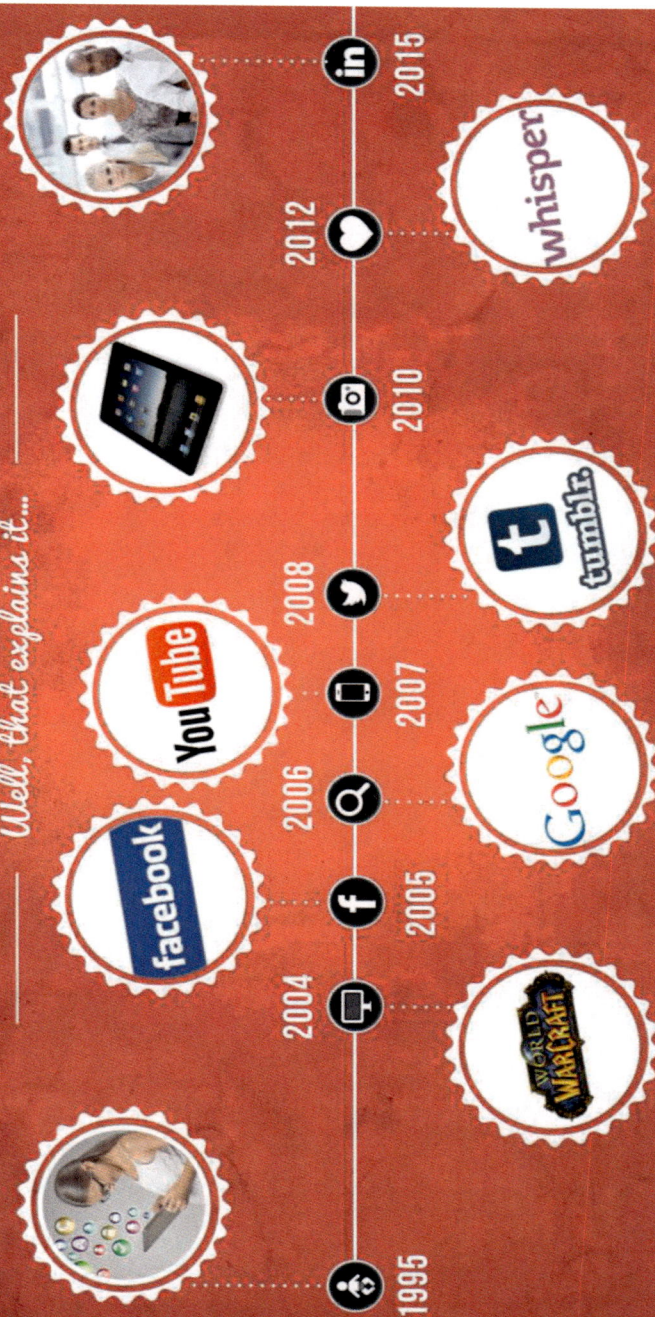

A GEN Z'S JOURNEY

Well, that explains it...

1995 · 2004 · 2005 (facebook) · 2006 · 2007 · 2008 · 2010 · 2012 · 2015

World of Warcraft · Google · tumblr · whisper

Our key findings
Gen Z are:

More global

"With how social media spreads news around, we are very educated in how the world is."

Female, 20, US

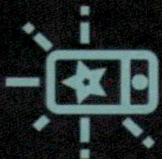

Under the influence

"I keep up with celebrities, influencers, and sometimes brands through Instagram."

Female, 17, US

More demanding

"Brands need to work more to retain their customers (since our choices have really gotten pretty limitless) – I would like it if they increased their offerings and make it easier to find things that you're looking for."

Eager to stand out

"Generation Z is more focussed on innovation and uniqueness."

Male, 19, China

After experiences

"The experiences I have had, they do define me in a way – not so that I can show off about them, but what they have taught me is really valuable."

Male, 20, UK

Pro social (responsibility)

"Ethics and message are most important to me... you cannot expect people to buy your products if your ethics are trash."

Female, 17, US

Generation Z by the numbers

86%
use the their smartphones multiple times a day

67%
would rather shop in stores than online

82%
of Gen Zers say they don't care about sexual orientation

73%
say that the brand they purchase is important to them

71%
of survey says they use facebook more than any other social network

70%
watch more than two hours of YouTube content each day

88%
say people are exploring their sexuality more than in the past

83%
say saving for the future is important

69%
watch motre than 2 hours of televison a day

YOUR STORY | INSPIRE INNOVATE IGNITE

THE CONNECTED GENERATION

As Gen Z takes to the road, already their always-connected, on-demand lifestyle is influencing vehicle design.

ABOUT GEN Z

Born 1996 to present

Make up about 25% of U.S. population*

Will account for about 1/3 of U.S. population by 2020*

The oldest members are seniors in college

There are more than 26 million licensed drivers younger than 25 in the U.S.**

First generation to grow up in an on-demand world

73% connect to the internet within 1 hour of waking up†

Spend 10% less time watching TV than Millennials††

Have an 8-second attention span – shorter than a goldfish‡

Called the on-demand generation for their music-listening, movie-watching habits

Despite reputation as ride-share enthusiasts, 92% own or plan to own a vehicle‡‡

35% list infotainment system as most important component when selecting a vehicle‡‡

Always-connected mentality drives in-vehicle technology like Wi-Fi, device charging, smartphone connectivity and Bluetooth

*U.S. Census **U.S. Department of Transportation ‡Wikia ††VisionCritical.com †www.statisticbrain.com ‡‡KBB/Autotrader

In a Room Full of Christians

What is the Conclusion and/or Point? Truly, those that believe the Bible in its Protocols of a coming Apocalypse, Resurrection-Rapture, 7-Year Tribulation, Genesis Creation, the Flood, Exodus, Jesus' Resurrection and the coming Rapture are but a hand-full that can be counted. It is sad that most other Christians pay no Mind to such things, but not the U.S. Federal Government. So much so, that these Type of End Time Watching Christians are on their Homeland Security 'Terrorist Watch'.

They are Watching the Watchers. Go figure. Most of these types of Christians find their Fellowship on Online End Times Websites as that is the only Platform where such Topics are discussed and Watches Fellowship, etc. Such a sad State of Spiritual Affairs of the Body of Christ on Earth to close-out the Church Age. The following is an oversimplification of how far the Apostasy has been pervasive in the Professing Protestant Bible Believing Church Denominations, of the USA, If the nearly 145 Million Protestants in the USA got together in a Proportional Ratio of 1 to 100, meaning 145 Million would equal 100 Christians on a Statistical Scale, then the following Calculus would approximate the Conclusion that one is bringing to Light.

Out of the 100 Protestant Christians in the Room, 50 of them, exactly Half would be Left of Center, meaning Pro-Abortion, Anti-Israel, Pro-LGBT, Same Sex Marriage, etc. Clearly steeped into the Teaching of the Spirit of Jezebel that Jesus warned about. Then out of the 2nd Half or 50 Protestant Christians in the USA, nearly 70% of this 2nd Half would constitute 35 Christian. These are what would be labeled as 'Evangelicals' who, for the most part are Pro-Life, Pro-Israel and Anti-LGBT, etc. This has changed now in the last 3 Years as more Mainline Evangelical Denominations are fast becoming 'Woke' and capitulating to the Jezebel Teachings of accepting the Gay Agenda.

Fall of the
United States of 'Sodom'

IMAGES OF THE COLLAPSE
2022+

Images of the Collapse of the Mighty Union of Sodom States. The Union was set up based on the Judeo-Christian Tenets of Freedom. That Freedom is based on Truth that results in Liberty and not Enslavement.

What happened is that the Left of Center, who ascended to the Positions of Power since the Nation was birthed, have worked to undermine the Judeo-Christian Moral Fiber that once United the States. Although not perfect it strived to be 'More Perfect'. However, it has not surpassed the Sins of Sodom and Gomorrah. The Sexual Sin of Perversion and Same Sex Marriage are not Celebrated and those not Affirming will 1 Day be Jailed. Following are from PxHere.

251

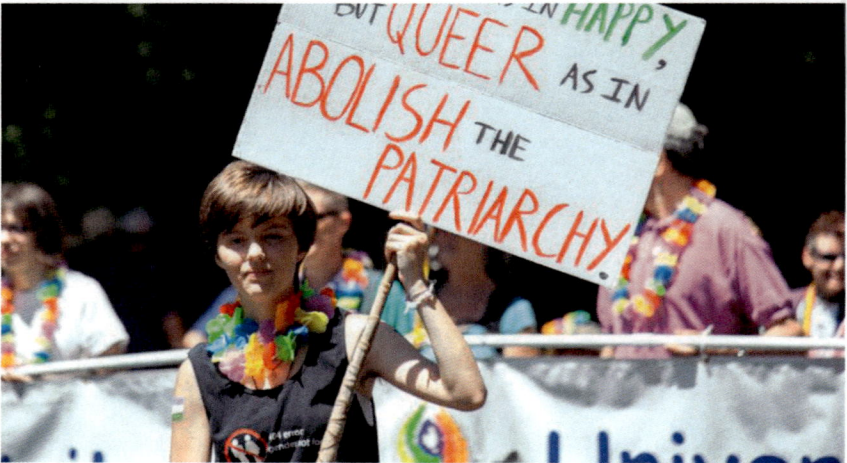

This would leave about 12 Christians in the Room from the 2nd Half that would be labeled 'Conservative'. Despite this number, recent Polls have determined that out of this so-called Conservative Persuasion, only about 3% are those that still hold to the Traditional Tenets of the Bible Teachings. Thus, out of a Protestant Denominational Gathering of 100 Christians in a Room, only 3 Christians would still hold to the belief in the Creation Account, the Flood, Exodus, Jesus' Miracles and Resurrection, the Rapture and the 2nd Coming, etc.

This is how far the Apostasy has become, Great. For sure, Christians are living in the Last Iteration of the Church Age, that of the Laodiceans to close out the Dispensation. Sad and just like it was for Israel. It is a Christ-Less Christianity. Just a Shell. And becoming 'Woke' is the Fruit. In particular, the intensification started in the early 1990s, one would say. It was with the Teaching of the 'Purpose Driven Life and then Church'.

It all sounded Biblical, and it sprouted-up the Mega-Churches and Seeker-Friendly types. Nothing wrong with being 'Friendly' but that meant, do not confront Sin. And the Pastoral Power was given over to the Laodiceans and Jezebels. They took over at least more than half of the Church Body in the USA that was not already on the Left. And now 30 Years later their Children, called the Y and Z'ers of that Generation in the USA reflect the latest Survey.

Less than 30% of them consider themselves Religious, go to Church or believe in GOD. What the Laodiceans did is that they Graduated Atheists. That was the Plan. One saw this 1st Hand being involved in one's Home Church in Bakersfield, California. In the early 2000s, the College and Career Ministry was solid. It had College/Seminary Level Teaching. But the Core Group was maybe 30-40 at that most. It reflected the 3% of all in that Age Ministry.

That was sad in that the majority of the Up-Coming Generations, did not want that type of Fellowship and Relationship with Jesus or his People. Yet, the High School Ministry had 100s of Students. But what happened when they graduated from High School, is that they also 'Graduated' from Church. In a lot of Student's lives, Christianity was just something their Parents forced them to do.

It was only a handful that would Transition to the College Group, the 3%. And why? Why not? The World was no different. Instead of the Church changing and influencing the Culture and Society, the Culture and Society Influenced the Church, as to not be 'offense'. One left the World to leave all that sort of Sin, but now it has come into the Church, and what is worse is that the Laodiceans and Jezebel's embrace it. But Jesus warned of this, in how it would look like in the 'End' of the Church Age.

In the Book of Revelation, Jesus sees it all, as He does in the USA. And the 2 main issues that plague the Professing Church are the Teachings of Jezebel within the Protestant Churches and the Teachings of the Nicolaitans within the Catholic and Orthodox Branches. It will either be full-on Wokeness and Sexual Perversion or a Pharisaical and Ecclesiastical Disposition, that in both cases are what Jesus hates.

Main Sources

30% of US evangelicals does not believe that Jesus is God.
https://evangelicalfocus.com/life-tech/7775/30-of-us-evangelicals-does-not-believe-that-jesus-is-god-survey-says

Just 2% of millennials hold a biblical worldview, lowest among all adults: study
https://www.christianpost.com/news/just-2-of-millennials-hold-a-biblical-worldview-lowest-among-all-adults-study.html

JUNE RAPTURE HOPE?
DR. BERRY AWE'S JUNE 15 DATE
A Critique of the Arguments

'Cooking for Jesus'… -Dr. Berry Awe

The purpose of this chapter is to present a Critique of a Video, entitled, 'Why our RAPTURE HOPE in JUNE is still alive!!!! SHAVUOT Ain't over! IT STILL AIN'T OVER!' by Dr. Barry Awe, off of his YouTube Channel, posted on June 9, 2022. The main Premise of this Teaching, is that he makes a Supporting Case for a June 15 Rapture Timing, in 2022. The reason one is presenting this Critique is that Readers of one's Website have asked for a Comment or Critique, as it has become now a custom.

The Requests come-ups when there is an interesting Video of Teachers presenting their Rapture Time-Lines and Charts, etc. In reply, one is of the Opinion that a Believer and Follower of Jesus is able to Discern on their own, of such Material and Teachings. And that one is, by no means out to 'Critique' the World or Fellow Watchman and Watchwomen. Everybody has a Natural Bias and Arguments about the Bible, This is especially the case with Hot Topic or Issues of Doctrine and Theology, like the Rapture, etc.

One believes that like the Bereans, one should be open and Scripturally Based and open, or should be of other's Teaching and Insights. Such Topics as the Rapture or when the Seals are Broken or if the COVID Shots are the Mark of the Beast are not a Salvation Issue in one's Mind. Although, those that do believe that the Injections will forfeit one's Soul would have an Argument about that. In such a case, one would Disagree. Nonetheless, as Brethren in the Body of Christ, one will Agree to Disagree, etc.

Now there are Serious Issues of Doctrine and Teachings that verge on either being Heresy, Error, Deception, Doctrine of Demons and Salvation. In such cases, if there is no Agreement, then it is Scriptural to separate from such Teaching and 'Mark those that cause Division', etc. All that to say, that the following Critique of Dr. Awe's Teaching of his June 15, 2022 Rapture Timing will be done in Respect and to note those Points in his Argument where one would and do agree and then those Points that are not agreeable. One's Critique does not, will not prove his or one's Counter Arguments.

It is not one's intention to sway or force anyone reading them to have to, 'Believe what one Believes'. And that is what Dr. Awe actually states also. Although one will admit that one has a strong Pre-Conceived Bias when it comes to Prophecy, and specifically, the Rapture Timing. It is because in one's Research and Understanding, it is 'Impossible' for the Rapture to occur in the Spring. Further information on this Argument will be given in the End Notes. How does a Follower and Believer of Jesus obtain Discernment?

Foremost, it is by the Scriptures. But what if portions of the same Scriptures are even used to Argue the Contrary of what one believes is the Opposite Teaching being presented? It is simple. The Bible then teaches to Seek Counsel, a multitude to find Wisdom on the Subject being Argued, etc. Then there is an issue of having a 'Witness' of a Confirmation in one's Spirit. If there is not that, given the Data, Arguments, and Presentation, then it is an Argument to just consider and keep an Open Mind about. But in one's Experience, it is when there is a 'Spiritual Resonance' that what is being presented is Truth. It is either confirmed through Scripture, foremost or a Confirming by Council or one's Spirit, in Communion with the Holy Spirit. If so, then that Teaching is to be acknowledged and accepted.

Ultimately, one can still be wrong, as it does not matter how many Years one has 'studied' Biblical Prophecy, etc. In doing such Critiques, one has to be Humble about it. Why? As the Measure one uses to Critique and measure someone else's 'Glass House', will be that the Spirit will use to measure one's Glass House. So, these are no 'Stones' being thrown here. In Summary, one does agree with a lot of Dr. Awe's Points presented in his Video Teaching. And his Insight is fantastic. But in terms of his overall Premise, of a June 15 Rapture Date? One does not agree. The Reason as to why not, have already been written about.

The Online Link to the various Articles presenting the case for a July Rapture, instead for 2022 will be given in the End Notes. Regarding Dr. Awe's Arguments for a June 15 Rapture Date? First, one thinks that one should address his Personality. There are those that Love Dr. Awe's Character and Style of Presentation. There are Testimonies of how People have turned around their Lives or Repented because of his approach. Then there are those that take him to task, as being a bit or a 'bat' more Irreverent in his 'Worldly Ways'. One would say, 'To Each Their Own'.

It is no different than having a 'Favorite' Teacher, Preacher and not all will sit well. One can say the same for one's Teaching of, rather a July Rapture, as such an Argument is rejected by most, etc. It is like that even in one's Job, how People will gravitate to certain Personalities that they are comfortable with, etc. As mentioned, one should listen to everyone's take on the issue of the Rapture 's Timing, as that is exactly what it is. As a fellow Researcher and Student of the End Times, one does appreciate the sharing of other's Teachings and Perspectives…about discerning the timing of when True Passover or Pentecost are, for example. Even with that, after either reading, listening or seeing all that is presented, there will be Points that one will agree on and not on others.

Let it be known though, that one is coming from a very 'Critical' Mind-Set, as one has it coming from Nature and Profession. Do to one's Profession, one has to be that way to evaluate, and 'Critique' more so than the average person would probably. Conclusively, those to study and seek the Deeper Things of Christ, can only trust the Holy Spirit to lead that Believer and Follower of Jesus into All Truth. It is for that precise purpose that Jesus sent the Comforter to be the Teacher to help the Body of Christ Discern, especially in these End Times. Thus, here are some thoughts that came to Mind as one listened to Dr. Awe's Teaching about the June 15, 2022 Rapture Timing.

As always, he makes very Good Points and some of his Understanding of Typologies are Top-Notch. However, he dismisses the Enochian Calendar. This, to some, is how the Great Pyramid of Giza was based upon. He is misunderstanding that both the Enochian and Essene Calendar start the New Years from the New Moons. One thinks that many People appreciate and resonate with his Excitement in that he also surmises that due to the present Sabbath Cycle, the coming one of the next 7 Year Cycle, could very well be Daniel's 70th Week. One would agree. That is why the Year 2022 is 'The Year', regardless of arguing the Rapture Timing.

But to agree also that, if one holds to the Pre-Tribulation Rapture Timing Scenario, the event has to occur before this next Sabbath Cycle begins. It is that close. Dr. Awe uses a lot of the Data, Information, Prophetic Type and Symbolism in his Teaching and Illustrations, which are great. But one does, however, find it a bit Comical, that he speaks of being 'Blind', yet the Truth is on his Board. For example, he goes to show how in the Hebrew Alefbet, the Letters have a Prophetic Meaning. True, one would agree. However, he calculates the Rapture event, being on June 15, in the month of Sivan, that being the 3rd Hebrew Letter, Gimel.

258

In one's Assessment, he is totally missing the 'Forest from the Trees' in that the 4th Month Hebrew Letter, the Dalet more precisely corresponds, Prophetically to the Open Door of the Rescue for the Bride of Christ. One would argue that it correlates also to the Book of Revelation Chapter 4 Marker of the Door being opened for the Apostle John, as a Typology of the Bride of Christ, etc. Then Dr. Awe talks about the Notion of when did that 40 Day Period of Jesus being with the Disciples occur. One would agree. It could have been instead, shifted to being counted after the Feast of Weeks and not pegged to the actual Resurrection Day, being Nisan 17, etc.

But here is where one Disagrees with the Logic he then used. Dr. Awe, in the 55 Minute Marker, states that the Ascension Day of Jesus was thus, on the 15th of Sivan or Shavuot. With no Disrespect, but this is absurd. It is Conjecture. At which point he does come off as a bit condescending in that he started out in the Video Teaching by essentially 'Castigating' all those 'not seeing it' his way and still being Spiritually Blind and 'Stuck in the Traditions of Men', etc. Yet one wonders what Teaching he will present next after June 15, 2022. Well, he did then say that he would consider the Feast of New Wine next.

That in his Mind, corresponds to Pentecost, or 1 of the 3 'Pentecosts' that he proposes in his Premise. 3 Pentecosts? Yes. In so far as he is counting 50-50-50 Days, he assumes the 49th Day of the Feast of Weeks was Pentecost, the 50th Day. This is not correct. But then the next subsequent 50 Day Count from the 49th Day, which one does agree with, would be the True Day of Pentecost: July 23, 2022. But here is another Error, in one's Assessment. It has to do with his Day Count of adding the 7 Days to the 40 Days Moses was called-up to then receive the Physical Tablets of the Law. In one's Study of Exodus, the 40 Day Count was All-Inclusive, from the Time Israel arrived at the Foot of the Mountain on the 60th Day.

The Day Count started on Nisan 15, which equated to the 15th Day of the 3rd Month, etc. Thus, the 40 Days since Sivan 15 = 99 Days. However, one can be wrong about this whole Day Count Assertion. But no, Shavuot is not a Pentecost and the Feast of New Wine is not Pentecost. For example, the Command to Count 7 weeks, or 49 Days has no Nomenclature associated with a Penta or 50 inference, etc.

Dr. Awe then makes the Statement that on the 5th Month was 120 Days as there were 120 Disciples in the Upper Room. Wrong. First, based on one's Research and Understanding, the 120 Disciples only initially meet behind Closed Doors for Fear of the Jews in the Upper Room. That is as much as the Upper Room could hold. And it was rather large for a Common Space in Jerusalem that is extremely compact, in terms of Meeting Spaces. Thus, the 5th Month does not add-up to 120 Days.

5 Months x 30 Day/Month = *150 Days*

One is of the Opinion, that Jesus gave a Direct Clue as to when the End of the Church Age 'Harvest' of Wheat was to occur, Month Wise. The Year, being still a Mystery, but it was on the 4th Month, or that of 120 Days. One suggests that Jesus made this Declaration in the Month of April, just before His Crucifixion.

(April + May + June + July) or (Nisan + Iyar + Sivan + Tammuz) = 120 Days
1   2   3   4   1   2   3   4

As to one's July Rapture Timeline? It is amazing that, as one noted in his prior Teaching Video...he has that July Rapture 'Answer' drawn right on his Board. One would agree that Dr. Awe is right about True Pentecost being associated when Moses came down with the Law Tablets and the Golden Calf Incident occurred.

260

And that is corroborated in how Aaron declared the Day before the 99th Day, that the next Day would be a 'Feast unto the LORD', etc. Although Dr. Awe is right about this Scenario, in one's Understanding and Research, he gets it wrong by not realizing that it was on the 4th Month, that of Tammuz, corresponding to the Hebrew 4th Letter, Dalet that this event took place, not Av as he has calculated, etc.

So, as to this Critique, one is seeing that in several junctures in his Arguments and Presentations, where he is forcing Day Counts and Months that do not align with his own Time Lines or Statements like, at the 1 hour Time Marker. He states that, 'It is like GOD being Drunk on Wine'. One would not go that far, even in his attempt to parallel the Sin Ham committed against Noah.

And how he associates the event surrounding the Feast of New Wine with the Drunkenness of Noah and his interpretation that it was Ham who laid with Noah's Wife, etc. He is also disparagingly, associating the 9th of Av, being an Evil Day, with that of the 'Pouring of the Holy Spirit' that came down on Pentecost.

It is perhaps 1 of the Greatest Days in Human History, aside from Creation, the Birth, Dead and Resurrection of Jesus. Thus, in one's Assessment, Dr. Awe is Flip-Flopping the Scenario and is Out-of-Sync for a June 14 Rapture, in one's Understanding. One can see his Logic in that he is attempting to assign that same event to the Anointing of the 144k Jewish Evangelist to come. However, one does not agree with his Scenario. Why not?

If the Rapture has to happen on June 15, that being, supposedly Shavuot, the Late Summer Wheat Grain is not yet ripe for Harvest. This goes totally contrary to his Scenario. He then teaches that 50 Day later, August 4, 2022, the Anointing by the Holy Spirit will come down on the 144K Jewish Evangelists.

This is impossible because this Anointing Event occurs once the Tribulation Period has started. And one is of the Understanding that what starts the Tribulation Period is when the 1st Daily Sacrifices are made. In order for this to occur, there has to be at least an Altar Build, Sanctioned and Sanctified. The Turn-Around Time for this to occur in merely an approximate Month from the writing of this Critique, is why it is Impossible. And this would leave out the 3rd Feast, that of Oil to then be associated and complete what Prophecy?

It is understood by many who study the Typologies of the Jewish Feasts believe that the Oil represents a Pressing and Stress, of a time of Tribulation. But for whom? National Israel. And that is what the 70th Week of Daniel is for, the Time of Jacob's Trouble, not that of the Church or Bride of Christ. Thus, Dr. Awe's 3 Feast Scenario does not hold, as he is inferring that the 1st 50 Days is when Jesus Ascended. Wrong.

Jesus rose on Nisan 17 as the 1st Order of the Resurrection. And shortly after, He presented the Barley First-Fruits as a Token, etc. This event had nothing to do with the 49th Day Offering. This is pure Conjecture. It is fine to do so, but it is an Error in one's Understanding to do so. And again, according to Dr. Awe's Interpretation, the 2nd 50 Day Count is when the Holy Spirit will come down for the 144K.

One is of the belief that it is at the 2nd 50 Day Count, rather that the Holy Spirit goes up, or that is, the Bride of Christ, as in the Resurrection-Rapture to conclude the Royal Commission of the End of the Church Age, etc. Now, the Holy Spirit will just be 'Set Aside' as that is what the Apostle Paul says the Restrainer will do. The Holy Spirit will still be on Earth and working through the Lives of the Tribulation Saints, but there will be no Body of Christ on Earth anymore.

And this is why, at this Place and Time, on Earth the Gates of Hell will Prevail over the Saints. What a dreadful Time it will be for Followers of Jesus after the Rapture event. Here is another Point of Disagreement. No, the Jews did not arrive on the 49th Day at the Foot of Mount Sinai. It was the 60th Day. That Day Count started from Nisan 15 to when the Jews arrived at Sinai on the 15th Day of the 3rd Month. It is Mathematically Impossible to have reached Mount Sinai on the 49th Day. So, that is why his Time-Line is off and will be.

Here is the next Observation. Despite his lecturing on those who hold to 'Traditions of Men', concerning some Prophecies or portions of Scripture, yet he is holding to the Traditional Interpretation of the Jews. How so? It is in how they state in the Encyclopedia Judaica that they Commemorate Shavuot on the 6th Day of the 3rd Month, Sivan and it is an Arbitrary Date chosen. They acknowledge that Israel had even yet arrived at Mount Sinai, but after 49 Days. And note that the Israelites had not yet even been given the Directive to observe the Feast of Weeks. Dr. Awe does acknowledge that it has been a Learning Journey and Experience for him and there has been a lot of Information and Teaching to consider. True. It has also been the case in one's Experience.

And one is in Agreement that one only seeks to know the Truth and share that with the Body of Christ, so 'All Good'. One believes it is just a matter of 'Iron Sharpening Iron'. One did like the Correlation of how the Raven was released by Noah on the 5th Month, that of Av. It would follow that if the Rapture does occur in July, the 4th Month as that is one's Argument, then the Month after is when the AntiChrist would appear, in the 5th Month. The 5th Month of Av is associated with Bad Omens, like the Bad Report of the 10 Spies and the 2 Temples being destroyed on the same Day, the 9th of Av, etc.

All this to suggest that, if the Rapture does take place on the 99th Day, as one suggests, that of July 23-24, being the 4th Month, it would appear to follow the Typology and Scenario of Noah, but it will remain to be seen. So, to reiterate, one believes Dr. Awe is off in that according to his Calculations, True Shavuot is June 15, 2022. One would Disagree. He, like most, is associating or taking for granted that 'Shavuot', the Feast of Weeks, being the 49 Days, is Pentecost. Incorrect. And that is why all Day Counts will not materialize when it comes to them associating the Rapture event.

Of course one could be totally wrong. One has gone back-and-forth in determining what 'Sabbath' is the Start Date. One also thought that it could be or was the Sabbath of the Regular Week, and then that would make any given Sunday, the Start Date. One agrees on how Dr. Awe has come to see that Jesus read the Isaiah Scroll on Yom Kippur, as that year, in 29 AD was the Jubilee Year. One does also like the fact that Dr. Awe entertains the Notion that there is a Pentecost Double Count after Shavuot. But more insightful is his Understanding that the Summer Season has 3 Minor Feasts of Grain, Wine and Oil. Most Students of End Time Prophecy are not aware of this.

And that they are exactly 50 Days apart, each. This is the Key, in one's Opinion. One also agrees that Dr. Awe does not hold to the Rapture being subject to the Doctrine of Imminence. In one's understanding, the Rapture will occur on a Feast Day, etc. But as mentioned before, one now leans more on the Sabbath Day to correspond to Nisan 15. Why? Nisan 15 was a 'High Day Sabbath' according to the Gospels. It was also how it was determined from the Exodus Day Count. It is then confirmed in how the Jews Count the Omer, that is the Day after Passover, that being the Nisan 15. Really, any Feast of YHVH is technically a Sabbath, etc.

But with the 3 main possible Sabbath Start Days, 2 of them complement each other and the 3rd would be just about a Week apart in Discrepancy. Now pertaining to the Double Count for determining True Pentecost? Consider the 3 Segments of 50 Days each: 50+50+50, etc. If one keeps to that Theory, in which for 2022, what one believes is True Pentecost will then be July 23-24, as the Day straddles the Jewish one, if one adds the 3rd Segment of 50 Days to July 23-24, a unique and familiar End Date emerges.

__July 23, 2022__ + 50 Days = September 11, 2022 (9-11) = 15th of Elul, 5782

Interesting. What to make of it? Not sure. Could be a Confirmation as this 3rd Segment of the 50 Day Count would thus correspond to the Feast of New Oil. The 2nd 50 Count would very well then be True Pentecost, and that of the Feast of New Wine, or thereabouts, but each Feast separate and distinct.

Here below is the Pentecost Matrix of Dates, based on the 1st and 2nd Day Count Options, Nisan 15 for 2022. What is also very fascinating, is that for 2022, both the Rabbinical and Gregorian Calendars match, to the Day. So, April 14, Passover was Nisan 14, etc.

From: NISAN 15 on a New Moon (Leviticus 23:15)

1. + 49 Days = June 3, 2022. This was Shavuot = 1st 50 Day Marker.
= New Grain Offering Feast.

2. + 50 Days = __July 23, 2022.__ This is True Pentecost = 2nd 50 Day Marker.
= New Wine Offering Feast.

3. + 50 Days = September 11, 2022. This is the 3rd 50 Day Marker.
= New Oil Offering Feast.

PENTECOST DOUBLE COUNT

WHEN IS THE END OF THE CHURCH AGE AND THE RAPTURE?

Date Calculator: Add to or Subtract From a Date

Enter a start date and add or subtract any number of days, months, or years.

Count Days   Add Days   Workdays   Add Workdays   Weekday   Week №

Start Date

Month:	Day:	Year:	Date:
5	/ 14	/ 2022	

Today

Israel's Independence Day

Include the time

☐ Repeat

Add/Subtract: (+) Add   **Years:** ∨   **Months:**   **Weeks:**   **Days:** 70

Include only certain weekdays

'In 70 more Days, the Wheat will be gone'.

[Calculate New Date]

From **Saturday, May 14, 2022**
Added 70 days

Result: Saturday July 23, 2022

= PENTECOST

1 JEWISH YEAR
=360 days

= 360°

Month of Tammuz
PENTECOST

5 6 7

1 2 3   4

THE DOOR

Spring Feasts of YHVH

49 Days
First Fruits +
49 Days + 1 Day

Fall Feasts of YHVH

50 Days
Mirror Count
Leviticus 23:16

As a Servant, as a 'Tree', a 'Memorah' before the Living
Waters of the Presence of YHVH before His Throne.

As an 'Almond Tree'

360

330

300

270   240

1. PASSOVER
2. UNLEAVENED BREAD
3. FIRST FRUITS
4. PENTECOST
5. TRUMPETS
6. ATONEMENT
7. TABERNACLES

Advertising

PENTECOST DOUBLE COUNT

WHEN IS THE END OF THE CHURCH AGE AND THE RAPTURE?

Date Calculator: Add to or Subtract From a Date

Enter a start date and add or subtract any number of days, months, or years.

Count Days   Add Days   Workdays   Add Workdays   Weekday   Week №

Start Date

Month: Day: Year: Date:

6   / 3   / 2022

Today

Rabbinical Shavuot

Include the time

☐ Repeat

[Calculate New Date]

From **Friday, June 3, 2022**
Added 50 days

Result: Saturday, July 23, 2022

= PENTECOST

'In 50 more Days, the Wheat will be gone'.

Add/Subtract: Years: Months: Weeks: **Days:**

(+) Add   ˅   **50**

Include only certain weekdays

Month of Tammuz
PENTECOST

1 JEWISH YEAR
=360 days

= 360°

1 2 3   **4**   **5 6 7**

49
Days
First Fruits+
49 Days + 1 Day

THE DOOR

50
Days
Mirror Count
Leviticus 23:16

Spring Feasts of YHVH

Fall Feasts of YHVH

As a Servant, as a 'Tree', a 'Menorah' before the Living
Waters of the Presence of YHVH before His Throne.

As an 'Almond Tree'

So, in one's Calculation, the highest Watch Time for any Year would be around Mid-July. That would coincide with that 2nd Count of 50 Days, in one's Estimation. And this Pentecost could correspond to the time of the Feast of New Wine then. And it is why in Acts 2, the Mocking Crowds suggested that the Disciples were 'Drunk on the New Wine', etc. Also, note that on that Day, 3000 Souls got Saved. This is to insinuate that a Massive Number of People were there in Jerusalem for a Major Feast as 3000 People were surely but a Fraction of the total number of Pilgrims there present, etc.

And one contends that the Descent of GOD the Holy Spirit on this Acts 2 Pentecost Event, as noted in other Studies, did not take place in the Upper Room. Then where? The Temple 'House'. If one has visited Jerusalem, no more than 120 People could ever fit in an average Home. At best, it would have had to have been a 'Conference Room' type, like the Upper Room, where the Core of the Disciples meet.

But it was after the Resurrection of Jesus, that they became emboldened by the Indwelling of the Holy Spirit, having come down on Pentecost, at the 50th Day after Shavuot, which is the 49 Days of Weeks, etc. The Bible clearly states that thereafter, they met Daily at the Temple. The only place in the entire Region of Israel where 1000s of People could be accommodated and gather in such Numbers is on the Temple Mount.

So, the 'House' that the Scripture is inferring to, is the House of YHVH or the Temple, in one's opinion. This was a 'Side Note'. But one would agree with Dr. Awe, that it is understood that 2022 is a Sabbath Year, starting in the Fall with Rosh HaShanah. And it will be a Reset. It is coming in September. The Luciferian Globalist Reset will happen. The issue is, will it coincide with their New World Order through Economic Collapse? Most likely.
Based on all the Geo-Political Trajectories and Financial

Trends, the so-called Experts are clambering that it is going to be the 'Big One'. Regardless of this Critique, as Dr. Awe stated, it is very exciting to watch it all play-out and if June 15, 2022 comes and goes, it is only a mere Month more to see if one's July 23, 2022 could rather be a more accurate Rapture Timing Scenario.

One would like to close with a 'Plug' for the July 23, 2022 Date in how a Reader sent an Email of the following Correlation or perhaps could be a Confirmation.
As it is known that the World is on the verge of Famine and that Wheat will soon be 'gone'. This is due to COVID and the intentional Disruption of the Supply and now Food Chains. There were 2 Reports that were made public that had some unusual Day Counts in themselves. The 1st one had to do with how the Headline read about the Wheat Famine to come.

It was reported on May 14, 2022 -which was Israel Independence Day, that 'There are only 70 Days until Wheat runs out'. If one adds 70 Days to May 14, 2022, the End Day is July 23, 2022. The Dire Situation that the World will shortly face, of the Issue of the Wheat Food Shortages has been the Headlines in another Reports. This time, the Date was June 3, 2022. This is the Date that many believed to be Shavuot, the 49th Day or Feast of Weeks, etc.

The Headline read, 'There are only 50 more Days until Wheat runs out in the World', Thus, if one adds 50 Days to this Day of June 3, 2022, it lands also on July 23, 2022. Coincidence? Synchronicity? Time will tell. But the Reader clearly understood the possible Prophetic Implications as the Believers are likened to Wheat and how at the End of the Church Age, at the Rapture, there will be 'No more Wheat-People left on Earth'.

Israel: *May 14, 2022 +* *70 Days =* *July 23, 2022*
Shavuot: *June 3, 2022 +* *50 Days =* *July 23, 2022*

Notice how from Israel's Independence Day in the Gregorian Calendar, the 70 Days echo when in 70 AD, Israel ceased to be a Nation and the Temple was Destroyed. Then for the June 3 Shavuot Date, notice how a 50 Day Count is what Pentecost is all about, the 50hh Day after Shavuot. Selah.

Main Sources

Why our RAPTURE HOPE in JUNE is still alive!!!! SHAVUOT Ain't over! IT STILL AIN'T OVER!
Dr. Barry Awe YouTube channel
https://www.youtube.com/watch?v=QZj5jN3Lylc

Articles

#609: SINAI PENTECOST
https://www.postscripts.org/ps-news-609.html

#630: WHEN IS PENTECOST?
https://www.postscripts.org/ps-news-630.html

#618: WHY 'PENTECOST' AND THE RAPTURE CANNOT OCCUR IN THE SPRING
https://www.postscripts.org/ps-news-618.html

WHY THE RAPTURE CANNOT OCCUR ON YOM TERUAH

A Critique in the Theory and Error that Watchers of the Rapture Event Keep Making

*'And when the Day of Pentecost was Fully Come, they were all with One Accord in one Place. And suddenly there came a **Sound** [Trumpet] from Heaven as of a Rushing Mighty Wind, and it filled all the House where they were sitting'. -Acts 2:1-2*

The purpose of this chapter is to circle back on a prior write-up, #637 The Great Apostasy. The main reason why one made that Info-Graphic that accompanied the Study was to illustrate just how bad it is with the Spiritual Condition of the Professing Protestant Church. And that the 3% that would be considered the Watchers in these End Times, because it is the End Times, is also in 'Bad' shape, Spiritually Speaking. How so. One would say that they do not have a sound footing or understanding of Prophecy.

In part, it is because it does take a lot of Years of Study and the differing Concepts, Premises, Conjectures, Speculations of what the 'Teachers' present as potential Timelines, Rapture Dates, etc., are not critiqued as they should be based on Scripture. It is not that one has 'Figured it Out', but the point is that Character Counts. The issue one has, is not that Speculative Rapture Dates are presented and come and go. That is how the Church is to Watch, Wait, and Test the Evidence and the Hypothesis, etc. It is about Character. Even though in one's opinion, it has been a 'Broken Record' Syndrome, as far as the Rapture Dates are surmised. It is because the same Premises keep being used in the Calculations. And the same Errors are made.

PENTECOST SUMMER FEAST

WHEN IS THE END OF THE CHURCH AGE AND THE RAPTURE?

CHURCH AGE - PENTECOSTAL INTERMISSION

Based on Leviticus 23:15

SPRING

Nisan	Iyar	Sivan	TAMMUZ	Av	Elul		Tishrei
1ST MONTH	2ND MONTH	3RD MONTH	4TH MONTH	5TH MONTH	6TH MONTH		7TH MONTH

FALL

1 - Passover
2 - Unleavened Bread
3 - First Fruits

4- PENTECOST

1 - Yom Teruah
2 - Yom Kippur
3 - Sukkot

49 Days

4 PENTECOST @ Sunrise

SUMMER

49 Days

1 - Passover
2 - Unleavened Bread
3 - First Fruits

4 - PENTECOST @ Sunrise

5 - Yom Teruah
6 - Yom Kippur
7 - Sukkot

Prophetic Symmetry of YHVH's Feasts

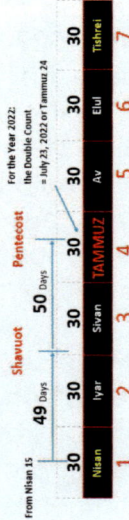

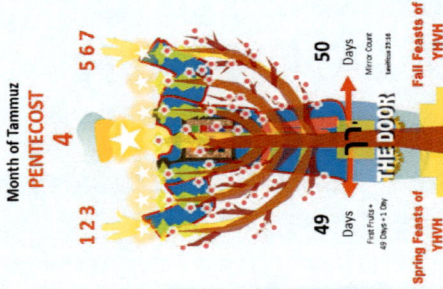

From Nisan 15

Shavuot — 49 Days
Pentecost — 50 Days

For the Year 2022:
the Double Count
= July 23, 2022 or Tammuz 24

	Nisan	Iyar	Sivan	TAMMUZ	Av	Elul	Tishrei
	30	30	30	30	30	30	30
	1	2	3	4	5	6	7

Spring Feasts of YHVH

49 Days
First Fruits +
49 Days + 1 Day

1 2 3

THE DOOR

4

PENTECOST
Month of Tammuz

5 6 7

50 Days
Mirror Count
Leviticus 23:16

Fall Feasts of YHVH

As a Servant, as a 'Tree', a 'Menorah' before the Living Waters of the Presence of YHVH before His Throne.

As an 'Almond Tree'

Do Not Drink the Kool Aid

For example, once the June 15, 2022 'Pentecost' Day of the Rapture came and went, the natural direction is to now go to the next Jewish Feast, that of Yom Teruah, or what many presume is the Feast of Trumpets. And this solely because it is the 'Last Trumpet' and that is when the Rapture will happen as the Apostle Paul alludes to. Right? No. But if that be the case, then that is the Time, Place and Feast that should be then solely focused on without wavering and 'Record Skipping' the gamut of all the Feasts of YHVH, starting from Passover, every Year.

The point is that what one finds disturbing is, again, not that Watchers, who Watch and Report of the possible Rapture Dates, but it has to do with the Watcher's Character. How so? As one would place oneself in that Community of the 3% that seeks to Watch, Discern, Hypothesis, Conjecture, Suppose, etc., when such a Premise of a possible Rapture Date is given, i.e., on a 99th Day from a Nisan 15 Date, being True Pentecost and perhaps the Rapture event, if that comes and goes for a given Year, one will say, 'I was wrong'. As for me, this has been one's Arching Argument, of a Double Count and that Pentecost is a Summer Feast, etc.

In one's Estimation and Understanding, the Rapture event is pegged to Pentecost, but at a Summer Wheat Harvest Season and past the Summer Solstice. The Point is that for the most part, the Watcher-Teachers that have insisted on a prior Watch Date, like June 15, 2022 do not allow Critiquing Comments on their YouTube Channel to be posted. But worse is that they still insist that, 'They were Right, but'…Even worse is that out of the 3% that supposedly are the Watchmen Community, they too are jerked-along with the 'Rapture Psychosis'. Here is a sample of this Madness in how they are 'Drinking the Kool Aid' that makes one run out the Door screaming.

It is not that one is 'Right', rather that others are 'Wrong'. But how Honest Critique is not accepted. Sure, it is easy, in Hind- Sight to Critique, but one was presenting the evidence well ahead of such Dates for how it is 'IMPOSSIBLE' to have a Rapture, if pegged to a Summer Wheat Harvest before the June 20-21 Summer Solstice. Here is my Point, in just how bad it is.

It is not just those who believed, for example, that June 15, 2022 was going to be the Rapture, up to a 99% Level of Confidence, but that the 3% Watcher Community also believed it too and are drinking their 'Kool Aid'. Here below is a Point made by a Commenter on the Unsealed.com Facebook Thread by a Rhonda R.

'I was watching/listening to the countdown to the Rapture with George at The Return of the King and want to share some thoughts. Right now for me it's getting close to 1:00 AM in the wee hours of the morning of the 15th of June. We are still here obviously. I think George was still correct in his timing but not in the Rapture itself but the countdown of the 7 days prior to the Rapture.

Remember in the account of Noah and Jesus said this time would like Noah's time. God gave Noah a 7 day warning before the flood started!!! Noah knew the flood was coming all those years but God told him exactly when only 7 days before it actually started raining. So, George is not wrong in his calculations I don't believe, he just forgot that mankind was going to get that last 7 day warning and the 153 fish were that.

Plus, the Song of Solomon chapter 2 tells of a spring time Rapture and 7 days added to the 14th brings us to the summer equinox. Jesus said the Rapture would happen when summer is almost here. Maranatha'. What this person basically said is that although the Rapture Date that was supposed to have happened, did not occur, it was 'Right'.

274

But really only 7 Days off now. And that the Rapture, being like a type of the Song of Solomon, is to take place in the Spring, but in the Summer Wheat Harvest. Are these People out of their minds? Do they not read what they are writing? It is called Plausible deniability. This is, to a degree, pure Rapture 'Cognitive Dissonance' and a Mental Dystopia going on here. One is not mocking or ridiculing, but just pointing out the absurdity of just how Potent the Rapture Kool Aid can be.

At the Feast of Yom Teruah, the Ram's Horn is blown.

And the point is that so long as the Watcher Community is not versed in Prophecy and the Bible, which would dispel all these 'Record Skipping', a lot less Blind Following would result. And in another aspect, the 3% of the Watchers would not be subjected to more ridicule and Resentment. This Resentment comes from within and without the 3%. But it is why the 97% of the rest of the Professing Protestant Christians, much less those outside Christendom do not even bother. One would not blame them. But as it is not just about pointing out the Faults or Errors, one always, as a Responsible Critic, will share the points, one believes why it is IMPOSSIBLE for the Rapture event to occur on a Yom Teruah, or how some mistakenly attribute that time to Rosh HaShanah for the Tribulation Period to Begin.

Evidence?

1-In Prophetic Time, the Feast of Pentecost is in the Present Tense. It is still occurring, as it began on Pentecost in 32 AD and will not end until the Church Age Commission comes to a close with the Resurrection-Rapture event.

To have the Rapture that is pegged to the Feast of Pentecost, to then have it occur in another Feast of YHVH, that being Rosh HaShanah, as the proponents of the Failed June 15, 2022 Rapture Date now has determined that Yom Teruah will be the Day of the Rapture, is absurd. If one studies the Passage in Acts 2, there was a 'Sound of the Trumpet', correcting it to the events, similar to those that occurred on Mount Sinai.

2. This same Watcher who now says that the Tribulation Period will start on Yom Teruah, because it is the Rapture is false. Where does he get the Information, Evidence or Scripture that the Rapture has to now occur on Yom Teruah? Where does he get the notion that the Rapture starts the Tribulation Period?

What starts the Day Count of the Tribulation Period, being 2520 Days or 2 Halves of 1260 Days, or 42 Months is the Daily Sacrifices commencing. This is determined in how the Scripture states that at the Mid-Point of the 7-Year Tribulation Period, that corresponds to the Revelation 12 Passage, thereafter, the Woman, that being the Remnant of Believing Israel, will be protected for 1260 Days.

And for the Daily Sacrifices to begin, the Jews need the Altar. And for the Altar to be Consecrated, they need the Red Heifers. So, one can see, no flippant Declaration of Rapture on Yom Teruah will occur, guaranteed.

3. The Church Age Period is an 'Intermission', meaning that it has no Prescribed Time, necessarily announced as to how long it will last. Consider when Jesus read on the Day of the Jubilee Year from the Scroll of Isaiah. It has been rightly noted that Jesus stopped at the point where it stated, 'And the Vengeance of our GOD' portion.

Jesus basically put a Comma in-between the entire phrase. And how long has this 'Comma' lasted? Nearly 2000 Years. The Point is that the Spring Feasts were fulfilled by Jesus in a matter of 1 Week, in the Spring.

The Fall Feasts, is when Jesus comes back at Yom Teruah and will be fulfilled in a matter of Weeks. But Pentecost? It is the Summer Feast that will conclude Pentecost, as it is still in motion and unfulfilled. It will be fulfilled when that Last Gentile is saved by Jesus, etc.

4. The Church Age is associated with Pentecost as that is when the Disciples, being gathered as it was their Custom, at the Temple 'House', in how the Holy Spirit came down and they began to Speak on Foreign Languages. Why?

It was because on Pentecost, it was 1 of the 3 In-Gathering Feasts were all Jewish Males of Military Age were to be presented before YHVH at the Temple, etc. This meant that the Jews came from all the Nations they had been taken to in the 1st Diaspora by the Babylonians.

It foreshadows the connection to the Nations as that is what has characterized the Prophetic Pentecostal Intermission. And to reiterate, that the Feast of Pentecost is presently in play, and not done. It will NOT, cannot be completed in another Feast of YHVH, in this case Yom Teruah. It is Impossible and absurd to think so.

But if the 3% of the Watchers that are left, Watching the End Days want to continue 'Drinking the Kool-Aid'? One is only pointing out the Counter Arguments and one is not asking for anyone to be convinced otherwise or to have to believe in what one is Arguing. But Character Counts. Thus, to reiterate, one is not faulting a Watcher/Teacher for considering possible Future Rapture Dates as seen in the Feasts of YHVH. One is engaged in the same Supposition and has presented one's argument, etc. What about Character?

For example, if one's July 23, 2022 Pentecost Date comes and goes, and the Rapture does not take place at that time, one will admit the Year was not then 2022. One is only highly suggesting that it could be a High Watch Date. And that is as far as one can say. As to Character, even so, if the Rapture event does not occur then, one will be the first to say, one was WRONG. And this is my point, I am disappointed that Fellow Watchmen and Watchwomen do not have the Character enough, and to Honor the LORD Jesus, to admit that they were 'WRONG' and carry on. No, instead they Double Down and worse, they insist that they were Right'.

And worse than that, all those that believed and believe the Kool Aid still believe he and other like-minded are 'Right'. Well, I find that to be so WRONG. And it is not that such Watchers and Teachers are accountable to this Critic, but they are to, not only the 3% of the Watcher Community, but to the entire Professing Christians or Body of Christ, and ultimately to Jesus Himself. One welcomes an Honest Critique of one's Work and Counter Arguments for a Rapture Date needing to occur on a Summer Season Wheat Harvest and on the 99th Day after a Passover, Nisan 15 Day Count.

Article

Evidence and Argument for a July Pentecost.

#609: SINAI PENTECOST CALENDAR CALCULATIONS
Determining the End of the Church Age
https://www.postscripts.org/ps-news-609.html

Additional Studies Related to Topic

#618: WHY 'PENTECOST' AND THE RAPTURE CANNOT OCCUR IN THE SPRING
https://www.postscripts.org/ps-news-618.html

#630: WHEN IS PENTECOST? ORIGINS OF CONFUSION AND COUNT
https://www.postscripts.org/ps-news-630.html

#632: WHY PENTECOST CANNOT OCCUR IN AUGUST
https://www.postscripts.org/ps-news-632.html

#634: JUNE RAPTURE HOPE? DR. BERRY AWE'S JUNE 15 DATE
https://www.postscripts.org/ps-news-634.html

#637: THE GREAT APOSTASY - COMPROMISED CHURCHES USA
https://www.postscripts.org/ps-news-637.html

WHEN IS PENTECOST?
ORIGINS OF COUNT CONFUSION
A Matrix Date Comparison of Various Concepts

The purpose of this chapter is to present the various Calendar Calculations that are used, as well as their Rationale based on Pharisaical Judaism and Church Tradition for determining when Pentecost is and how it is counted. As the Summer Months approach each Year, many who are Watching for the Blessed Hope, surmise that Pentecost could be a Prime Candidate for the Rapture event to occur, at such a Season.

The portion of Scripture that 1st mentions and gives Ecclesiastical Instruction about Pentecost is found in Leviticus. Pentecost is very much tied to Moses, Sinai, a Rebellion, a Golden Calf and Redemption. There is a Debate that has been as old as when Pentecost 1st started but one does believe it has not ended or completely been fulfilled. How so?

The present Church Age is what comprises this amazing Time. But Jesus stated that 1 Year, 1 Day and 1 Hour, the Church Age of 'Pentecost' will end. Although the exact Timing may never be known, Jesus has left enough Clues and Prophetic Patterns to conjecture. Although it is Speculation on one's part to do so, one can sense that in studying all the major 7 Feasts of YHVH, one would say that out of all of them, Pentecost is the most fitting for the Church Age and what Jesus is presently doing on Earth.

This is not to say that all other 6 Feasts could not be a Candidate, just the same. They all do, in fact, have a Rapture Element to them that can be argued. And it is assumed that one is ascribing the Resurrection-Rapture event to be fulfilled at a Feast, or 'Appointed Time'.

What one has persistently and consistently presented in various Articles, Charts and Studies is that if the Rapture were to occur on a Feast Day of YHVH, Pentecost would most likely be it. And thus for the past Decade or more, one has surmised that at any given Year, Pentecost is the height of the Watch Times. And this only because one is then inferring that in determining when True Pentecost is, then perhaps the Rapture event might correspond to it.

Moses on 99th Day, or 40 Days from Sivan 15. Dore.

Thus, one cannot with 100% Confidence, as others do, say that the Rapture will occur on a Pentecost Day. One can only suggest a High Watch Day, as every Year, when calculating the Double Count Theory from Leviticus, which is what one focuses on, no more, no less. It is in the Book of Leviticus that the Protocols of Pentecost are laid-out. And this is where the 'Confusion' starts. How so? It is about what is the True Count and from when? One would agree, in general, that if the Resurrection-Rapture event is to occur, it would or could most likely happen on a Feast Day of YHVH and not just on a random Day and Time. Before going any further, one will present the various pre-conceived Notions, Suppositions and Interpretations as to why one believes the current concept of what is Pentecost and how to count it is not what is presently understood.

Suppositions

The 1st Supposition is about the word itself, Pentecost. It simply infers the Number 50. The Root Word comes from the Greek, Penta or 5. The Jews, up to the Birth of the Church on Pentecost in the Year 32, as one calculates, counted the Day after the Feast of Weeks. But there is now Evidence, as surmised by Ken Johnson, who studies the Dead Sea Scrolls that the Jews had observed 3 Minor Feasts during Summer to culminate with the Feast of Wine, and that correlated to when Pentecost occurred.

The 2nd Supposition is how Pentecost is incorporated in the Economy of YHVH's Feasts in that it is 1 of the 3 Main Feasts Israel was to Gather. That is, all the Military-Age Men would be required to present themselves in Jerusalem and the Temple. It was sort of a Military Drill of 'Reporting for Duty' and being Counting in the Ranks, etc. Ken Johnson surmises that the Jews, upon comprehending the significance of the Pentecost Age being initiated, after the Resurrection of Jesus, re-interpreted the Term from being the 99th Day, to the Day after the Feast of Weeks, called Shavuot.

The 3rd Supposition is that, as it stands now, the Traditional Interpretation of when is Pentecost and how to count it, is predicated on what one does believe, how the Pharisaical Jews re-defined what and when Pentecost is and when it occurs. Further, the Roman Catholic Church has continued in this Rendition of the Day Count that just adds 1 Day after the Feast of Weeks or Shavuot.

Herein lies the problem, in one's estimation and the following Evidence and Rationale will be presented. These Suppositions not to try and convince People to stop Believing and Practicing the Celebration of the Traditional Pentecost as it is presently understood. But the main focus of such a Rationale, does go contrary to the Tradition of the Church, at least since the Roman Catholics.

It is to just present the Arguments as to why one believes that the True Count of Pentecost is what one and many others have come to understand is a Double-Count of 49 Days plus 50 subsequent Days. It is adding to the Feast of Weeks an additional 50 Days that determines True Pentecost. This would then be a total of 99 Days. But from what time?

The 4th Supposition is that Pentecost, as the Jews Count the Feast is derived from then the 'Sabbath after the Morrow' is defined as. The Jews, considered Passover as a High Day Sabbath, and that is corroborated in the Gospels. This is why any 'Criminal' Crucified on a Cross, had to be 'Died' before Sunset or else all of Israel would be Cursed. This is why the Romans were ordered to break the Bones of the Men, so that their Frame could collapse and not be able to exhale and thus Asphyxiate and die. But when they came to Jesus, He was already Dead and 'No Bone was Broken', as that is what Prophecy foretold about the Messiah, when put to Death, etc.

The 5th Supposition is that the Jews use the 'Counting of the Omer'. It had to do with the Barley Harvest. This has been the Traditional Jewish Starting Point of the Day Count. But only the 1st 49 Days plus the 50th Day, etc. The 7 Sabbaths or the 49 Days are counted from the Day after a Passover. Then adding just 1 Day, is thus considered 'Pentecost'. To add the additional 50 Days would Verify and Legitimize the Church Age.

The 6th Supposition, even based on this Logic, is clearly discerning in that the 7 Sabbath Count or the Feast of Weeks, Shavuot is not Pentecost. Pentecost is not part and parcel to this 49 Day Count. Presently, Pentecost, obviously is attributed to and Celebrated by the Jews and Traditional Church on this Day after, the 50th Day. This is how the present Count of Pentecost is derived from.

It is about Legitimizing the Church Age

One will not be emphasizing the Calendar Debate, in so much as one is only attempting to focus on the Day Count itself.

The 7th Supposition is that, in so much as Calendars go, the prevailing Notion of the Seasons and how they are corresponding to the Feasts of YHVH are without Argument, except when it comes to Pentecost. Here is the current Logic used. The Spring Feasts of YHVH, Passover, Unleavened Bread, and First Fruits occur in the Spring. Ok. Then the Fall Feasts of YHVH, Yom Teruah, Yom Kippur and Sukkot occur in the Fall. Ok.

This leaves Pentecost as some arbitrary, unassigned 'Season', but is then 'Tagged' to the Spring Feasts as that is when the Feast of Weeks occurs, still within a Spring Season. Thus, Pentecost is always attributed to a Spring Fulfilment. This is an error. Here is where one presents the Argument that Pentecost is a Summer Feast Celebration.

The 1st Supposition is that the Day Count as interpreted by one, is to be an Additional 50 Day Count and not just 1 Day after the Feast of Weeks. This will always put True Pentecost in the Summer Season, some Time in July Wheat Harvest of Tammuz.

The 2nd Supposition is that YHVH uses the Astronomical Calendar to Delineate and Calibrate the Seasons of the Year into 4 Quadrants of Time for this precise reason. What He created and uses are the Demarcations of the Solstices and Equinoxes. These also were to be for Appointments of His Feasts and for Signs. Thus, the various Cycles of Planting and Harvesting were also pegged to these Yearly Demarcations as Israel's Agriculture depending on it, as well as the World for that matter.

The 3rd Supposition is that the Astronomical Demarcations of Time, is what dictates the True Calendar of YHVH. And in so understanding, it is how the Feasts of YHVH are to be determined. It is not based on some Physical Observation of when Man thinks any Grains are Mature enough to then start a Calendar. This is absurd.

The 4th Supposition is that the Feasts of YHVH were also pegged to these 4 Quadrants of Time. Meaning that the Calendar, as far as YHVH is concerned, defines the Start and End of Seasons, and Feasts. This is to suggest that the 1st Month of YHVH, as instructed to Moses, is determined by the New Moon after the Spring Equinox.

The 5th Supposition is that by correctly delineating the Calendar Year by such Astronomical Bench-Markers, the Feasts of YHVH will always be in sync with the Seasons. Thus, the Spring Feasts occur after the Spring Equinox of March 20-21. The Summer Feasts, that of Pentecost, will always occur in the Summer after the June 20-21 Summer Solstice. And the Fall Feasts will always occur after the Fall Equinox, etc.

The 6th Supposition is that the current Jewish Calendar, the Hillel 2 is only based on the Lunar Cycles that are Mathematically calculable but are not in sync with the Solar 4 Season Time Markers as outlined above. This is why, in any given Year, the Jewish Feasts, as celebrated by the Jews, currently and the Church to some extent, will always be off. This means, that for example, the Fall Feasts may occur before the Fall and thus, the 'Fall' Feasts are technically still Summer Feasts.

The 7th Supposition is that, purely based on the Day Count of Exodus, of when the Hebrews and Company left Egypt, Nisan 15, the Scripture Accounts exactly determine how long it took for the Multitude to reach Mount Sinai, 15th Day of the 3rd Month. This was 60 Days total.

What is the Starting Day?

According to YHVH's Command, the Trek and Day Count started the Day after Passover. And the Bible is clear as to what specific Month and Day it took. With this Pattern and that of the Prophetic Pattern of the Menorah, one believes that Pentecost occurred on the 99th Day (40 Days Later) for the following reasons.

This portion of the Study will focus on why Pentecost occurred on the 99th Day, once the Hebrews and Company arrived at the Foot of Mount Sinai, in Arabia as the Apostle corroborates this Supposition that is still debated within the Church, etc. First, one has to state that this Double-Count Theory can have 3 End Dates, based on the Start Dates. The 1st Day Count is strictly taken from the Exodus Nisan 15. The determination of when Pentecost truly occurred is based on the following Day Counting.

The Exodus Account in the Bible states that it was on the 15th Day of the 3rd Month, Sivan that Israel arrived at the Foot of Mount Sinai. This means that it took 60 Days or 3 Months of 30 Days each to accomplish that feat. Notice that the Feast of Weeks passed, being the 49 Day and not yet arrived at Mount Sinai for another 20 Days. The Feast was not even known, given or observed by Israel at the Time.

Then once at Mount Sinai, a Preparation of 3 Days elapsed, as that is when YHVH came down in Full Glory to 'Meet' Israel. It was from Sivan 15 that the 40 Day Count starts and Moses goes up the Mountain. He does not return until that 40th Day corresponds to the 99th This is corroborated in how Aaron proclaimed in Exodus 32:5 that the Next Day would be a Feast. The 60th Day was neither Shavuot nor Pentecost. What it was is the Marriage Proposal by YHVH to Israel. YHVH basically Proposed, by figuratively saying, 'Ok, I Rescued you, now will you Marry Me?' Israel said 'Yes'.

Prophetic Pattern

This is amazing as no Peoples or a Nation has this Relationship-Status as only Israel does. However, due to its Messiah, a Son of theirs by Birth, Jesus and the Son of GOD, by Divine Decree, has made it possible for Individual People to enter this 'Marriage Covenant'. Although there is a Delineation in who is the Groom and who is the Bride.

Meaning that this Marriage Contract made by Jesus and the Disciples at the Upper Room constitutes the 'Bride' for the GOD the Son. It is Israel that is the 'Wife' of GOD the Father, etc. This to say that GOD the SON has a Bride and that is now composed of all those individual 'Stones' or 'Jewels' that make-up the Church Age Believers. And this includes Jews and non-Jews, up to when the Commission is completed at the Rapture.

This Completion of the 'Bride of Christ Jesus' will occur at the Last Day when the Resurrection-Rapture will conclude this 'Pentecost Intermission' as GOD the Father, YHVH deals then with His wayward Wife, Israel in the Last Sabbath Cycle. And so, the Rationale is that it will be at a Pentecost Feast Day, that would most likely have the Resurrection-Rapture event occur. Why? It is because of the following Suppositions.

1st, based on the Menorah Typology, the Prophetic Symmetry of YHVH's Feasts must maintain their 'Prophetic Symmetry'. In the Menorah, there are 3 Branches on either side of the Center 'Servant Stem'. It is what brings Balance and Equilibrium to the whole integrity of the Form.

If any side is stacked, it will collapse. This is the same Prophetic Principle dealing with the Feasts of YHVH and their corresponding Prophetic Fulfillments. This to say that Pentecost cannot be assigned to the Spring Feasts.

288

2nd, based on this Symmetry Principle, the Feasts of YHVH in the Spring, start after the Spring Equinox. The Fall Feasts start after the Fall Equinox and this would then stand to reason that the Summer Feast of Pentecost, corresponding to the Servant Stem, that being Jesus really occurs after the Summer Solstice of June 20-21. This is why any assertion of the Rapture corresponding to the Traditional 'Pentecost' that occurs before June 20-21 will always fail to materialize

3rd, based on these Assertions, this is why, every Year, those that are seeking and expecting a Pentecost Rapture are 'Half-Right'. In one's Assessment, they have the Right Feast but the Wrong Time. One has to also emphasize that the Day Count on the Jewish Calendars, as far as Day Counts are concerned, always stay the same. Or in other words, the Jewish Calendar Count is more standardized as Nisan 1 and the 14, being Passover is always the same. It is when the Jewish Calendar Count is transposed onto the Gregorian Calendar that it adds a layer of further Confusion. Why? It is because it is Solar based and the Jewish Hillel 2 is Lunar based.

4th, based on the Jewish Calendar, regardless of when it is determined to start, is fixed in so much as the 1st Month has fixed Days of 30 Days each. But there are Discrepancies even in this consideration due to the Hillel 2 Calendar. Some Jewish Months have 29 Days, etc. But in Theory, the Months should have 30 Days each.

5th, based on this Supposition, as noted, the Jewish Feasts are always on a Prescribed Day. Meaning that Passover always is and will be on the 14th Day of the 1st Month. Yom Kippur will always be on the 15 Day of the 7th Month, etc. What complicates the issue, is how the Jewish Months translate and correspond to the Gregorian Calendar.

Traditional Interpretations

6th, based on these Assertions, so far, there are those that would rightly argue that Jesus only spent 40 Days right after His Resurrection and Ascended into Heaven on the 40th Day, just 10 Days prior to the 50th Day. But what if the 40 Day Time-Span pertained to a different start Day other than when Jesus resurrected? Nonetheless, one argues that the 50th Day was not Pentecost nor were the Disciples at the Upper Room with only 120 when the events of Acts 2 occurred, rather at the Temple.

7th, based on the Traditional Interpretation of these Scenarios above, it would mean that all of the Male Fighting Men of Israel, not only had to present themselves during Passover, but now, just 49 Days out, just over a 1 Month period, they had to all return again to Jerusalem. This would not make sense as a great Financial Burden would be required, that one does not think YHVH would have Sanctioned that.

Thus, based on all these prior Points of Argument, one leans more to Comprehend that Pentecost, 1st corresponded in the Mount Sinai Narrative, that being 99 Days from when they left Egypt, the Day after Passover, Nisan 15. They reached Sinai on the 60th Day and from there, on the 3rd Day, YHVH came down to proclaim His 10 Commandment. But the 2 Tablets were not presented to Israel by Moses at that Time.

There were 7 more Days to prepare and then Moses went up to meet with YHVH, Face-to-Face for a duration of 1 Week. All these Day Counts were the Period of 40 Days. The Total Days surmised since Nisan 15 were 99 Days. This is why Israel grew weary of waiting for Moses, being gone for over a Month and thus turned to the Golden Calf as their New God, etc. It was on the 99th Day then that Moses came down the Mountain with the 2 Tablets of the Law.

However, it was the occasion of the Golden Calf and how Moses struck the Tablets because of it and 3000 People Died. Here is why one then corresponds this 99th Day with being Pentecost or what would be celebrated thereafter, the Giving the Law and a Marriage Covenant, etc. It is why the connotation of Sinai being connected directly with Pentecost in the 'Giving of the Law' is correct. This part is True, but not the actual Day Count.

Tradition holds that the Feast of Weeks was when YHVH came down and the Day after was Pentecost. This does not 'add-up'. Given this precise Jewish Day Count, the 99th Day will always fall on Tammuz 23-24 in any given Year. Now it will vary when that Day is transposed onto the Gregorian Calendar. For example, in the Year, 2021, that 99th Day corresponded to July 20. In the Year 2022, it corresponds to July 23, etc.

Now to reiterate, the Double Count Theory is based on the 49 Days and then the +50 Days to determine True Pentecost. However, this Pattern will then vary when being transposed onto the Gregorian Calendar also. And again, it will depend on which Day one will use to determine the 'The Morrow after the Sabbath'. What is this Day, the Day of Unleavened Bread? Was this Day, the Sunday, after the Sabbath in which Jesus rose in the afternoon, corresponding to the 72 Hour Count, precisely?

Or is the Day Count to start on the Sabbath, the Week following? Thus, the following Matrix will be provided to show these 3 Primary Day Count Assertions based on the Evidence presented. At the end of the 'Prophetic Day', the Discrepancy is just over 1 Month of a difference. However, based on one's understanding, as it still stands and how most Christian Watchmen discern the Timing of Pentecost, still connected to the old Pharisaical Jews and Roman Catholic reckoning of Time, will always be wrong, in one's Assessment.

Pentecost Day Matrix

Although one whole-headedly agrees that if the Resurrection-Rapture event is to take place, it will occur on a Pentecost Feast Day. To reiterate, one believes that the current Interpretation of when Pentecost is really to be determined has been obfuscated, deliberately recalibrated to take-away from what Pentecost signified in the Book of Acts. Why? Pentecost is a Harvest Festival. It is the ingathering of the Summer Wheat Harvest.

Jesus alluded the World as a Wheat Field and a Harvesting of Souls at the End of the Age. What Age was that? The Church Age. In anything that all the different Pentecost and/or Rapture Camps would agree on, is that the World is ready now for this Harvest, this Transition back to Israel.

Many, even in the World are sensing a coming Climax, a Transition, a 'Birth' as the World is spiraling out of control. Precisely. The following is the Pentecost Matrix of Day Counts. Realize that the 99th Day Count Theory, will fall on 3 different Dates, but within a Weeks' difference only in this consideration. And finally, to surmise that the Resurrection-Rapture event does not have to correspond with a Feast of YHVH, that being primarily, Pentecost and it could happen at any Time or Day. This is the Doctrine of Imminence, but one doubts it.

Those that are teaching that Pentecost, in 2022 is on June 15 and that is when the Rapture will take place will be disappointed. First of all, from Nisan 15, the 49th Day corresponds to Sivan 3-4. There is a 13 Day Count Discrepancy. As one can perceive, the Day Count is off by 13 Days. This Day Count would not even correspond to any of the 4 Day Count Scenarios that are used to determine when Pentecost would occur.

Calendars Synchronize

From: *June 15, 2022*
Subtracted: *49 Days*
Result: *April 27, 2022*
https://www.timeanddate.com/date/dateadded.html?m1=6&d1=15&y1=2022&type=sub&ay=&am=&aw=&ad=49&rec=

1. Pentecost Sinai Pattern: from Day after Passover in Egypt.

Nisan 01 Spring Equinox   *New Moon.*
Nisan 14 Passover Nisan   *Full Moon.*
Nisan 15 Feast of U. Bread   *Starts Day Count of 49 Days = Sivan 7 But*
Israel is still in Route to Sinai.
Sivan 15 Arrival at Sinai   *Jewish Days start prior Day, the 14th at*
Sunset and staddle Gregorian.
Sivan 14,15,16   *Prescribed 3 Day of Consecration. Start of*
40 Day Count.
Sivan 17-23   *7-Days Moses consults with*
Elders/Instructions/Preparations.
Tammuz 23/24   *40 Days later, on the 99th Day Moses*
came down with Tablets, Golden Calf.

For the Year 2022, Tammuz 23-24 = thus **Pentecost is on July 23, 2022.**
(A 49 day + 50 Day Count) Scenario.

2. Pentecost Omer Count Pattern: from Day after Passover Hillel 2.

Nisan 14 Passover Nisan   *Full Moon.*
Nisan 15 Feast of U. Bread   *Starts Day Count of 49 Days or 7 Weeks.*
Sivan 3 Feast of Weeks   *Traditional Date ascribed. Date Varies in*
Gregorian Calendar.

For the Year 2022, Sivan 3 Feast of Weeks = thus **Pentecost on June 2, 2022.**

3. Pentecost Sunday Count Pattern: from 'Morrow after Sabbath'-Sunday

Nisan 14 Passover Nisan   *Full Moon.*
Nisan 18 Morrow after Sabbath *Starts Day Count of 49 Days or 7 Weeks.*
Sivan 6   *Traditional Date ascribed to Feast of*
Weeks. Date Varies in Gregorian Calendar.

For the Year 2022, Sivan 6 Feast of Weeks = thus **Pentecost on June 5, 2022.**

4. Pentecost 1 Week Count Pattern: from Sabbath of the following Week.

Nisan 14 Passover Nisan   *Full Moon.*
Nisan 25 1 Sabbath Later   *Starts Day Count of 49 Days or 7 Weeks.*
Sivan 13   *Traditional Date ascribed to Feast of*
Weeks. Date Varies in Gregorian Calendar.

For the Year 2022, Sivan 13 Feast of Weeks = thus **Pentecost on June 13, 2022.**

The point is just to show that those who are teaching that June 15 will be the Rapture are starting the 49 Day + 1 Day Count on April 27, 2022, or Nisan 27. This does not make sense and the Rapture will most likely not correspond to this Day Count either, unfortunately. Note that for the Year 2022, amazingly, both the Jewish Hillel 2 Calendar and the Gregorian Calendar are in sync. Jewish Days start on the prior Day, the 14th at Sunset and staddle Gregorian Calendar by 2 Days.

14 April 2022 After Sunset = 14th of Nisan, 5782
י״ד בְּנִיסָן תשפ״ב
Ta'anit Bechorot
Erev Pesach/Parashat Pesach
Show Hebrew Nekudot

Convert from Gregorian to Hebrew
Day: **14**
Month: **April**
Year: **2022**
After Sunset: **Yes**

Convert from Hebrew to Gregorian
Day: **14**
Month: **Nisan**
Year: **5782**

https://www.hebcal.com/converter?gd=14&gm=4&gy=2022&gs=on&g2h=1

In summary, one is only conveying why one has come to believe Pentecost is a Double Count, based on the 49 Days and then a subsequent 50 Day Count. It is the Minority Opinion and does go against Centuries of both Jewish and Christian Tradition. With each passing Year, one surmises that Pentecost corresponds to the Mount Sinai event of the Tablets of the Law being brought down by Moses. And that this Day corresponds to the event and circumstance of the Book of Acts.

And that in any given year, this 99th Day Count, starting 1 Day after the Passover is more precisely the correct Day Count. To reiterate, it is understood and proclaimed by those Watching for the Blessed Hope that the Law was given on Pentecost. This is the Key Truth. Yes and No. YHVH came down on the Mountain and iterated the 10 Commandments on the 3rd Day of their Assembly.

It was the Marriage Vows. No Stone Tablets from Moses were presented that Day. This was not Pentecost. It was 40 Days later, that Moses went-up to Receive the Physical 'Receipt' or 'Certificate' of the Marriage between YHVH and Israel. Being absent so long, that is why the People gave-up on Moses and built their Golden Cave instead.

This 50th Day, which would be the 99th Day since Nisan 15 and one argues, is Pentecost when Moses came down with the 2 Tablets. It symbolizes the Judgment that is coming upon those of the World that will be 'Worshiping' the 'Golden Calf' of the AntiChrist instead. This will occur during the 7-Year Tribulation Period as a 'Golden Image' will literally be built by the Orders of the 2nd Beast. This will be the Abomination of Desolation and occurs at the Mid-Point of the Sabbath Cycle.

This Double Count is just a Theory that seeks only to consider and determine the true Date of Pentecost. It is assuming a lot of Variables, like Shavuot is not Pentecost, that there is Prophetic Symmetry in the 7 Feasts of YHVH and the Argument is based on 3 main facets or 'Witnesses'. There is the Astronomical Delineation of Time. There is the Start Date of being either the Day after Passover or the Morrow after the Sabbath. And that if the Rapture event were to occur on a Feast of YHVH, Pentecost would most likely be it. If not in 2022, then the Double Count Theory persists and will be applied to 2023, 2024 and so on.

Main Sources
Wikipedia.com

Articles

#609 SINAI PENTECOST
https://www.postscripts.org/ps-news-609.html

#618 WHY 'PENTECOST' AND THE RAPTURE CANNOT OCCUR IN THE SPRING
https://www.postscripts.org/ps-news-618.html

#439 CALENDAR RECALIBRATIONS
https://www.postscripts.org/ps-news-439.html

Charts

Sinai Pentecost Countdown
https://nebula.wsimg.com/6213e89f48e2493921463e7ac2489e64?AccessKeyId=D40106E1331C24ABD7C3&disposition=0&alloworigin=1
Calendar Recalibrations
https://nebula.wsimg.com/a37cd5a303bc434e6743faf222cda550?AccessKeyId=D40106E1331C24ABD7C3&disposition=0&alloworigin=1

Sinai Great Pyramid Pattern - 2022
https://nebula.wsimg.com/4681687251d5ddd5af3915eb655e2991?AccessKeyId=D40106E1331C24ABD7C3&disposition=0&alloworigin=1

Videos

Tour of the Golden Calf Worship Site
https://www.youtube.com/watch?v=YDyArvioJ6w

Drone video Golden Calf Altar & Graveyard at the Real Mount Sinai in Arabia
https://www.youtube.com/watch?v=iarB1RjV2hk

Book of Exodus - Part 2
https://www.youtube.com/watch?v=b0GhR-2kPKI

RAPTURE PLANET PARADE?
COUNTDOWN TO A DIVISION
Great Alignment of an Occultation and Separation

The purpose of this chapter is to examine the June 24, 2022 Great Planetary Alignment. It consists of all the recognized Planets. There are 5 Planets that are visible to the Naked Eye and 2 Planets, Uranus and Neptune that are obscure. One needs either a Telescope or Powerful Binoculars to see them. The last Great Planetary Alignment that occurred with all the Planets lined-up was back in December 2004, some 18 Years ago. There was a Planetary Parade in April-May of 2022 but the Planet Mercury was absent.

There will be 2 Observations, in particular that will be highlighted in this Great Planetary Alignment. One Observation in how the Visible Planets, 5 in total are ordered in their Respective Distance from the Sun. This is amazing. The other observation is that all the Planets, both Visible and not, are to the Right Side of the Sun, from a Top View of the entire Solar System. This is also amazing. The rest of the Observations have to do with how such an

Alignment may have Biblical Implications as part of the Signs that occur in the Sun, Moon and the Stars, per the Prerogatives of YHVH in the Bible. What would be some of such Signs? The following well suggest possible Interpretations that one believes could have implications for the End of the Church Age and the occurrence of the Resurrection-Rapture event. How so? Consider the following subsequent Observations. The Planetary Parade is different from the last one in December of 2004 in that the Planetary Parade did not occur in their relative Natural Order as it is on June 24, 2022.

GREAT PLANETARY ALIGNMENT

Uranus is the 7th Planet from the Sun. Its Name is a reference to the Greek God of the Sky. At the precise Day and Peak on the Alignment, the Moon will pass or Eclipse Uranus, as to make it 'Disappear', 'Vanish'. Note that the Astronomical Sign for the 7th Plant is a Motif signaling a Upward Trajectory. As it is in Earth's Position, is it signaling the Rapture event to come in the Sky?

June 24, 2022 - 4 Days after Summer Solstice

Planetary Parade led by Orion - Signaling Out Earth's Position with a Disappearance and Rapture Typology

June SsCutldS

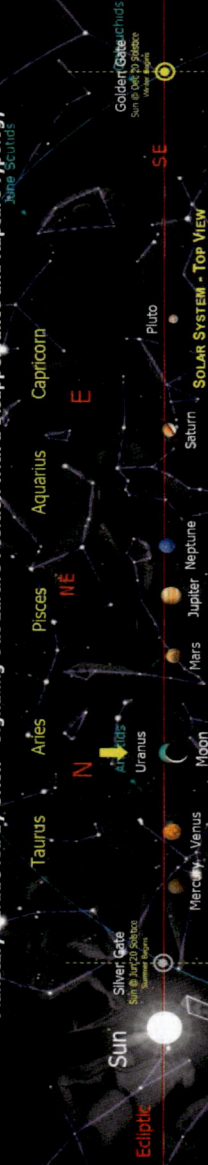

Golden Gate SsCutldS
Sun @ Dec 29 Solstice
Winter Begins

Silver Gate
Sun @ Jun 20 Solstice
Summer Begins

Sun

Ecliptic

Taurus · Aries · Pisces · Aquarius · Capricorn

ORION

N · NE · E · SE

Mercury · Venus · Uranus · Moon · Mars · Jupiter Neptune · Saturn · Pluto

Arkids

MOON

June 24
Waning Crescent
Illumination: **18%**

18 = 6-6-6

37.751, -97.822, 0 m   FOV 168°   17.9 FPS   2022-06-24 20:40:30 UTC+02:24 (LMST)

A DIVISION

SOLAR SYSTEM - TOP VIEW
June 24, 2022; Planetary Parade

1-Mercury
2-Venus
3-Moon / Uranus
4-Mars
5-Jupiter
6-Neptune
7-Saturn

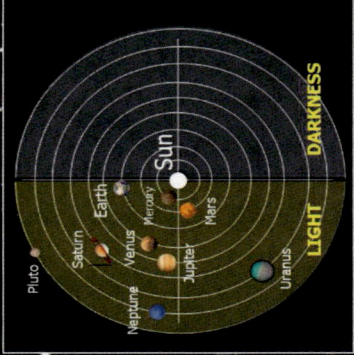

SOLAR SYSTEM - TOP VIEW

Sun

Mercury · Venus · Earth · Mars · Jupiter · Saturn · Uranus · Neptune · Pluto

LIGHT · **DARKNESS**

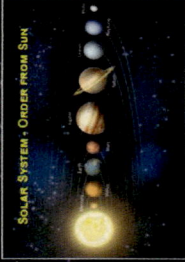

SOLAR SYSTEM - ORDER FROM SUN

LAST PLANETARY PARADE
December 2004 - 18 Year Ago (6-6-6)
And not to re-align until 2040

And neither are all the Planets on 1 side of the Sun. What is interesting, is that based on one's Double Count Pentecost Theory, that being 49 Days + 50 Days per an Alternative Interpretation of Leviticus 23:16, the proposed true Date of Pentecost is July 23, for the year 2022. How the Great Planetary Alignment fits into the Prophetic Equation is that it is exactly 1 Month or 30 days out from this Projected Date.

June 24, 2022 Parade + 30 Day = July 23, 2022
Excluding End Date

One wonders if this is the Last 'Line-up' before the Rapture even to close-out the Church Age. What do all the Planets, this Time being on 1 side of the Sun mean? One would suggest that the meaning suggests a 'Division' or Separation is being made or will be: Biblically Speaking? 'Goats to the Left, Sheep to the Right'? Or perhaps, the 'Raptured Saints' over here, those of the World to stay, over there? It was Jesus and then the Apostles that taught that those Followers and Believers of Jesus are the Sons of Light, and not the Sons of Darkness. And Light does separate Darkness.

This is a clear indication, one would strongly suggest is then possibly Prophetic as the Meaning of Uranus is associated with the God or the Sky. And that is where the Rapture will take place, in the Clouds, the 1st Heaven, etc. Specifically, Uranus is the 7th Planet from the Sun. Its Astronomical Symbol is a Dot within a Circle having an Arrow pointing up to the Sky. Thus, this is now relevant the Rapture Typology is, in that it corresponds to Earth's Position and Time in the Line-Up, to suggest that the Great Planetary Alignment is specifically 'signaling-out' Earth. That a certain 'Event' is to take place, a 'Disappearance', that is there and then it is gone on Earth, etc. And what would that be?

Sons of the Light

The Sons of Light being 'Raptured', gone? This is not to say that the Rapture occurs on this Date, as the Sign is not the Event. So, this rare Great Planetary Alignment or 'Line-Up', in the 5 Visible Planets being in their Natural Order from the Sun, is a Once-in-a-Century event. And such an Alignment will not re-align until 2040. The next Astronomical Observation has to do with Orion. How so? If one plots the Planets in the Line-Up along the Ecliptic, one will see that just 3-4 Days after the Summer Solstice the June 24, 2022 Alignment reached its Peak Configuration appear to be led by Orion.

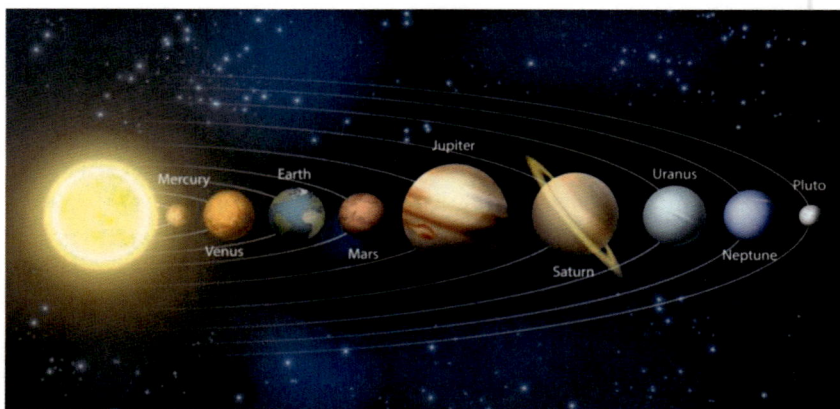

Solar System showing the Natural Order from the Sun.

In the depicted Outline of the Motif of the Constellation of Orion, his gaze is opposite the direction and inclination of the rest of the Constellations where the Planetary Line-Up is occurring. The point is that the Anthropomorphic attribute of Orion is that of a 'Conductor'. How so? Orion is appearing as the 'Light to the Worlds' as is Jesus, the Light of the World. Orion has the Sun as its 'Torch', orchestrating the Planets. So, the possible Prophetic Overtones is that, on one Hand, this Orion Motif is acting like a Christ-Like Figure. How so? It is Orion, like Christ Jesus, the Light of the World that is Illuminating the Way, leading the Line-Up of the Planets.

But he is designating Earth's Place in particular as mentioned of a Disappearance that is forthcoming. A Heavenly Light will go out with the Moon Eclipse that is Earth's Position. Again, this denoted by the Moon's Occultation of Uranus, the 7th Planet. It could infer being that of the 7 Churches of Asia.

Thus, the Disappearance of the Church Age Believers, being 'Lights' also as Jesus called His Followers will insure. At the Resurrection-Rapture event, they 'Disappear', from the Earth. It is as though their 'Lights go Out', as far as the Earth is concerned, will be left in Spiritual Darkness, ready to go into the 7-Years of Tribulation Darkness. When? That remains to be seen as the Sign, is not the Event.

But as some have suggested, perhaps a 30 Day Countdown to the July 23 proposed true Pentecost Date could be that Time. This is pure Thought/Conjecture, but in terms of a 'Departure', what happens to the People as they are ready to Board the Plane as the Announcement is made for the Pre-Boarding Call? The Passengers get Lined-Up. So, is this unique Planetary Line-up, Jesus' way of signaling, 'Hey' Line Up', one is about to board Flight 777 for Departure? That is to rendezvous in the Sky, as in Uranus? It could just be Wishful Thinking and one may be reading too much into this Alignment of the Century.

But it could be a Sign, Prophetically Speaking of how Jesus is to separate the Children of Light from the Children of Darkness, on Earth, as that is what the Resurrection-Rapture is all about, a Division, a Separation.
It will be as an Occultation that will see Jesus' Followers one Moment and gone the Next. So, it is just one of those topics that show the Wonders and Mysteries of the Sun, Moon and the Stars in how everything has an order and sequence, but also for Signs and Seasons, a Call.

Main Sources
SolarSystemScope.com
Stellarium.org
Wikipedia.com

All Planets Have Aligned In The June Sky And You Should Not Miss This Show
The Secrets of the Universe
https://www.youtube.com/watch?v=78crD1I1sCA

Article

#639: 7 REASONS WHY ISRAEL WILL GO TO WAR WITH 6 ENCIRCLED MUSLIM ENEMIES THIS SUMMER
https://www.postscripts.org/ps-news-639.html

#625: PLANETARY PARADE 2022
https://www.postscripts.org/ps-news-625.html

#630: WHEN IS TRUE PENTECOST
https://www.postscripts.org/ps-news-630.html

#618: WHY 'PENTECOST' AND THE RAPTURE CANNOT OCCUR IN THE SPRING
https://www.postscripts.org/ps-news-618.html

#609: SINAI PENTECOST
https://www.postscripts.org/ps-news-609.html

Summary

This is one's contemplation of the June 24, 2022 Great Planetary Alignment of the Century and one does see possible Rapture Connections. It is important to consider and report. One does not think the Rapture occurs there and then, as the Sign is not the Event, but no Objections if that were to be the case.

To reiterate, it is established that there is a 33 Day and 30 Day Count leading-up to July 23, 2022 Date. But as to the Great Planetary Alignment having a Rapture Connection, here is what one has observed and reported.

1. It has been established that the Planetary Alignment has not occurred since December of 2004, 18 years ago. This has a 6-6-6 Time Sequence.

2. What is also different this time around, since 2004 is that ALL the Planets, to include Pluto are on the Right Side of the Sun. It is essentially dividing the Universe between the 'Lights' on 1 side and Darkness on the other.

3. The Moon will be Occulting or making Uranus 'Disappear' or 'Vanish' right in the Position that the Earth should be, given the Natural Order of their Distance from the Sun. The Moon will be Wanning at 18% Illumination. Another 6-6-6 Sequence of Time.

4. The Astronomical Symbol for Uranus is a Dot within a Circle having an Arrow point up. One thinks that this Motif is befitting that is pointing to the Sky, as that is what will happen at the Rapture.

5. The Mythological Meaning of Uranus is attributed to being the GOD of the Sky. Yes, in the converse, it could allude to the Prince of the Power of the Air.

But it could have a Dual Meaning that is being signaled of who is to come. But in the affirmation, it is the palace, in The Sky, were the Rapture Rendezvous will occur.

6. *Orion, still being 'Illuminated' by the Sun as his Torch, is as a 'Conductor' leading the Parade of the Planets through the Silver Gate. In this Metaphorical rendition of the Celestial Motif, he is as Jesus, the True Light of the World. And we are His Lights, but notice how in Earth's Position, there will be that 'Vanishing' Effect by the Moon.*

7. *Out of all the Planets in the Celestial Line-Up, Earth's Position will be taken up by her Satellite, the Moon that will then Eclipse Uranus that is there, but not 1 of the 5 Visible to the Naked Eye Planets.*

Thus, one surmises that this Occultation of Uranus by the Moon, to have it 'Appear one moment and then disappear the next', could allude to how the Light of the World, our Greater Orion is Lining-Up the Planets in their Order to signal-out the Earth that a coming 'Vanishing' to the Sky is forthcoming, on Earth.

That the Lights on Earth, as mentioned prior, is how the Separation and Division will occur as that is what the Rapture event will be. And then how the Darkness that is left will set-up the 7-Year Tribulation of the Kingdom of Darkness. So, it is very Significant and Important to watch and consider.

PS: one received an Email from Work alerting that one's User Password will expire…Guess what Month and Day that will be? July 22, 2022, just before the Infamous July 24, 2022 Speculated True Pentecost Day and perhaps Rapture to go along with it.

---

xxxxxxx@sonoma.edu
xxx AM
(3 hours ago)

Hello,

Your Seawolf UserID account password will expire on 09-JUL-22.

Please change your Seawolf UserID password soon to avoid a disruption of service. Your Seawolf UserID, also known as your LDAP ID, is used to access SSU Online Services.

It sure would be nice to never have to change another Password again. 'Passwords? I don't need no Stinking Passwords', where the Raptured Saints are going, right? So, I thought that was neat but could be just pure coincidence.

RAPTURE RETROSPECT'S

CAN THE RAPTURE DATE BE KNOWN?

A Study in the Various Argument concerning the Blessed Hope

The purpose of this Chapter is to consider, in a Philosophical manner, the Rationales behind one's Notion, if the Rapture Timing can be ascertained. Usually, the most common response is that 'No one knows the Day or the Hour'. One is of the Understanding that the Context of the Passage from where the Verse comes from is not pertinent to the Rapture, as Jesus was Debriefing the Disciples. They were a Representative of Israel during the Tribulation Period. It was a Flash Forward Retrospect to the Abomination of Desolation, as spoken by the Prophet Daniel, as Jesus noted. That Phrase is probably the most known Bible Verse aside from John 3:16. It is usually used to dispel and negate any Possible Rapture Timing Scenario.

Aside from that, one takes a Scriptural Position, that for Centuries, since the Church started on Pentecost in 32 AD, the true counting of how to determine True Pentecost got 'Lost in Translation'. And? This misappropriation of the Timing has ensured that any and all possible Rapture Timing Scenarios would and will be off or incorrect. How so, and what is one's Solution or Argument for the correct Rapture Timing? Study Exodus and consider the Double Count Pentecost Theory. Leviticus 23:15. One has come to Understand, but may be wrong, that the Church has to delineate Shavuot from being Pentecost. They are not the same Feast. This is where all will and are mis-calculating the Rapture Timing, and will, in one's opinion. Can the LORD reveal the Timing of the Rapture to just 1 person? Yes, Jesus can. And he has.

If one sees the Rapture as a 'Coming' of Jesus, which it is, consider the Experience of a Young Boy named Daniel. He was from Judah as the Tribe was being led Captive to Babylon. There in the Mix were Daniel's 3 Friends. It is purported that Daniel might have not been more than 14-15 Years Old at the time. Consider that, also at that Time on Earth, there were not more than 1 Billion People on the Planet. Let us use 1 Billion. The Point? It is that out of 1 Billion People, YHVH chose 1 Young Man, out of the whole Planet to reveal when Jesus was coming. 1:1,000,000,000. Daniel 9:26.

What are the Odds? And then it is known, in Principle, from the Old Testament Prophetic Protocols of YHVH, that He promised not to do anything, as in major Judgments, Movement or in Changes in Dispensations(?), without first Telling His Prophets. Amos 3:7. Now granted, there is an Argument if there are even 'Prophets' in the Church Body today. One would agree that at least, in the Spirit and Office of a Prophet or Prophetess, for sure. To Speak the Gospel, for example, is to Prophesize. Yet, one would not dare say one is 'A Prophet'. So that is for another Discussion. Then there are those that believe that 'God' literally speaks to them.

Many People have and are receiving Rapture Timing in Dreams but revealing the Date of the Rapture in a dream? One would agree that it is possible. Reveling of Understanding and/or Information in Dreams is Scriptural. Such occurrences just add to the 'Overall Equation' in one's Estimation as to the Timing of the Rapture. But this, one can say, is also Scriptural regarding all such types of 'Revelations', that they need to be Tested though. Are they all coming from the Same Source, that is Jesus/Holy Spirit? If so, there will be no Contradiction. The Bible teaches that YHVH is not the Author of Confusion but that the Holy Spirit is the one who Teaches and leads to all True, etc.

Of Dreams and Visions

This to say that a lot of what People believe or claim to 'Hear the Voice of GOD', because of Dreams are not of Christ. So, just because one has a Dream about the Rapture? One has to Test the Spirits. And especially in these Last Days, Months as the Doctrine of Demons is profound. And one may chime in on Dreams about the Rapture's Timing, based on one's Singular Rapture Timing Dream Experience. As some may know, it was in 2021 that one had, what one would say was a Dream-Vision. A Blank White Canvas appeared and a Brush swooshed across it. With a Stroke, it revealed the Number 723 that appeared. That was it. Did not think much of it. Then the Next Night, the same thing happened.

So, then one took note. One is not the type who has never had such occurrences, except when one experienced a Near Death Experience. The only thing one could do was to report it to one's Revelation 12 Daily Blog Watcher Family. The consensus was that it was a Date, and one agreed on 7-23 as July 23. But as the Day and Month came and went, one thought, 'Oh well, just a Dream'. One kept the Article up on one's Website. But perhaps it was a 1 Year Warning? One then started in 2022 to study the Exodus Account, in detail, down to the Days. One was still investigating the Double Count Pentecost Theory, etc.

One was shocked that from Nisan 15, the Day after Passover, and then applying the 49 Day + 50 Day Pentecost Double Count Theory, that being 99th Days, it landed on 7-23, July 23, 2022. So, that got one's attention. And it was Reported. Then People started to inform that there were 70 and 50 Day Countdowns to the July 23, 2022 Date exactly. The 1st Countdown was from Israel's Independence Day and the Rabbinical Shavuot, Feast of Weeks. And that a Subsequent 50 Day Count from the July 23, 2022 Date would land on September 11, 2022. What to make of it? One can only Report it and see.

But what if Christ did show the Rapture Date to 1 Person. Consider that as most Teachers and Watchers are looking for the Shavuot Pentecost, they will not be expecting the Real One in July. And is that not what the Scriptures says, that it will come when one will least expect it? Now, circling back to Daniel's Revelation of when Christ was to Appear.

In one's Studies on the other Theory of the Sabbath Cycles, it was echoing in one's Mind and Heart the Sentiments of many who are eagerly waiting for the Blessed Hope are excited to see how events and the Timing have become clearer in more Focused. In what way?

Could this coming 7-Year Sabbath Cycle in the Fall of 2022 be Daniel's 70th Week of Years? The following is a List compiled that has some unique Day Counts that lead-up to the July 23rd Date. Some were Emailed, some were posted on the Blog one frequents and the others are from one's own Discernment, etc. Does it prove the Rapture will occur on July 23? No.

Then a Thought entered one's Mind, not sure if it was Impressed or just a Self-Induced, but it went something like this.' Do you realize that out of all the People on Earth, it was YHVH that revealed to Daniel precisely when the Day and Month the Messiah was to have come?' One thinks Christ heard one's Heart's Question in that one was Questioning, 'What did Daniel get out of all his Experience'…Looking back, it was a very Presumptuous Thought. But one did not grasp the Awesomeness in that to Daniel, the exact Date of when Jesus was to have Appeared was given to him.

1- June 2021:
Dream-Vision of a 723 Number across Canvas twice, thus a July 23 Date. Rapture Timing?

2- April 2022:
Study in Sinai Pentecost where the 99th Day, based on Lev 23:16 Interpretation is July 23.

3- May 2022:
Informed that 70 Day from Israel's Independence to reported 'End of Wheat' is July 23.

4- June 2022:
Informed that 50 Day from Rabbinical Shavuot and end of Wheat on Earth' is July 23.

5- June 2022:
Calculated that a subsequent 50 Day Count from July 23 would be September 11.

6- June 2022:
Calculated that a subsequent 33 Day Count from June 20-21 Solstice would be July 23.

7- June 2022:
Informed that a subsequent 30 Day Count from June 24 Planet Alignment would be July 23.

8- June 2022:
Informed that on June 22, one's Work Password would Expire, the day before July 23.

Level of Confidence?

This pattern of Thought came up because as one left for the Summer, one's Testimony was given about the Near Death Experience to a Colleague over Zoom. And one shared how Jesus worked through that. One was also able to share one's Testimony of how as a Young Man, one also identified as a 'Daniel' in a lot of Aspects as one read his Book. One said in one's Mind and Heart, that one committed to be like a Daniel. But what did that mean? It meant that with such a Commitment, perhaps YHVH would also reveal the exact Day and Month Jesus would be coming for His Bride? May it be so Jesus.

The Bride is Tired, Sick, and Weary. It has Little Strength left. Jesus, come quickly. Jesus, your Bride longs for You and is Calling for You. So, here is the point, the Thought in one's Mind said then, 'Will YHVH reveal the Date of when Jesus is Coming, just as He did to Daniel?' Well ok then. We shall see. One is in no way elevating oneself to the Level of the Prophet Daniel. All this is being shared that is Personal as one did initially with the 7-23 Dream-Vision, with apprehension, now as one had then. One can only Report and see what happens. If anything, one has held firm to a 49 Day + 50 Day Pentecost Rapture Timing. If this is the case, it would be, will be an Extremely High Watch Day. This is the Clue to the possible true Rapture Timing and not determined to be on Shavuot.

Thus, Personally, the Highest Rapture Day of the Year will be July 23, based on the Double Count Theory. But one cannot say or go beyond that. As one has said from the very beginning, that Speculating and Calculating are fine as that is how it is to Watch, by Observation, etc. Regarding the July 23, 2022 Date? One can say, based on the Exodus Studies, is that one believes and can say with Scripture, that Pentecost is to occur on the 99th Day since Nisan 15. This is Scripturally Provable. Now if one Conjectures that this is the Greatest Candidate for the Rapture?

One has to Test the Premise each Year. But with the Sabbath Cycle Theory converging, what year would it have to occur on? The 7th Year of a 7-Year Sabbath Cycle, which is 2022. That is one's Speculation, nothing more as the Bible does not say. But what if it has been impressed that the Holy Spirit might indeed 'tell' or 'show' 1 Person out of 1 Billion on Earth? There are for sure more, and many Worthy and Holy Saints in this Last Generation like Daniel and his 3 Friends.

So, one has wanted to explain one's Philosophical Rationale with some Personal Perspective, regarding the possible Rapture Timing. But one cannot say, will not say with 100% Confidence that July 23 will be the Rapture event. If today and tomorrow come and go, and so will July 23, the Watch continues as the Bride has that much more Time to be about our Father's Business, no? What about the Fall 2022-Fall 2029 Timeline?

The Speculated Timeline Starting on October 18 after Shemini Atzerets. One's Rationale is Conjecture but based on Scriptural Precedence of how at that Time, the Kings of Israel and Zerubbabel read the Law after the Altar of Sacrifice was Dedicated. It would be a Convocation of all of Israel, in which it echoed what Israel agreed to at the Foot of Mount Sinai as YHVH recited the 10 Commandments, as a Marriage Proposal to them and Israel said 'Yes'.

Even though Weeks later, not even, did they fashion the Golden Calf instead. But that has been Israel's Besetting Sin. And thus the Reason for Jacob's Troubles, not that of the Church. But one surmises that in like Fashion, the coming False Messiah, once accepted by the current Nascent Sanhedrin and having given the Authority to rebuild the 3rd Temple, will then Commemorate the Start of the Daily Sacrifices on this Day, of the Consecration and Re-Dedication of the Altar of Sacrifice and Temple.

It will be as what Solomon did in his Dedication of the Temple and Altar. This is where and when Fire came down from YHVH to consume the Sacrifice. One conjectures that Satan as part of his Lying Wonders and Signs will have this occasion demonstrate that he is the 'Messiah'. The Daily Sacrifices will be replicated and performed by the False Prophet and AntiChrist. It will be as the same Protocols during Solomon's Dedication, as the Daily Sacrifices started. This event is what starts the 2520 Day Count of the Tribulation Period.

This event will deceive all of Israel and the World, as Israel will now be under Mosaic Law, but worse is that for all the Non-Jews of the World, they will be under the Noahide Law. And? The 1st Commandment will condemn all Christians to Death. How so? It is written in the Noahide Law that the Sin of Blasphemy for Saying that 'Jesus Is LORD' or is GOD will be Capital Punishment. In what form? Guillotine. Look it up.

So, this Dedication, in turn will start the 1260 + 1260 Day Count. Its End Day, being September 11, 2029, which happens to be Yom Teruah. This is why one is adamant that it is not the Rapture that starts the Tribulation Period as most suppose or even when that Covenant is 'Confirmed' or Strengthened, etc. But that if it is this Year 2022, and at this Pentecost Day, the 99th Day since Nisan 15, most who have already dismissed that Pentecost has 'come and gone', will fulfill Prophecy, in that they will not see it coming, as such a Month is not expected or being considered. The following is the Fall 2022 to Fall 2029 Tribulation Timeline.

Possible 7-Year Tribulation Timeline – Fall 2022 to Fall 2029
Based on 2 Halves of 1260 Equal Day Counts

Beginning:	*Shemini Atzeret on*	*October 18, 2022?*
Midpoint:	*Passover on*	*April 1, 2026?*
End:	*Yom Teruah on*	*September 11, 2029?*

Tribulation Timelines

It has been anything but and would be 'Least Expected'... June, August, September, sure but not July. It reminds one of that same 33-Day Countdown, from the Great American Eclipse in August of 2017 and how it led-up to the Revelation 12 Sign. The Theory will be put to the Test. If July 23/24, 2022, comes and goes, then the Theory was wrong, at least for the Year 2022. But as we all could agree, as Lyn Melvin wrote in her Blog, the Other Shoe is about to drop, has to, based on all the Signs that are now Flashing 'Rap Con 1' as Bro Chooch from his Thinking Out Loud TOL YouTube Channel would call it.

All the Preparations on both sides, up to now are not for Nothing. To reiterate, what strongly supports that the Rapture 'has' to be 'This Year', 2022, is the Sabbath Cycle Theory, or as it is widely known as the Shemitah Year, which is the Year 2022. And according to some, it is the 70th in a Counting, pegged to the Anniversary of the Queen of England and thus a Jubilee of Shemitah's on top of it all.

The Platinum Jubilee of Elizabeth II is being celebrated in 2022 in the Commonwealth of Nations to mark the 70th Anniversary of the Accession of Queen Elizabeth II on 6 February 1952. Remember, that one and a few others are Clambering that the Year, 1952 is the more accurate Countdown Year, being a Shemitah Year to then apply the Psalm 90, 7-Year Generation Template.

Notice that it is the Platinum or Silver Alloy associated with the Year, and how the Orion Circle highlights the Summer Solstice that occurs at the Silver or 'Platinum' Gate. As one can ascertain, the Celestial Signs are 'Screaming' that after June 20, things on Earth will start to 'Light Up'. A Turning Point will have been reached and a Door of Opportunity will ensue. One hopes that Door is of the 4th Month, of the 4th Feast of YHVH and of the 4th Chapter of Revelation wherein John as the Type of the Bride is Called-Up.

Pentecost is associated with the Long Silver Trumpet Blasts of Mount Sinai and on Pentecost. The Trumpet Blasts at Yom Teruah are that of a Military Campaign, of War, as that is what Jesus will be bringing to Earth, on Yom Teruah. But leading all to that Daily Sacrifice Dedication are all the Financial, Economic, Social and Military Pundits 'screaming' that by this Fall 2022, the World as we know it now, will cease to exist, as far as it current Framework is concerned, i.e., the Great Reset.

But as a fair Critique, the 'Fall' Feasts in 2029 occur before the Fall Equinox of September 20-21. So it breaks one's Template and Theory that the Fall Feasts have to start at the sighting of the New Moon after the Fall Equinox. Now with the New Year's Beginning in the Spring, one can say, with 100% Confidence that it is true and it is Scriptural.

But realize that no Verse or Section/Passage in the Bible tells the Jews when to start their New Year, Date wise, except in the Palms and how during the Exodus, YHVH instructs Moses to make Nissan the 1st Month of the Year. But how does one determine that? Yes, there are many Theories but the true calculation, pegged off of the Spring Equinox, is found in Psalm 81: 3. (2-4)

'Lift up a Song, strike the Tambourine, play the Sweet-Sounding Harp and Lyre. Sound the Ram's Horn at the New Moon, and at the Full Moon on the Day of our Feast [Passover]. For this is a Statute for Israel, an Ordinance of the God of Jacob'.

This is the verse concerning how to determine Passover, that being the 1st New Moon after the Spring Equinox. Thus, one would agree that the 1st Half of the Premise regarding the Fall 2022 to Fall 2029 Timeline is strongest at the beginning. It does appear to be solid and corroborated with Scripture.

So, what one did is to then just flip that Spring Equinox Pattern and apply it to the Fall, using a Corresponding Logic to mirror the 1st Half of the Argument. One can say that this Template is Astronomically Correct. But true, the Fall Feast New Moon to determine the Fall Feasts does not necessarily have to be the one after the Fall Equinox but perhaps the Nearest one. For example, Ken Johnson believes that it is the 'Nearest New Moon' that determines Nisan 1, etc.

Or in other words, regardless of when the Jews say the Yom Teruah is, Astronomically, the 7th Month is already pre-determined by the Spring Equinox. So, the Timeline is based then on the equal halves of the 1260 Day Counts. This is how one then arrives at the halfway Marker, that being Passover, on the Rabbinical Calendar, which one thinks is amazing and confirming.

And mind you, the Feast Days are reckoned based on the current Rabbinical Calendar. So, Passover occurs on April 1, 2026, exactly 1260 Days from End of Shemini Atzerets on October 18, 2022. And now as of the latest, just 7 Days from October 25, 2022 is when Israel is now going to have its 5th National Elections.

And one conjectures that the Passover Feast would be the Optimal Time for the AntiChrist to Desecrate its significance and stop the Daily Sacrifices. So, yes, then 1260 days later is September 11, 2029 and Yom Teruah on the Rabbinical Calendar, Amazing.

But it could be significant in some other way, if it is not the Return of Jesus or if the Fall Feasts are off. Regardless, because using this sole Day Count Template, the 2nd Half does have to have the same 1260 Days, no matter what Day or Feast that is. It is rather amazing, one would think, that it does happen to be Yom Teruah on the Rabbinical Calendar, September 10-11th.

But true, it will be before the Fall Equinox which would make it Technically still be a Summer Feast and go contrary to one's Logic and Timeline. This is where one is at in the Prophetic Learning Curve.

Or one might not understand completely that the Fall Feasts occur based on the Day Count and not necessarily on any Astronomical Observations, aside from the Sighting of the New Moon on the 7th Month in the Rabbinical Calendar. That would be the only way to rectify the Timeline.

_____

Articles

#517: 723 VISION OF THE RAPTURE DATE?
https://www.postscripts.org/ps-news-517.html

#609 Article of the Sinai Pentecost Study for Reference
https://www.postscripts.org/ps-news-609.html

WHY PENTECOST IS IN JULY/TAMMUZ
END OF THE WHEAT HARVEST
After the Summer Solstice

The purpose of this study is to chart the Timeline leading-up to July 23, 2022. The Chart Illustration format will give a better Visual of the various Factors that will be presented as Evidence for a July/Tammuz true Pentecost Date. In the Timeline, one also superimposed a 40-43 Week Human Gestation Period to it. It is very interesting in what correlates to the overall Theory of when true Pentecost is, and in turn could be the Place and Time when the Rapture occurs. It looks 'Promising', but it has to be Tested to see if the Theory is correct. If it is, the Bride has Arrived. The Wheat Harvest concludes as the New Wine Commences and a 'Birthing' as come to Term, etc.

One finds it very suspicious and Interesting how now that the Israeli Government has collapsed, it will be run by the Interim Prime Minister, Lapid. But as some Political Science Pundits have rightly assessed, there can be a Government formed, if they wanted to, but it has not been decided for that. Instead, Israel will be left without a 'Leader' or Ruler until Elections on October 25, 2022. Interestingly, this Date is just 7 Days from one's suggested and possible Tribulation Timeline. One wonders if 'They' are leaving the Spot for the 'Ruler'? Which at that time, all Power and Authority will be given to Rule Israel and then the New 'Reset' World Order.

October 18, 2022 (Shemini Atzerets)
+ 1260 Days = April 1, 2026 (Passover)
+ 1260 Days = September 11, 2029 (Yom Teruah)

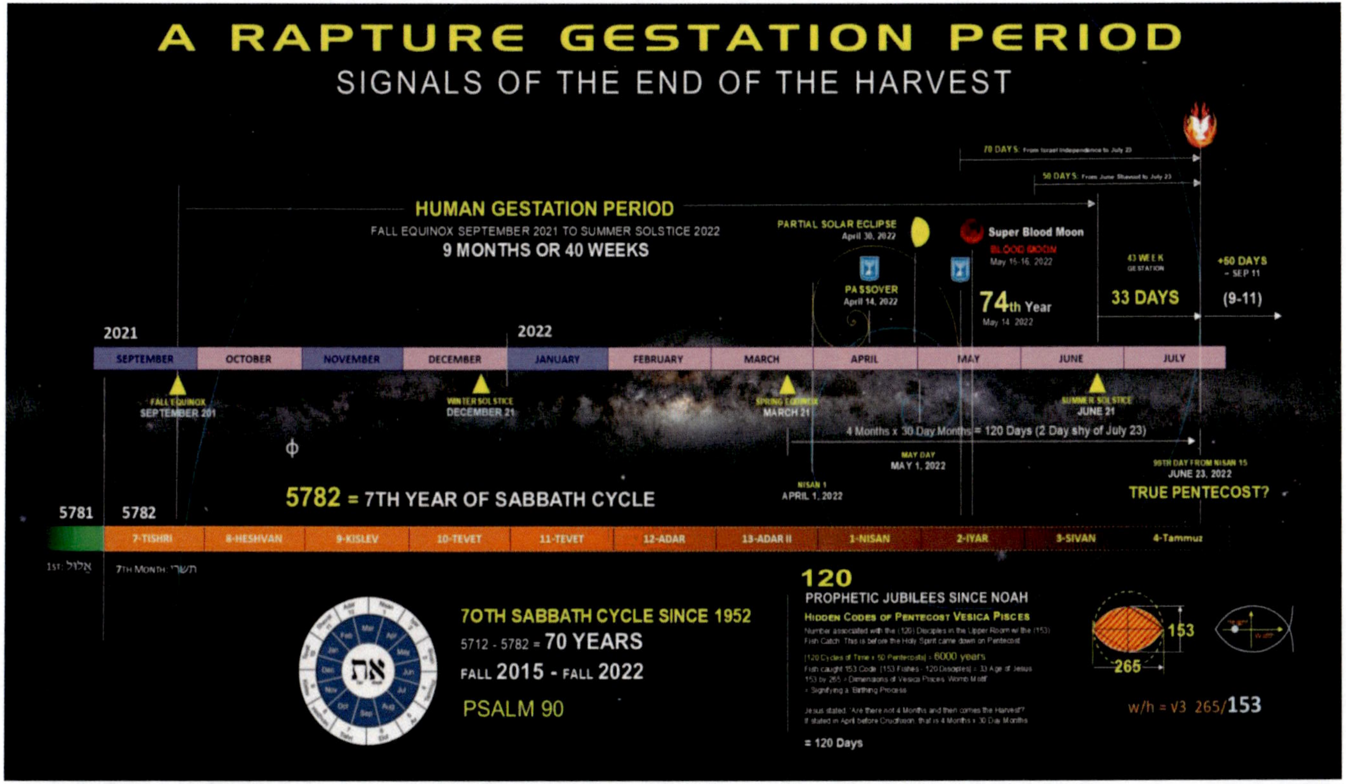
A RAPTURE GESTATION PERIOD
SIGNALS OF THE END OF THE HARVEST
70 DAYS: From Israel Independence to July 23
50 DAYS: From June Shavuot to July 23
HUMAN GESTATION PERIOD
FALL EQUINOX SEPTEMBER 2021 TO SUMMER SOLSTICE 2022
9 MONTHS OR 40 WEEKS
PARTIAL SOLAR ECLIPSE
April 30, 2022
PASSOVER
April 14, 2022
Super Blood Moon
BLOOD MOON
May 15-16, 2022
74th Year
May 14, 2022
43 WEEK
GESTATION
33 DAYS
+60 DAYS
– SEP 11
(9-11)
2021
2022
SEPTEMBER
OCTOBER
NOVEMBER
DECEMBER
JANUARY
FEBRUARY
MARCH
APRIL
MAY
JUNE
JULY
FALL EQUINOX
SEPTEMBER 201
WINTER SOLSTICE
DECEMBER 21
SPRING EQUINOX
MARCH 21
SUMMER SOLSTICE
JUNE 21
4 Months x 30 Day Months = 120 Days (2 Day shy of July 23)
MAY DAY
MAY 1, 2022
NISAN 1
APRIL 1, 2022
99TH DAY FROM NISAN 15
JUNE 23, 2022
TRUE PENTECOST?
ϕ
5782 = 7TH YEAR OF SABBATH CYCLE
5781
5782
7-TISHRI
8-HESHVAN
9-KISLEV
10-TEVET
11-TEVET
12-ADAR
13-ADAR II
1-NISAN
2-IYAR
3-SIVAN
4-Tammuz
1st: אלול
7th Month: תשרי
70TH SABBATH CYCLE SINCE 1952
5712 - 5782 = 70 YEARS
FALL 2015 - FALL 2022
PSALM 90
120
PROPHETIC JUBILEES SINCE NOAH
Hidden Codes of Pentecost Vesica Pisces
Number associated with the (120) Disciples in the Upper Room w/ the (153) Fish Catch. This is before the Holy Spirit came down on Pentecost
(120 Cycles of Time x 50 Pentecosts) = 6000 years
= 120 Days
153
265
w/h = √3 265/153

A Matter of Synchronization

The following are just some more tid-bits as to why one believes and is convinced the true Pentecost is in July or the 4th Month of Tammuz in the Array of the 7 Feasts of YHVH. And as to one's Correlation that the Resurrection-Rapture event could thus occur at such a time, that will remain to be seen. What strengthens the Argument of 'But what Year?' Question, is the Fact of the Sabbath Cycle Patterns. Out of all prior Years since 2015, the point is that the Rapture Timing could not have occurred or even thought of until 2022, in Hind-Sight.

But that the Rapture event would materialize, only in the Year in which either a New End/Beginning Sabbath Cycle would occur. Perhaps. That logic would be why no Year since 2015, could have the Rapture occur, but in 2022, and this is the Year now. It is now a real possibility, but still Conjecture and an Educated Guess as the Rapture 'Window', is ascertained to be in the 4th Month, based on the 99th Day Count from Nisan 15, etc. So, this means that out of all the prior 6 Years in the Sabbath Cycle, none but 2022 could be even considered to be a High Watch Year, as it is then for 2022.

All this is based on one's Estimation and Calculation. The Chart will show that the Feasts of YHVH follow the Agricultural Seasons of Sowing and Planting and that they are pegged to the Solstices and Equinoxes, in one's Understanding. Realize that this Time Reckoning is solely based on the Sun, as opposed to the Rabbinical Calendar that is solely based on the Moon. That is why there is a Discrepancy and Confusion in the overall Day-Counts. Before the Jewish Diaspora, by the Romans and the Temple being destroyed, a Solar-Lunar Calendar Matrix was used to Synchronize the Sun and Moon Times; to know when exactly to Calibrate and Celebrate the Feasts of YHVH, etc.

The Hillel Calendar was then Mathematically formulated, based on only the Lunar Cycles as the Sanhedrin disbanded and this Rabbinical Calendar became the next best Instrumentation to go by. It was because the Jews were scattered throughout the Nations, as the Bible said this Last Time they would be. This Calendar served to keep their Identity and Unity. And this Rabbinical Time Reckoning is aside from the Torah Calendar, the Enochian Calendar and the Creation Calendar, and the Essenes Calendar.

But also take note that the Enochian, Essenes and the Creation Calendars use the Solar Cycles, based on the Equinoxes and Solstices, to varying degrees. Here is the example of why, on average, at least in the Northern Hemisphere and in particular, North America, the Summer Wheat Harvest begins right after the Summer Solstice of June 21. It should be noted that it is an Average as certain Regions may have had their Wheat Harvest ready for Harvest early, by as much as 2 Weeks, etc.

Nonetheless, the point is that the Summer Solstice kicks-off the Summer Wheat Harvest. See Video Link for a Visual and Commentary at end. Why this is important, and why one seeks to tie it to or make a Prophetic Link to the Rapture Timing, is that consider the following Day Counts below. Realize that the Wheat that is being Harvested, starting around, after the Summer Solstice of June 21, on average is really what is called the Winter Wheat. The Wheat Crop was planted back when?

Around the Fall Equinox of September 21 of the Prior Year. And guess how many Months will that have been? 9 Months. This is the same Time-Frame as that of a Human Gestation Period. And? The Point and Correlation is that the Wheat Harvest staring in the Summer typifies this Spiritual Analogy that even Jesus inference, as to the Harvest of Human Souls on Earth being 'White for Harvest'.

A Spiritual Gestation

Remember the 120 Numerical Coefficient. 4 Months x 30 Days = 120. This has a Prophetic Inference to the 120 Jubilees set for Mankind, as revealed by YHVH in the Old Testament. And it is based on the Number of Sabbath Cycles of 7 Years, etc.

Also have in mind, that in considering all of this, most Watchers and Students of the Bible and End Times would agree that the End of the Church Age will be likened to a Harvest and a 'Birth'. That is what is currently happening and has since Pentecost started the Commission to 'Go out into the Harvest, to Sow, Water, and Reap Souls'.

This is why the Prophetic Fulfillment of Pentecost is on-going. But there is another Key Prophetic Typology of this Present Pentecostal Intermission. There is another Spiritual Typology, that of a Man-Child that is to be 'Born'. This has direct implications to the Revelation 12 Motif. Here are the possible 'Rapture' Human Gestation Equations.

September 21 Winter Solstice to a June 21 Summer Solstice = **273 Days**

Or **9 Months** *Excluding the End Date. (39 Weeks)*
Human Gestation Period is 9 Months or on average of about **42 Weeks.**

But if one uses the Winter Solstice of September 21, 2021 to see how long it would be to the July 23, 2022 Speculated true Summer Pentecost, and thus possible Rapture Date, the following Day Count results.

= 10 Months or **43 Weeks**

According to Research, 'the Average Gestation Period of Humans is 280 Days or 40 Weeks. The Gestation Period begins on the 1st Day of the Woman's Last Menstrual Period.

Full-Term Babies are Born from 37 Weeks to 42 Weeks of the Estimated Date of Birth. The Stages of Human Gestation are broken into 3 Trimesters that are 3 Months Long Each'. - Reverence.com

'Can a Pregnancy be 43-Weeks-Plus? Yes. Even when the Doctors are sure of the Dates, some Pregnancies last longer than 40 Weeks. After about 42 Weeks, Doctors get real antsy about it, though. The Key is Placental Function and Baby's Head Size, both of which can usually be determined by Ultra-Sound'. - Quora.com

It is understood that, based on the Teaching of the Apostle Paul, he linked the Bride of Christ to that of a Baby, in the Spiritual Process of a Gestation Period. And what is being 'Formed or Birthed? This is Paul's Perspective: 'My Children, for whom I am again in the Pains of Child-Birth until Christ is Formed in you'... -Galatians 4:19. Paul even identifies as a sort of Mid-Wife that is seeing that the 'Delivery' is on Schedule and to be completed to its 'Term'.

If this be the Spiritual Case, then the Spiritual Typology is to follow in now there is some sort of Spiritual 9-Month Human Gestation Variable at work. And? That his Time Sequence will lead-up to the 'Harvest an 'Birth' with the Resurrection-Rapture Timing. This is why one is emphatic that, here comes an 'Impossible Word' Alert... It is Impossible for any other of the Spring or Fall Feasts of YHVH to be associated with a Harvest Feast and Gestation or Pregnancy coming to 'Term'.

Well, aside from Tabernacles of Sukkot, but that is emblematic of the Year's End Harvest. Many Watchers do believe Sukkot is a likely Candidate for the Rapture because of this. But not in comparison to the many Typologies given as Innuendos and Clues about a Summer Wheat Harvest and a Gestation-Birthing Process that is tied to the Wine Harvest 1 MONTH later after the Summer Solstice. How so?

A Birthing Process

Here is where one has the Statement of Jesus, to the fact that in 4 Months, there will be a Harvest or a 'Birth'? It is assumed that He made that statement just prior to the Crucifixion in the very Month of the Spring Equinox, being March 21. Thus if one counts 4 Months of 30 Days each from March 21, the Day Counts are as follows.

March 21 to April 21   *= 1st Month*
April 21 to May 21   *= 2nd Month*
May 21 to June 21   *= 3rd Month = (A Trimester of Time)*
June 21 to July 21   *= 4th Month*
                      or 120 Days Total

All that, to infer as to why true Pentecost took place and will take place in the 4th Month of Tammuz or in a Mid-July. The Point? In approximately 1 Month after the Summer Solstice, the Grape Harvest begins. This would be starting in the Mid-July 20s and why the Apostles were then accused of being 'Drunk on New Wine' as that was being then Harvested.

One cannot say the same of Tabernacles/Sukkot or any other Fall Feast, as Yom Teruah or Yom Kippur. But again, all these Day Counts and Suppositions are based on there being a Double Count (49 Days + 50 Days) to determine true Pentecost, in the 4th Month of Tammuz (July). One cannot prove that 100%.

Although one is convinced of this Hypothesis, based on both the Day Count, how Israel left Egypt on Nisan 15 from the Exodus Account. Then from the Counting of the Omer, results in the same Day Counts. Traditional Pentecost is pegged to the Rabbinical Calendar and in one's Opinion, based on a False Mis-Understanding that 'Pentecost' is just the 50th Day after Shavuot or the Feast of Weeks.

Nonetheless, it will be interesting to see what the 1 Month Countdown or the 30 Days to July 23 for the Year 2022 will bring from the Summer Solstice. The following Section will attempt to explain the Chart Illustration. First, note the Phi Ratio Time Correspondences based on the Feast Days of YHVH. The Chart reiterates that true Pentecost occurs on the 99th Day after Nisan 15 in the 4th Month of Tammuz.

This would put the Pentecost, based on a Double Count of 49 Days + 50 Days in Mid-July of a Given Year. For 2022, it would be July 23. What is highlighted is how from the Fall Equinox of September 21, 2021 to the Summer Solstice of June 21, 2022 is 40 Weeks or 9 Months. Is it suggesting a 'Birth' Innuendo, which could be Prophetically synced to the Rapture Timing?

Is not Pentecost the event where a 'Birth' was insinuated of the Church Age and that of a Royal Commissioning to go into the 'Wheat Field' of the World? What one wishes to highlight from the Chart are the following Observations. Notice that for 2021, the Rabbinical Calendar was off by 1 whole Month or approximately 29 Days as that is the Lunar Cycle difference needed to re-align with the Solar Cycles.

It so happened that for 2022, the Jewish Lunar Calendar synchronized with the Gregorian Solar Calendar. This proves that the Rabbinical Lunar Calendar 'drifts' and as a result, for 2021, a 13th Month had to be added. Note that based on the Sabbath Cycle Theory, 2022 is the 70th Sabbath of Sabbath Cycles, meaning that it has been 70 Years since 1952, which one argues is the true Start Date for the Countdown to Daniel's 70th Week.

This Assertion then would mean the End of the Church Age. This of course necessitates the Resurrection-Rapture event, if one holds to a Pre-Tribulation Rapture Scenario. And this means that the Rapture Timing Window is but at most 3 Month out to the start of the New Sabbath Cycle.

SOWING AND HARVESTING TIMES IN MODERN ISRAEL AND THE CLIMATE

March 19-21: Spring Equinox • September 22-24: Fall Equinox

		1	2	3	4	5	6	7	8	9	10	11	12
		Nisan	Iyyar	Sivan	Tammuz	Av	Elul	Tishri	Cheshvan	Kislev	Tevet	Shevat	Adar
Seed	Harvest	April	May	June	July	August	Sept	Oct	Nov	Dec	January	February	March
		March												
Barley														
Wheat														
Oats														
Millet														
Flax, Linseed														
Grapes														
Figs														
Pomegranates														
Olives (oil)														
Rain mm	97,9	31,5	2	0	0	0	0,2	23,6	67,8	110,3	143,4	113,3	97,9
T.Max Ø °C	15,9	21	25,2	27,5	28,8	28,8	27,9	24,8	18,9	13,7	11,9	13,3	15,9
Temp. Ø °C	11,1	15,2	18,8	21,4	23	22,6	22,1	19,2	14,2	9,7	8	9	11,1
T.Min Ø °C	6,3	9,5	12,4	15,2	17,2	17,3	16,3	13,7	9,5	5,7	4,1	4,6	6,3

The sowing and harvesting times (according to O. Borowski 1987) compared with the climate data (according to ClimaTemps) correspond to the Gregorian calendar. All biblical feasts have a relation to the three main harvest seasons in spring (1st month, Passover, barley), summer (3rd month, Pentecost, wheat) and autumn (7th month, Feast of Tabernacles, grapes/fruits/olives). In biblical times, the barley harvest began from the middle of the 1st month on the 16th of Abib/Nisan with the first sheaf (first fruits) offered in the temple as a wave offering. After 50 days (Pentecost), the wheat harvest began with another wave offering of the first fruits at the beginning of the 3rd month (5th-7th Sivan). Depending on altitude, the barley harvest extended for several weeks into May and the wheat harvest into July. In Israel today, the harvesting rules described in the Bible (Torah) are usually not observed, so that barley is harvested before Passover and wheat before Pentecost. The spring and autumn feast days are always in the area of the spring and autumn equinox.

End of the Church Age

Then note how from the Spring Equinox of March 21, 2022, adding 4 Month or 120 Days results in July 21, 2022, just 2 Days shy of the Supposed true Pentecost Day that is arguing for 2022. As noted, the Numerical Coefficient of 120 is an Inference to the Jubilees that are based on the Number 50, as is Pentecost.

It is in reference to what YHVH told Noah in that there would be only 120 Year allotted to Mankind. It is directly tied to Humanity's Judgment in the Days of Noah and so will it be after the 'Harvest' or 'Birth' of the Bride of Christ when the Rapture event occurs. Some Bible Researchers have assumed a Double Entendre in that if one dissects the Mathematics, it would be the following.

120 Cycles of Time x 50 Pentecosts = 6000 Years

This Prophetic Equation, to some, signifies the period Humanity has in relation to the 6 Days of Creation Pattern. It leaves the 7th Day or the Sabbath to correspond to the Millennial Kingdom once Jesus returns to Earth. The Numerical Coefficient of 120, as mentioned is also the Time Duration that is also directly associated with the Disciples in the Upper Room. They had returned from 'Going Fishing' and had caught the 153 Fish in the Net. This Exact Numerical Coefficient also alludes to the End of the Church Age. But more, is the Mathematical Fact that it relates to what is called the Vesica Pisces.

If one takes the difference of 153 from 120, the result is 33, the Age of Jesus. Then, in Mathematics, the 153 Numerical Coefficient is a Factor of the Vesica Pisces. And? It is a Motif of the Womb in that it infers a Birthing Process. And that is perhaps what the Timeline is suggesting in the Gestation Period that will end in a 'Birth'. The Chart will also note how there are significant Day Counts leading-up to the Supposed true Pentecost Day of July 23, 2022.

There are 70 Days from Israel's Independence Day, on May 14, 2022. There are 50 Days from the Rabbinical Day of Shavuot of June 3, 2022. There are also 33 Days from the Summer Solstice. And 50 Days out from July 23, 2022 will be September 11, 2022. This has also a direct connection, if the start of Daniel's 70th Week does begin sometime in the Fall. How so? The 7-Year Timespan, that ending in 2029, on Yom Teruah will be September 11, 2029, etc.

And to reiterate, the Chart will show how one believes that YHVH 'Clocks' Time in Phi Ratio. Consider that from September 21, 2021, being the Fall Equinox to the July 23, 2022 supposed true Pentecost Date, the Phi Ratio delineations match April 1, 2022 as being Nisan 1. And it would correspond to when the Partial Solar Eclipse occurred on April 30, 2022. Then to Triangulate when Israel celebrated its 74th Independence Day.

There is another Phi Ratio correspondence of Nisan 1, or April 1, 2022 which corresponds to April 14, 2022, being Passover to then triangulate to the May 14, 2022 Independence Day of Israel. Coincidence? No, if one understands Mathematics and Sacred Gematria in Motion, and how it is applied to Prophetic Time. All this to strongly suggest that July 23, 2022 is significant as far as all the pieces of Evidence are concerned.

In some cases, they are but Circumstantial, but nonetheless, for one personally, July 23, 2022 is the Highest Watch Date of the Year for the Rapture. And only because one is pegging it to the supposed true Pentecost Date. It is only that from there, one is projecting the Supposition that, if and when the Rapture would or could occur, Pentecost would be the Prime Candidates to Close out the Church Age with as it began, a 'Harvest', and as a 'Birth'.

Articles Related

#640: RAPTURE PLANETARY PARADE?
https://www.postscripts.org/ps-news-640.html

#638: WHY THE RAPTURE CANNOT OCCUR ON YOM TERUAH
https://www.postscripts.org/ps-news-638.html

#632: WHY PENTECOST CANNOT OCCUR IN AUGUST
https://www.postscripts.org/ps-news-632.html

#609: SINAI PENTECOST
https://www.postscripts.org/ps-news-609.html

#618: WHY 'PENTECOST' AND THE RAPTURE CANNOT OCCUR IN THE SPRING
https://www.postscripts.org/ps-news-618.html

#595: TRIBULATION PERIOD 2022-29?
https://www.postscripts.org/ps-news-595.html

#590: 70TH WEEK OF YEARS
https://www.postscripts.org/ps-news-590.html

#564: SHEMITAH'S OF ISRAEL
https://www.postscripts.org/ps-news-564.html

#549: THE 70TH SHEMITAH
https://www.postscripts.org/ps-news-549.html

#517: 723 VISION OF THE RAPTURE DATE?
https://www.postscripts.org/ps-news-517.html

#480: SABBATICAL CYCLES PATTERN
https://www.postscripts.org/ps-news-480.html

#444: 70TH WEEK OF DANIEL
https://www.postscripts.org/ps-news-444.html

#434: SIGN OF THE SON OF MAN
https://www.postscripts.org/ps-news-434.html

#439: CALENDAR RECALIBRATIONS
https://www.postscripts.org/ps-news-439.html

Books

RISE OF THE WHORE
https://www.lulu.com/shop/luis-vega/rise-of-the-new-world-order-whore/paperback/product-7m99zz.html?page=1&pageSize=4

DAYS BEFORE THE RAPTURE
https://www.lulu.com/shop/luis-vega/rise-of-the-new-world-order-whore/paperback/product-7m99zz.html?page=1&pageSize=4

REVELATION BROKEN SEALS
https://www.amazon.com/dp/1716326354?tag=nice04f-20&linkCode=ogi&th=1&psc=1

END OF THE CHURCH AGE
https://www.amazon.com/dp/1716290252?tag=nice04f-20&linkCode=ogi&th=1&psc=1

Videos

Oklahoma Wheat Harvest Update - June 18, 2022
https://www.youtube.com/watch?v=W5KT4Jqath4

Countdown to the Apocalypse: The Four Horsemen Portend Doom
https://www.youtube.com/watch?v=wtgW5DKIFTI

The Universe: Constellations & The 13th Zodiac Sign
https://www.youtube.com/watch?v=o3OSe8HaRyw

JUBILEE OF THE UN-BORN
SUPREME COURT DECISION
Prophetic Implications for Church and Rapture

'The Word of the LORD came to me, saying: Before I formed you in the Womb I knew you, and before you were Born I set you Apart and Appointed you as a Prophet to the Nations. Ah, Lord GOD, I said, I surely do not know how to Speak, for I am only a Child!' -Jeremiah 5:4-6

The purpose of this chapter is to provide a Commentary of the U.S. Supreme Court's Ruling to overturn Roe vs. Wade that legalized and Federally protected Abortion-On-Demand. The Title, 'Jubilee of the Un-Born' is taken from Mark, who follows one's Work online. He suggested that this is what is going on, Spiritually, Biblically, Eschatologically. He also shared the exact Time Span from when the Law went into effect, until June 24, 2022. One would whole-heatedly agree.

The following will be some Observations as to why the Decision was made on a particular Day, that is Astronomically linked to the Great Planetary Alignment and has a 9-Month 'Gestation' Connection to it, as one surmises. One will also interject an Eschatological Frame-Work of possible Biblical Interpretation as it relates to how close the End of the Church Age of Grace is and liken it to a Gestation and a Birthing Process itself.

It is tied to another Keen Observation another Follower and Blog Contributor from Revelation 12 Daily, named Stephan made concerning the possible Fall 2022 to Fall 2029 Tribulation Period Timeline. And this deals with another 'Birthing', that of Israel. One finds it very interesting and 'timely' that the Supreme Court Decision to Reverse Roe vs Wade came on the Day that the Great Planetary Alignment reached its Maximum.

And Reasons for possible Prophetic Implications as surmised in the prior Study presented. Also tied to the Decision is how it happened right after the Summer Solstice that again signifies a 'Turning Point'. The following are the 3 Factors that have an Astronomical Correlation, as seen by some and that of a Human Gestation Typology in itself.

1. Great Planetary Alignment, calculated to not have happened in over 1000+ Years.

2. Decision pegged right after the Summer Solstice of June 21.

3, Inferring a 9-Month 'Gestation' Decision since the Fall Equinox of September 21, 2021.

And how one assessed, not really having in mind the Supreme Court Decision, but how from the Summer Solstice, minus a 40 Week or 9 Month Human Gestation 'Birthing' is eerily inferred, perhaps. So, Abortion or Murder of Defenseless Babies in the Womb, on Demand is no longer Federally Protected under the U.S. Constitution. However, Abortion or the Murder of Defenseless Babies will continue in the States.

What is the Big Deal? Realize that the Primary Reason why Roe vs. Wade was passed, was that it was argued that Abortion was to only be considered in case of Rape, Incest, Medical Complication to the Mother, etc. But in fact, what it became and still is, is that it is the Prime Method of Birth Control.

One received this from a Follower of one's Work online. He asked, 'A Jubilee Year for the Un-Born?' One thinks this is brilliant in how, indeed, it is a sort of a Reprieve, or 'Jubilee' Type. It is in the 50th Year that a Decree is made. In theory, the Un-Born are 'Free' from the Evil Doctor's Scalpels.

Jubilee Year

Here is the specific Day Count from when Roe vs. Wade was passed to the Great Planetary Alignment of 2022.

January 22, 1973 (Roe vs Wade) to June 24, 2022 (Great Planetary Alignment)
= 18,050 days
*= **49 years, 5 months**, 2 days excluding the end date.*
= 593 months, 2 days excluding the end date.

But one suspects that all this is also about a continued Psyop of Demoralization and Division of the USA, in particular. As the Left will Protest and Riot, forthcoming, it echoes the Summer City Riots that burned-down innocent Business, due to the Floyd Incident. At that time, many Democrats came out in direct support and even some Congresswomen incited the Crowds to Violence, which is a Crime in itself. Did the Justice Department do anything then? No.

As the News of the possible Supreme Court overturning of the Abortion Rights Law 1st were 'Leaked', Pro-Life Pregnancy Centers and Churches have been Fire-Bombed. These are Acts of Domestic Terrorism. But had the Justice Department acted as fast as they wanted to Investigate Concerned Mothers and Fathers who showed-up at Local Board Meetings to question the Pro-LGBT Agenda? No.

They rather label and put Mothers on Domestic Terrorist List, along with Christians who believe in the Rapture and End Times Scenario of the coming 7-Year Tribulation Period and Apocalypse. They are joined by Returning Veterans, Gun Owners and those who believe in the Constitution, etc. And the Orchestrated Mass Shoots will continue as it is coming out that the Shooting in South Texas was again, allowed to happen. It has been now reported that one Mother that could have saved their Child and others was detained from going in.

It took over 1 hour for the Police with Equipment to do anything to prevent the Murders. That was the Plan. And in another case, the actual Husband of 1 of the Teachers that was murdered, who was a Policeman, in hearing of the incident, as he was proceeding to enter into the situation had his gun taken away from him and was detained.

And how can a confused, Trans-Questioning Adolescent, mocked for being 'Odd', Weird and Poor acquire the $10,000+ Dollars' worth of Guns and Ammunition to carry out this act, with such marksmanship as the Police waited? If one believes in 'Gun Control', great. And that Guns should be confiscated and rid-of.

One would agree then, but that it also includes the Federal Government. One is not worried about Criminals that acquire Guns, regardless of No Gun Zones. See California. But it is the Government that has the Guns that one is worried about. It is when the Government starts to take away the Guns, look out. All you need to take care of Bad People with Guns, shooting-up Schools is to have Good People armed with Guns killing those Bad People with Guns.

So, on 1 Hand, the Great Planetary Alignment has signed that this 'Delivery' of the Supreme Court Decree, 'Gestating' for 40 Weeks or 9 Months was not to be 'Aborted'. And that it is on the 50th Year running, the Decree is likened to a 'Jubilee' of the Unborn, Free from the Evil Doctor's Scalpels.

And to one's surmise, it has then a direct connection to Pentecost, i.e., '50'; of a coming Supernatural Delivery of the Man-Child that will NOT BE ABORTED perhaps at a Pentecost, on a 50th Year? Thus, could it be then that the 'Man-Child' that the Evil Red Dragon, Lucifer and his Minions have tried to 'Abort' the 'Birth' of the Bride of Christ, of the coming Rapture Date.

A Pentecost

How will the coming Resurrection-Rapture event will be like? It will be like a Birthing for Theological and Eschatological reasons pointed-out in the prior Post. On the other Hand, the Powers-That-Be, exactly calculated the Decision to occur on such a Monumental and Celestial Day. In part, it is to maintain the Tension of Conflict, especially in the USA, as it is just a 'Move' in their Luciferian Chess-Board Reset Agenda.

The Abortion Decision will continue to foment the Great Divide, especially since the 2017 Great American Eclipse. It was an Omen of Division and Separation that cast its literal Shadow upon the USA. But the coming Demonstrations will also serve as an outlet for the Frustration on the Left, in particular due to Biden's less than Stellar Achievements.

And also, to deflect from the Left's Questing and Doubt now of all those still dying as a result of their Obedience in receiving the Dangerous New mRNA Injections. Remember, to the Left that deny YHVH, the Creator and Jesus, the Savior, they have to replace that 'Void' and Savior. At this Place and Time, it has been 'Science' and Politics..

Thus, Biden and People like Bill Gates and Anthony Fauci are the 'Gods' and Saviors of the Left. They have to be right and obeyed at all costs. They cannot be False nor really telling Lies in disguise that actually want to Kill and 'Abort' all those in the Left. Consider this Dichotomy.

Yes, the U.S. Supreme Court may have overturned the Abortion on Demand as a Constitution and Protected 'Right'. 'My Body, My Choice'. Great, yet it does not apply with the Government Mandated Injections that also infringe upon the Bodily Sovereignty of one's Body, regardless of Issue or Reason. But as the Left is known for, 'Rules for Thee, not for Me'.

They are Hypocrites and delight in a Double Standard of 'Social Justice'. It is a Farce. Conjecture? The FDA approved, unanimously to approve the Dangerous mRNA Injections for COVID to Babies now. The Point? Such a large-scale Injection Schedule, already on top of the 30-50 Injections to be given to Babies by the time they reach 2 Years of Age.

It will ensure an 'Abortion' Like Outcome will continue, as millions will die because of it, if not to be damaged for life. That is the Plan of the Evil Luciferian Eugenicist, Globalist that to Contaminate, Cull and Control all Humanity, to enslave it. With this context, the fellow Watcher named Stephan as mentioned, from the Online Blog Revelation 12 Daily made an interesting Observation from Nisan 1, 1949.

He surmised that the 1952 Platinum Jubilee Year, 2022 would not only fulfill Psalm 90's 70 Year Countdown to Daniel's 70th Sabbath Week but as Stephan has pointed-out, at the end of the 1st Year (Nisan 1, 1949) Israel returned to the Promised Land, although in Unbelief and as a Secular Nation would be 80 Years to the Year, Nisan 1, 2029.

1. *Fall 1952* + *10 Sabbath Cycles of 7 Years* = *Fall 2022* *(Platinum Jubilee)*

2. *Nisan 1, 1949* + ***80 Generation*** *having 'Strength'* = *Nisan 1, 2029* *(80 Years)*

One would totally agree and the Mathematics would appear to fit into the overall 'Equation'. Furthermore. As one holds to the current Timeline one is looking at: Fall 2022 to Fall 2029 has the exact 1260th Day Mid-Point on April 1, 2026, which will be Passover. But Passover on April 14, 36 Months later, will be exactly also on Passover, April 14, 2029.

From Israel's 1st Year commemorated in the Promised Land:

March 31, 1949 (Nisan 1) to April 1, 2029 (Passover)
= 29,221 Days

*or **80 Years** Exactly*
or 960 Months

Thus, as then one's Timeline suggests, 1260 Days from April 14, 2029, will be September 11. Yom Teruah finishes as it is a 2-Day Observance and Excluding End Date. So, yes, amazing Calculations and it does seem to 'Line-up'. May this be the Last Rehearsal as the Church Age have entered Rap-Con 1 Alert Status per Brother Chooch's Terminology at Thinking Out Loud YouTube Channel.

Main Sources
Chabad.org
Rev12Daily.BlogSpot.com

Articles

#637: THE GREAT APOSTASY
https://www.postscripts.org/ps-news-637.html

#635: THE LAODICEANS
https://www.postscripts.org/ps-news-635.html

#633: GOD DAMN AMERICA
https://www.postscripts.org/ps-news-633.html

#619: MY BODY MY CHOICE?
https://www.postscripts.org/ps-news-619.html

Videos

Radical Pro-Abortion Group Declares "Open Season" Against Pro-Life Groups
https://www.youtube.com/watch?v=BfrfenQ-OQ4

Pro-life group offers reward for information on firebombing
https://www.youtube.com/watch?v=1PeXdmAhICA

'The Five' reacts to attacks against pro-life groups
https://www.youtube.com/watch?v=sxOSaLAjiUU

Why this former anti-abortion activist regrets the movement he helped build
https://www.youtube.com/watch?v=25JyC5Whhvc

75TH DIAMOND JUBILEE
JEWELS IN THE CROWN OF CHRIST
Prophetic Significances of the Great Planetary Alignment

The purpose of this chapter is to expand on what the Great Planetary Alignment of June 24, 2022 Prophetically Signifies, perhaps and to encourage the Brethren because if it. This is especially the case for the USA, as the Supreme Court reversed Roe vs. Wade on that Date. This will be the context as the Decree deals with the Gestation of a Human Being in question. It is a Monumental Victory for those who are Pro-Life and believe in the Sanctity of Life in the Womb.

For the Left, it will be a Rallying Cry for Bodily Autonomy as in their Rationale, the Womb must continue to be the Tomb for Millions of Unborn Human Beings, etc. But how was that Decree tied to the Great Planetary Alignment? Planetary Alignments, in themselves, are not uncommon. There are many Conjunctions with 2 or 3 Planets coming together on a frequent basis. But what makes it more 'rare' is when all the 5 Visible Planets (Mercury-Venus-Mars-Jupiter-Saturn) are involved and all in Alignment as it is the case now.

What is more Rare is when ALL the Planets, + Uranus and Neptune, to include Pluto are in Alignment, which is the case now. This is why this is indeed 'The Great Planetary Alignment' This type has not happened since 947 AD, according to Research. For example, the last Time, only the 5 Visible Planets were in Alignment was back in December 2004. In fact, the 5 Planets align roughly every 19 Years, and some say all eight planets align every 170 years. Now, again to reiterate, what makes this Great Planetary Alignment for June 2022 is that ALL the Planets to include Pluto are aligned.

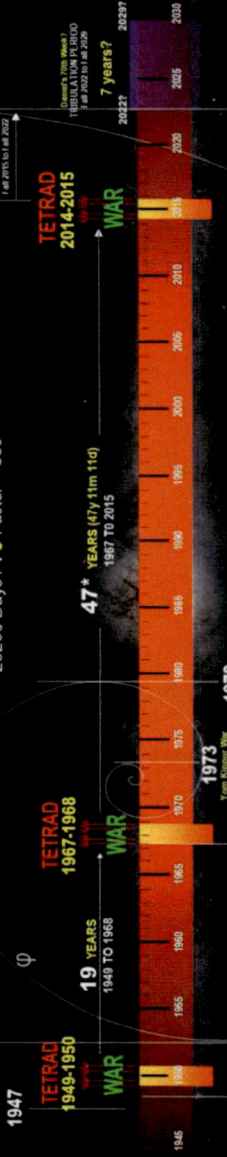

70-YEAR OLD FIG TREE

PROPHETIC COUNTDOWN TO ISRAEL'S RESTORATION AND THE START OF DANIEL'S LAST WEEK OF YEARS

1952

70 Years: Fall 1952– Fall 2022 (10 Sabbath Cycles of 7 Years)

25200 Days / 70 Factor = 360

5782

1947

TETRAD 1949-1950

WAR

φ

19 YEARS
1949 TO 1968

TETRAD 1967-1968

WAR

47* YEARS (47y 11m 11d)
1967 TO 2015

TETRAD 2014-2015

WAR

10th Sabbath Cycle
7 Years
Fall 2015 to Fall 2022

Daniel's 70th Week ?
TRIBULATION PERIOD
Fall 2022 to Fall 2029

7 years?

2022? 2025 **2029?** 2030

1979
Camp David Accords
Peace with Moslem Egypt

1973
Yom Kippur War

RESTORED NATION

May 14, 1948
Independence
"The Fig Tree"

RESTORED CITY

('19 + '48 = '67) 1967
Jerusalem Reunited

From AD 70
(2nd Temple destroyed)
+ 1948 years
= 2018

Order of Ordained Destruction - Count-up
1 Temple
2 City
3 Nation

Order of Ordained Restoration - Count-down
3 Nation 1947
2 City 1967
1 Temple 2017 Jerusalem Made Capital
Revelation 12 Sign

2022
(B.Han) Countdown to Flood from Lamech who
Died at 777 Years Old)

TETRAD PATTERN
1. Passover
2. Sukkot
3. Passover
4. Sukkot

RESTORED TEMPLE

?

Fall 2022
3rd Temple Event?

1945 1950 1955 1960 1965 1970 1975 1979 1983 1986 1990 1995 2000 2006 2010 2015 2020

Good Report

But note that it is only the 5 Visible Planets from Earth that are in their Correct Order from the Distance of the Sun. And then you had that 'Disappearing' or Occultation of the Moon, the Proxy of Earth, going through Uranus, where the Earth corresponds in the Planetary Alignment Order. Many who calculate the Alignment say this one is a 1 in a 1000-Year Occurrence. One would agree. That is extremely Significant and perhaps Prophetic as one has alluded to in the prior Posts and Studies. Perhaps it could be the last Celestial Sign before the Rapture, etc.

Consider also how this '1000-Year' Factor is also occurring in tandem with World Wide Record Heat and Droughts, not seen in '1000-1200-Years'. This is amazing and Biblical in one's opinion. Consider this, the 1000-Year Factor is half the Time the Church Age or Body of Christ has been 'Alive' going about the 'Harvest' and 'Gestation' Processes, on Planet Earth. Meaning?

If the last Great Planetary Alignment of ALL the Planets occurred 1000 years ago, in 947 AD, that means that 1000 Years + 947 = 1947 Years. **A** And? Here is a possible Prophetic Correlation to Israel's 'Birth' and the Great Planet Alignment. Being that it is the Year 2022, and the last time the Alignment of All the Planets occurred in 947 AD, consider then that if one adds 1000 years to 947 AD = 1947. This year, from Creation is presumed and believed to be when Abraham was Born.

Thus when the last Great Planetary Alignment occurred in 947 AD, it would be exactly 1000 Year or '1 Prophetic Day', per the Apostle Peter wherein, Israel would be 'Born', 9 Months from the UN Report. And how Watchers know that in 1947 is the Year that the United Nations ratified the Partition Plan that created the State of Israel, then ~9 Months later, on May 14, 1948, on the Eve of Shavuot, the 49th Day from Nisan 15, Israel was 'Born'.

70 Years is a Factor of 25200 days that pertains to 360 Degrees in a Circle of Time.

947 AD + 1000 Year Coefficient = 1947 (75 Years from 2022)

Consider that the Origins or 'Genesis' of the Partition Plan was made into a Report and submitted in August of 1946, exactly 9 Months from May 14, 1948. The following was stated from Research:

'In August, after 3 Months of conducting Hearings and a General Survey of the situation in Palestine, a Majority Report of the Committee recommended that the Region be Partitioned into an Arab State and a Jewish State, which should retain an Economic Union. An International Regime was envisioned for Jerusalem'.

August 1947 Report to Partition Land to Israel Birth May 1948 = 9 Months (40 Weeks)

Meaning? One believes that the End of the Church Age approaches and the Transfer of Dispensation from Grace to the Law is forthcoming. As Israel experienced their 'Birth', their coming to 'Term' and Delivery, although in War; Blood, Sweat and Tears, so it will be with the 'Birth' of the Bride of Christ that concludes the Royal Commission as the 'Harvesters' are summed to 'Fall Back'.

It will be a Command to 'Retreat' as they Hear the Trumpet Call. It will be that of the Silver Trumpet to Assemble....unto Jesus in the Sky. So too will the Bride of Christ reach her 'Term', Delivery and Presentation. In a Traditional and General sense, is that not what occurs once a Baby is Born, it is presented to the Father?

1947 UN Partition Plan for Israel to End the Church Age? 2022 = 75 Years

Consider the Prophetic Significance of a 75 Year Anniversary. A 75th Anniversary is called the Diamond Anniversary. It is sometimes referred to as the Diamond Jubilee and is considered the 'Pinnacle' of Anniversary Celebrations. Diamonds are the strongest substances on Earth, as well as one of the most desired, and therefore represent such an Esteemed Celebration. Anniversaries have long been marked by a Traditional Gift that is specific to each Year celebrated.

These Celebrations get their root from Medieval Times when a Husband would Crown his Wife with a Silver Wreath for 25 Years of Marriage and a Gold Wreath at the 50th Year. Even today, People refer to the 50th Anniversary as the Golden Anniversary. Is Jesus, as the Groom about to Crown His Bride with the Diamond, Jewels Prepared to be given at the Presentation to the Father on this 75th Year Anniversary?

If the Church Body on Earth was 'Born' on Pentecost of 32 AD, the Year one has calculated to be the correct Time-Frame of the Crucifixion, Death, Burial, Resurrection and Birth of Church Age, to 2022, and if the Rapture does close-out the Church Age, then the Church Age would have lasted for exactly 1990 Years.

July 23, 32 AD (Pentecost presumed) to July 23, 2022 (Pentecost, presumed).
*=**726,834 Days** (Notice '**726**', which in the Greek is Harpazo, Strong's #726.)*

*or **1990** Years*

'At that Time those who Feared the LORD spoke with one another, and the LORD listened and heard them. So a Scroll of Remembrance was written before Him regarding those who Feared the LORD and Honored His Name.

*They will be Mine, says the LORD of Hosts, on the Day
when I prepare My Treasured Possession. And I will spare
them as a Man spares his own Son who serves him. So
you will again distinguish between the Righteous and the
Wicked, between those who Serve GOD and those who do
not'. -Malachi 3:16-18*

*'The LORD of Hosts will Shield them. They will destroy and
conquer with Slingstones; they will drink and roar as with
Wine. And they will be filled like Sprinkling Bowls, drenched
like the Corners of the Altar. On that Day the LORD their
God will save them as the Flock of His People; for like
Jewels in a Crown they will Sparkle over His Land. How
lovely they will be, and how beautiful! Grain will make the
Young Men flourish, and New Wine, the Young Women'.
-Zechariah 9:15-17*

So, how all this is tied to Israel has to do with the 70 Year
Generation of the Fig Tree also. How so? It has been
presented that the Fall of 1952 was the 1st or Start of the
70 Year Countdown to Daniel's 70th Week of Years or the
Tribulation Period. As one has presented in prior Theories.
The Key is the Olivet Discourse. Jesus gave the Sequence
of Israel's Destruction but also of its Restoration, in verse
order. Jesus set forth the order of Destruction, that being
from the Inner-Most Sanctum of the Jewish People.

The Omen started 1stt with the Temple, then the City of
Jerusalem, then the Nation of Israel. And this is exactly
what transpired under the Command of the Roman Prince,
Titus that later became Emperor. But the Key to Israel's
Redemption would have such Elements reconstituted, in
reverse order before Jesus could return. Thus, the Nation
of Israel had to be Reborn. This occurred in 1948. Then the
City of Jerusalem had to be Recaptured. This occurred in
1967. The last Factor, that of the 3rd Temple has yet to
occur.

One believes that there is a Numerical Pattern that accompanies these Restorations of Israel in the Modern Era. In actuality, the Concept of Israel was 'birthed' in 1947. Then in 1967, Jerusalem and the Temple Mount came under Jewish Control, not since 70 AD. But, then in 2017, a monumental and Prophetic Event took place.

The Capital of Israel was recognized by the USA and other Nations as Israel's Eternal Capital, etc. The Point? They all ended in a '7' and this goes back as far as 1917. That Year, 1917 is when Jerusalem was Liberated from the Muslim Rule of the Ottoman Turks. But what about the Temple? Here is where one's Theory of a the 5-Year Countdown to it is derived from.

It has to do with Lamech, the Grandfather of Noah. In what way? Since Israel returned to the Promised Land, although in Unbelief as Ezekiel foretold, being a Secular Nation, 3 Major Factors contributing to its Road to Restoration as stated by Jesus in the Olivet Discourse has to do with a Triple 7 (777).

Realize that 1947-1967-2017 all ended with a 7, as noted and by themselves are a Triple 7. And? What Year in the Life of Lamech did he Die? It was in his 777th Year. Ok. But how is that connected to Israel and the Temple? The Old Testament Account notes that 5 Years after the Death of Lamech, the Food of Noah came.

The Flood spoke of a coming New World Order, a 'Reset' and judgment as in the coming 7-Year Tribulation Period, etc. And? The Temple has to be built for that time. Thus 5 years from 2017 when Jerusalem was recognized as Israel's Capital will be 2022.

2017 Israel Capital Decree *+ 5 Years* = *2022*

This strongly suggests that the Fall of 2022 synchronizes then with the Sabbath Year since 1952 and now with the 5-Year Countdown based on the 5-Year Countdown from the Death of Lamech, who died on his 777th Year. And?

Also, the Great Sign of Revelation 12 appeared Astronomically as a Wake-Up Call of the Pending Rapture Event that would also occur in Tandem to a 5-Year Countdown to the start of the Tribulation Period.

Main Sources
NASA.gov
TimeAndDate.com
Wikipedia.com

Resources

Rare planet formation lights up sky for the first time in 1,000 years (947 AD)
https://www.news.com.au/finance/rare-planet-formation-lights-up-sky-for-the-first-time-in-1000-years/video/0a3d61ce749ced37fe03be41987936e9

LIVE Telescope view of Jupiter, Venus, Mars, & Saturn
https://www.youtube.com/watch?v=5jdSnREyPRM

Planetary alignment | Line up last occurred 1,000 years ago
https://www.youtube.com/watch?v=BCqn1MhClbc

REFERENCES

Biblegateway.com
BibleHub.com
Calander-365.com
Chabad.org
CFR.org
CIA.gov
CIFWatch.com
Concordatwatch.eu
DebkaFiles.com
FemaCamp.com
GlobalSecurity.org
Earth.Google.com
Guardian.co.uk
Hebcal.com
IDF.il
JewFAQ.com
MissingPeace.com
NASA.gov
SecularHumanism.org
ShadowStats.com
StockCharts.com
TrendsResearch.com
Trivisonno.com
Stellarium.com
TimeAndDate.com
UN.org
UPI.com
WHO.int
Wikipedia.com

ABC's OF SALVATION

The ABC's of Salvation explain the Way of Salvation through Faith in Jesus Christ alone in 3 Simple Steps. Jesus Himself Stated the following for context and need of Salvation. Jesus came from beyond the Stars, from Heaven as the True Creator, with the True Gospel and as the only True Savior. There is none other, and no other 'Savior' can Redeem one's Soul, Spirit and Body. YHVH created Man and Woman on Earth. Each person has a unique Genetic Code that is like a 'Combination Key'.

There are no 2 alike. YHVH knows each and Genetic Code that is attributed to the Body but is tied to one's Soul and Spirt as well. All 3 Aspects need to be Redeemed or 'Bought Back'. Why? One only has this Life to make the Choice of where one will spend in Eternity after one Dies. And by the way, YHVH did not design Adam and Eve to 'Die'. But He gave Humanity Free Will. The Human 'Experiment' has been Contaminated. Lucifer wants Humanity destroyed, Genetically, Spiritual and for Eternity.

This is called Sin and caused by Sin. Sin resulted from being Disobedient to YHVH by choosing to Reject Jesus and turn one's back on Salvation. Humanity was fooled into thinking it can be or are 'Gods'. This is 'The Lie'. A Time is coming where Lucifer will mandate the Mark of the Beast. This will change one's DNA enough to cease being fully Human and thus not Redeemable.

ADMIT YOU HAVE SINNED

A person might think they are 'Good' and deserve to go to Heaven. Many are trusting in how 'Good' they are or what they have done. The truth is that all Humans all 'Sinners', meaning one can never be 'Good Enough' to earn their way to Heaven or do enough Good to out-weigh all their Bad.

For all have Sinned and fall Short of the Glory of GOD
– Romans 3:23

For whoever shall keep the whole Law, and yet stumble in one Point, he is guilty of All. – James 2:10

As it is written: There is none Righteous, no, not one.
– Romans 3:10

The Bible clearly teaches that ALL Humans have Sinned and have broken YHVH's Commandments. Since the Creator, YHVH is a Holy and Just GOD. Sins against a Holy Creator must be Paid for and Punished. The Bible teaches that the 'Wages or Payment for Sin is Death'. This means that it will cost you Eternal Death and Divine Separation from the Living GOD in a place called Hell.

However, a Loving, Merciful GOD, YHVH does not take pleasure in the Death of the Wicked, it states in the Bible. Nor does YHVH desire any to Perish and go to Hell. YHVH devised a Plan to Redeem or 'buy back' Humanity. The 1st Step thus in being 'Redeemed' or bought back is to acknowledge that one is Sinner.

BELIEVE ON JESUS CHRIST

However, YHVH had a Plan of Salvation that involved sending Jesus, GOD the Son to Pay for the Sins of Humanity. Admitting one is a Sinner also involves wanting to Repent, that is to 'Change Directions'. In the Bible, both John the Baptist and Jesus Himself began their Preaching with the word, 'Repent'. Jesus stated, 'Repent, for the Kingdom of Heaven' is at hand.' –Matthew 4:17.

For GOD so loved the World that He gave His Only Begotten SON, that whoever Believes in Him should not Perish but have Everlasting Life. For GOD did not send His SON into the World to Condemn the World, but that the World through Him might be Saved. – John 3:16-17 NKJV

So, they said, Believe on the Lord Jesus Christ, and you will be saved, you and your household. – Acts 16:31

And this is His commandment: that we should Believe on the Name of His Son Jesus Christ and Love one another, as He gave us Commandment. – 1 John 3:23 NKJV

'For I delivered to you first of all that which I also received: that Christ Died for our Sins according to the Scriptures, and that He was Buried, and that He Rose again the 3rd-Day according to the Scriptures.' – 1 Corinthians.

Believing is a 'Work'. Why only Jesus? Jesus Christ is presented by YHVH, the Creator as a Perfect, Sinless 'Lamb of God'. But contrary to forced Animal Sacrifices, Jesus stated that He came willingly because of the Love toward GOD the Father.

CALL UPON THE NAME OF JESUS

Jesus laid down His Life and took the Penalty or 'Consequences' meant for every Human on Earth. He literally took the Judgment upon Himself on the Cross of Calvary in one's Place as Isaiah 53:6 teaches.

Jesus paid the Debt no Human can ever come close to paying and Redeemed one's Spirit, Soul and Body. Why not? The 'Payment' requires 'Sinless Perfection'. YHVH, through the Work of Jesus made the Salvation of one's Soul, Spirit and Body possible and easy for Humanity, but it cost the Son of GOD everything. Jesus made Believing in Him not just based on Aimless and Empty Faith or Meaningless Religious Works.

If one then recognizes that Jesus is the Only Way to obtain Salvation of one's Soul, Spirit and Body eventually, one has to act upon this Understanding. One must agree and apply this Truth to one's Life. How? One has to Call upon the Name of Jesus and declare this Truth. But GOD, who is YHVH is a Respecter of Humanity's Free Will. He will not force People to be 'Saved' or call on His Name.

...that if you Confess with your Mouth the LORD Jesus and Believe in your Heart that GOD has raised Him from the Dead, you will be Saved. For with the Heart one Believes unto Righteousness, and with the Mouth Confession is made unto Salvation. – Romans 10:9-10

For I am not ashamed of the Gospel of Christ, for it is the Power of GOD to Salvation for everyone who believes, for the Jew first and also for the Greek [Non-Jews]. – Romans 1:16

354

Not sure how to receive this Salvation?

YHVH did His part by sending His One and Only SON to die in one's place on the Cross of Calvary. Jesus now offers every person on Earth not only the Forgiveness of Sin as a Free Gift, i.e., Salvation, but Eternal Life and a place with Him in Heaven. However, this 'Gift' must be received as one would extent that to a person. How is this done? One must confess that one is a Sinner, no matter how Good or Bad of a Sinner.

To reiterate, one must then Believe that Jesus Died, was Buried but was Resurrected from the Dead as the Bible teaches and there were 1st account Witnesses to this event. Then, one must confess with one's Mouth -if physically able to as GOD requires an Outward, Public Action. Why? Jesus Died Publicly, Naked on the Shameful and painfully on a Wooden Cross for the Sinner. The least one can do is to not hide this Free Gift of Salvation as a 'Secret' and live with a Fearful Type of 'Faith' in Jesus.

The Gift of Salivation is operated by way of a Prayer. If one is not familiar with Prayer, it is simply 'Talking to GOD' Openly and Honestly. In ones' own words, Confess or state that you admit you are a 'Sinner', are Repenting and want Forgiveness. YHVH already knows that one is a Sinner but wants one to agree. Prayer is just opening up a 'Channel of Communication' to verbalize the obvious.

Then, ask for Jesus' Gift of Salvation by declaring that you believe in Jesus' Finished Work on the Cross of Calvary, in that Jesus shed His Blood for one's Sin. And that Jesus Rose from the Grave on the 3rd Day. Confess or accept that Jesus as the Only Savior and Lord of one's Life. This Commitment to Jesus should be considered that thought about carefully. It is not an 'Insurance Policy from Hell' as many do see it. Or, just to not have a Guilty Conscious but knowing that one will Return to a Lifestyle of Sin.

The Bible teachers that if one genuinely wants to come to Jesus for Salvation and Redemption, one will see a True-Life Change. If one is unsure of what and/or how to Pray, one can Pray something like the following 'Template'.

Father in Heaven,
I know that I am a Sinner before a Holy Creator. I realize that the Penalty for Sin is Eternal Death, being Separated from your Love and Life. I believe that Jesus, you shed Your own Sinless Blood on the Cross of Calvary so that I could receive His Righteousness by Faith in what He finished and Paid for. I Confess that I am a Sinner and ask Jesus for Your Forgiveness. I believe that you Died and Rose again so that I can be Forgiven and Live Forever with Him. Jesus, here and now, I surrender my Life, my Soul, Spirit and Body to you to be used for Your Purpose and Glory from now on. Jesus, Thank You for coming as the SON of GOD, to Die in my Place. I Ask and Pray all this in Your Name, Jesus. Amen.

If you have said this Prayer or something like it to Jesus, genuinely and from a Repentant and Sincere Heart, then you are Saved! Welcome to the Family of Jesus! The Bible teaches that a Follower of Jesus is saved by Grace through Faith'... not of Works. Realize that YHVH, GOD sees One's Heart and He cannot be fooled. But one is not 'Saved' by simply saying some Special Words in a Formal Prayer.

One is Saved when one Says and Lives the Prayer of Salvation by the Power of the Holy Spirit Jesus gives now into one's Life as a result. This is and will be the 'Proof of your Salvation. However, the Bible does teach that this Saving Faith produces 'Fruit'. One way one will be able to tell if one is 'Saved' is that one will be Forever Changed from that point forward. The Bible teaches that GOD the Holy Spirit will come in 'Dwell' or Live in one's Spirit to help live-out this required 'Holy Life' in Obedience to the Will of Christ Jesus until Death comes or the Rapture occurs.

I PRAYED TO RECEIVE JESUS CHRIST! IS THAT IT?

Becoming a Follower of Jesus means that one's Life will be Forever Changed as a New Journey of Faith begins in you. It is now a Relationship. Begin by Reading the New Testament and then the Old Testament to get a Perspective of how YHVH dealt with People and see Examples of Good and Bad types of 'Faith'. Then meet with other Followers of Jesus to Encourage one another. Then grow in the Understanding of Jesus. Then be Baptized if possible.

Likewise, I say to you, there is joy in the presence of the Angels of GOD over 1 Sinner who repents. – Luke 15:10

Realize that as the Gift of Salvation has paid for one's Spirit, Soul and Body. Presently, the Body is not yet Redeemed. So, one is this present Evil World and will still be subject to the Temptations of Self, Sin, Satan and the World. However, Jesus Christ has not left His People alone on Earth. As mentioned, Jesus sent GOD the Holy Spirit to help you be Convicted of Sin and have Power over it. One Day, the Bible states that Jesus is to Return to Earth to Extract of 'Rapture' His Bride and then 'Make All Things Right'.

In the meanwhile, the Journey of one's Faith with Jesus has begun. Like a Newborn, one must be Feed, Cared For and Grow in Stature, Knowledge and Understanding that is found in Jesus. This is the 'Walk of Faith' as now Jesus, whom is your Savior and LORD desires you to reach 'Maturity'. How is this achieved? In part, it is finding His Will for your Life and applying one's Purpose and Role in being used by Jesus until He Returns.

…'to equip the Saints for Works of Ministry, to build-up the Body of Christ, until we all reach Unity in the Faith and in the Knowledge of the Son of GOD, as we mature to the Full Measure of the Stature of Christ.' – Ephesians 4: 12-13

COMMITMENT TO JESUS CHRIST FOR SALVATION

I made a Pledge to be Saved and receive the Gift of Salvation only found in Jesus Christ.

__Yes   __Not Yet __Need for info

If Yes! Whom prayed with?

__Self __Group __A Person

I,_____ Prayed to Receive Jesus as my Savior and LORD. Born unto the Kingdom of Christ Jesus, on this

Date:_____   Place:_____

PLEDGE?
I pledge to be a Follower of Jesus from now on and live a Life worthy of His Holy Name.

__Yes   __Not Sure __Not Yet   __Need for info

I pledge to read the New and Old Testament to grow in my Faith and tell others about the Saving Work of Jesus on the Cross.

__Yes __Not Sure __Not Yet __Need for info

Book Resources

If one would like to read further content, the following Books are 6x9 inches Paperback. The topics range from the Geo-Political, Biblical Prophecy, End Times, the Occult and so-called Conspiratorial Subject Matter.

These Books can be purchased for a Study Reference, Personal Interest or a Gift to others. Nonetheless, it is an attempt to provide a Resource in Hand.

The Books are also in PDF format and can be downloaded with a Donation off the Author's webpage. A OneDrive Account is not required for such an option.

The links to the DOWNLOAD W/ DONATION Buttons, takes you to the Public Files where the Books are publicly accessible in PDF Format.

https://www.postscripts.org/books-1.html

COVID RELATED

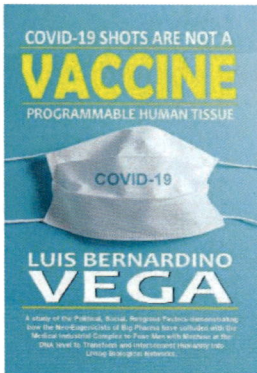

COVID-19 SHOTS ARE NOT A VACCINE
Programmable Human Tissue
The COVID-19 Injections are not a 'Vaccine'. The Culling of Humanity has begun, 1 COVID Injection with Liquid Metal, 'Black Goo' at a time.
ORDER ON AMAZON BOOKS

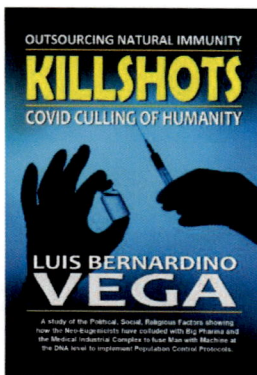

COVID KILL SHOTS
The Great Culling of Humanity
How do you kill 6 Billion People on Earth? You lie to them. Neo-Eugenicists have colluded to fuse Man with Machine at the DNA level to implement Population Control Protocols.
ORDER ON AMAZON BOOKS

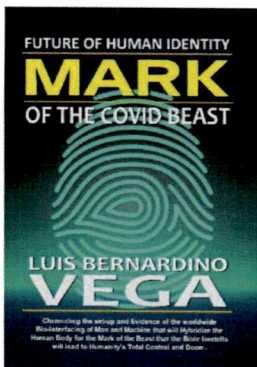

MARK OF THE COVID BEAST
The Future of Human Identity
The purpose of this Book is to note how the Gene Editing mRNA COVID-19 Shots are dangerous and will be catastrophic but will construe the necessary Genetic Scaffolding to make humans Biological Computers to program Living Tissue.
ORDER ON AMAZON BOOKS

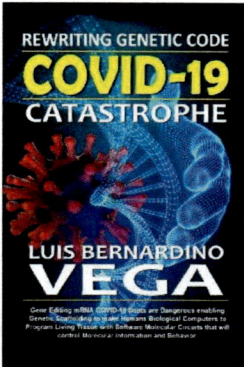

COVID CATASTROPHE
Rewriting Genetic Code
The purpose of this Book is to note how the Gene Editing mRNA COVID-19 Shots are indeed changing DNA. The Book will present several Key and very important interviews with Doctors and Virologist denouncing the re-Creation of Adam 2.0 where Man merges with Machine.
ORDER ON AMAZON BOOKS

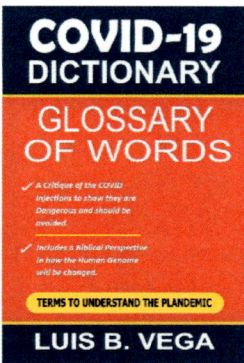

COVID-19 DICTIONARY FOR THE PLANDEMIC
Glossary of Words
The objective is to have a better sense of what the COVID Words, Terms, and Concepts mean. It is to be better educated in understanding such content to make a more informed decision as to reject the new mRNA Shots.
ORDER ON LULU BOOKS

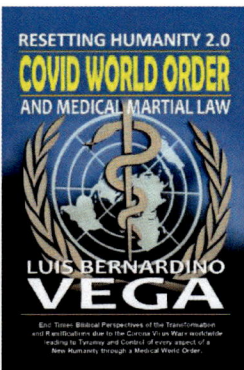

COVID WORLD ORDER
And the Medical Martial Law
The studies presented in this Book will consider the various sources that strongly suggest that the release of COVID-19, although real, is being abused to foment the need to undergo and implement the Global Economic 'Reset'. Medical Passports will be required.
ORDER ON AMAZON BOOKS

New World Order

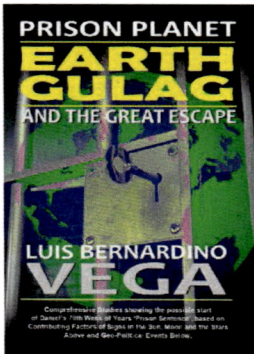

EARTH GULAG

Rise of the Prison Planet   Events, Places, People and Issues that are making Earth into a Prison Planet. In fact, it already is. This Book will present various chapters of Topics, Events and or Occurrences that deal with Geo-Political, and Theological Constructs.
ORDER ON AMAZON BOOKS

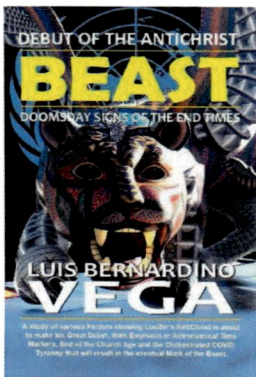

DEBUT ANTICHRIST BEAST

Doomsday Signs of the End
What is the 'Beast'? Who is or will be the 'Beast'? Why does the Bible call this coming Man, the 'Beast'? Several Factors will show how the Spirit of Lucifer's AntiChrist has risen in the World and about to make his Great Debut.
ORDER ON AMAZON BOOKS

FALL OF THE PHOENIX

Master Plan for America
The Fall of the Phoenix chronicles the Code of the 33 'Economic' Sabbatical Cycle Countdown since 1776 for America's Demise. Various Celestial Signs are taking place that appear to also be signaling a Prophetic Countdown to the Fall of the Phoenix, America.
ORDER ON AMAZON BOOKS

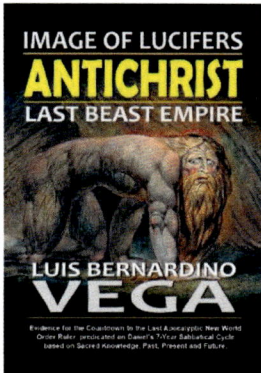

IMAGES OF ANTICHRIST
Last Luciferian Beast Empire
This Book examines the case for the Countdown to the coming Apocalyptic New World Order that will be tied to Daniel's 7-Year Sabbatical Cycle of the Terminal Generation based on Sacred Knowledge, past, present and future.
ORDER ON AMAZON BOOKS

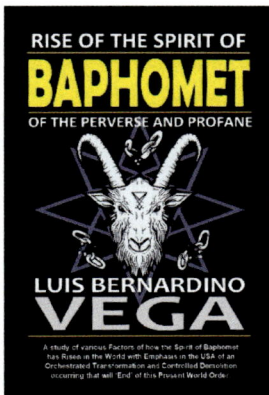

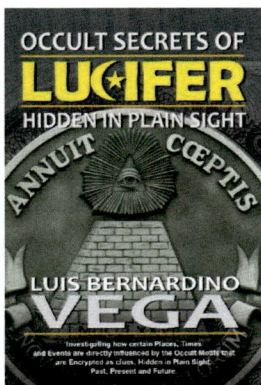

RISE OF THE SPIRIT OF BAPHOMET
Prepare for the End of World
The purpose of this Book is to ascertain several Factors of how the Spirit of Baphomet has risen in the World and in the USA in particular. It is a Spirit of Perversion that has reversed and undermined all Human Moral Institutions, Ethics, etc.
ORDER ON AMAZON BOOKS

SECRETS OF LUCIFER
Sacred Coordinates & Measurements
The purpose of this Book is to investigate and ascertain the possible Prophetic Mathematical Calculations that are related to People, Places, and Times related to meaning hidden in plain sight.
ORDER ON AMAZON BOOKS

Mars Star Gates on Earth

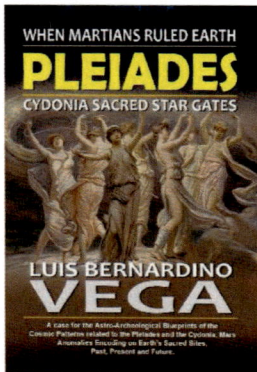

PLEIADES CONSPIRACY
When Martians Ruled Earth
The purpose of this Book is to ascertain the Cosmic Motifs of the Pleiades and Orion as they pertain to the pyramid designs of the ancient Sacred Sites on Earth, past, present and future.
ORDER ON AMAZON BOOKS

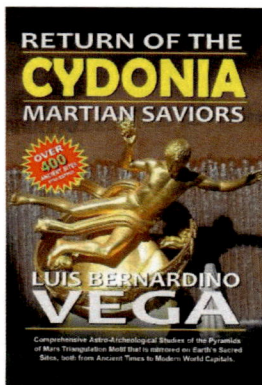

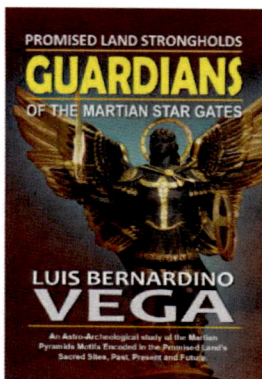

RETURN OF THE CYDONIA MARTIAN SAVIORS
Unmasking of the Rebel King
The purpose of this Book is to present a case for 'unmasking' who is behind the 'Face of Mars' from a Biblical point of view. This coming Deception that the Bible speaks about will be in part, the 'return of the Martian Saviors'.
ORDER ON AMAZON BOOKS

GUARDIANS OF THE GATES
Possessing the Portals

This Book will show how such Martian Motif Triangulations served and serve as 'Gates' and/or 'Portals' on one level and Luciferian 'Spiritual Strongholds'.
ORDER ON AMAZON BOOKS

End of Days

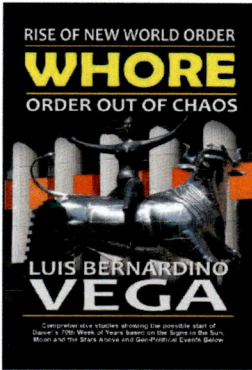

2022 - RISE OF THE WHORE
Mystery of Iniquity
The purpose of this Book is to present an array of comprehensive studies spanning over a decade of Eschatological Research suggesting that 2022 is the Probable Year of the start of the Tribulation Period. The studies strongly suggest a Convergence in 2022.
ORDER ON AMAZON BOOKS

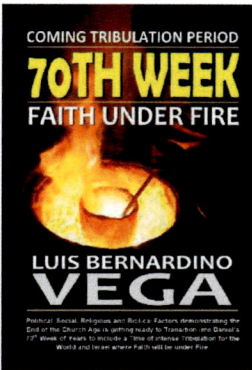

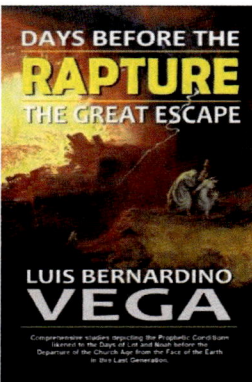

70TH WEEK OF YEARS
Coming Tribulation Period
The purpose of this Book is to provide a comprehensive study of the Political, Social, Religious and Biblical Factors demonstrating just how close the end of the Church Age is and ready to Transition into Daniel's 70th Week of Years.
ORDER ON AMAZON BOOKS

DAYS BEFORE THE RAPTURE
The Great Escape
The purpose of this Book is to chronicle the Last Days leading up to the Rapture event and what that will look like. There will be a variety of topics discussed and presented from Political, Social, Religious and Esoteric sources in such a context.
ORDER ON BARNES & NOBLE

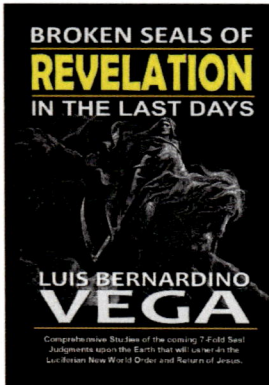

REVELATION BROKEN SEALS
In the Last Days
The purpose of this Book is to chronicle various precursory events leading-up to the breaking of the Seal Judgments in the Book of Revelation. Such events are inevitably leading-up to the collapse of the current World Order.
ORDER ON AMAZON BOOKS

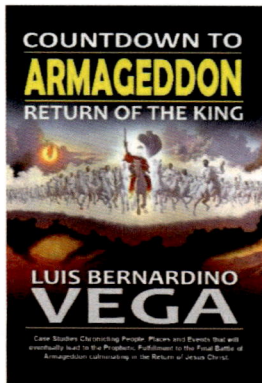

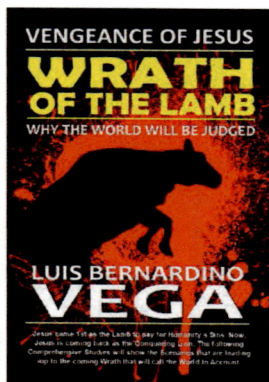

COUNTDOWN TO ARMAGEDDON
Return of the King
The purpose of this Book is to investigate and ascertain the possible Prophetic Variables that will lead to the ultimate Battle of Armageddon. The presumption is that certain events in the Middle East, in particular will be centered in Israel and Jerusalem.
ORDER ON AMAZON BOOKS

WRATH OF THE LAMB
Vengeance of Jesus
The purpose of this Book is to Chronicle the Reasons, Evidence and Events that will cause the Wrath of the Lamb to fall on Humanity. The Wrath of what Lamb? Jesus. One will present the Evidence and Clues of what that will look like.
ORDER ON AMAZON BOOKS

Israel

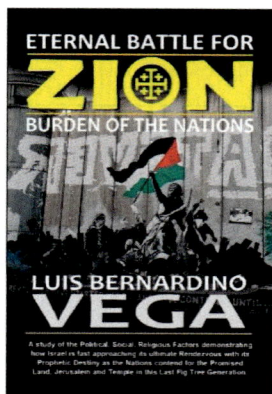

ETERNAL BATTLE FOR ZION
Burden of the Nations
The purpose of this Book is to ascertain events surrounding Israel as the Fig Tree Nation and how it is being contested by the Nations and coming from the Muslim Arabs who call themselves 'Palestinians'. It is a 'Battle over Zion' as the 'Winner takes All'.
ORDER ON AMAZON BOOKS

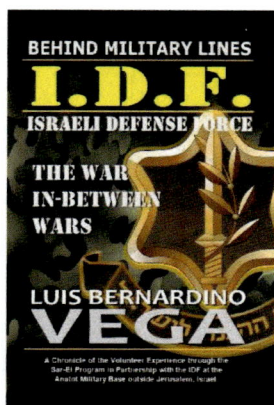

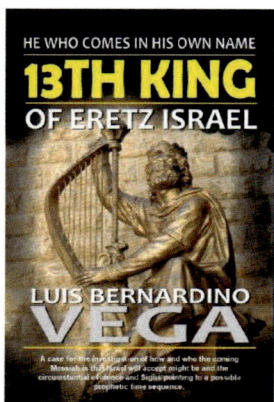

BEHIND IDF MILITARY LINES
The War In-Between Wars
The purpose of this Book is to chronicle the volunteer experience through the Sar-El Program in partnership with the Israeli Defense Force, the IDF at the Anatot Military Base outside Jerusalem, Israel. The following are items documenting the short incursion to Israel in 2019.
ORDER ON AMAZON BOOKS

13TH KING OF ISRAEL
He Who Comes in His Own Name
The purpose of this Book is to correlate the first 13 Kings of both the Kingdoms of Judea and Israel with that of the first 13th 'Kings' of Modern-Day Israel in terms of its Prime Ministers since 1948. This study suggests that perhaps the 13th Person will be the AntiChrist.
ORDER ON AMAZON BOOKS

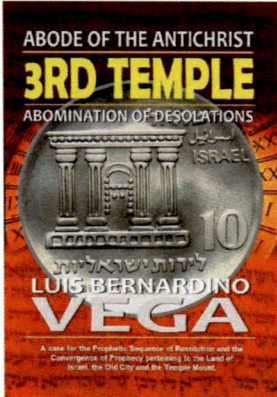

THE 3RD TEMPLE

Prophetic Keys to Israel's Restoration

The Olivet Discourse basically consisted of a Prophetic Outline or Blueprint that would involve the restitution of 3 Factors that have to be in place before the LORD's 2nd Coming. The Factors disclosed by Christ start with the Temple, then Jerusalem and ended with Israel.

ORDER ON AMAZON BOOKS

Biblical Astronomy

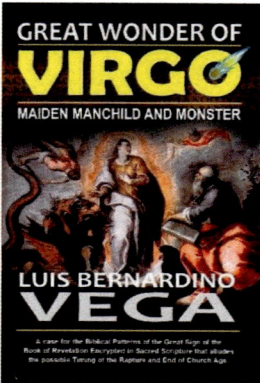

GREAT SIGN OF VIRGO
Maiden, the Manchild and Monster
Revelation chapter 12. The main argument will be that such a Sign to occur prophetically matched the Astronomical Configuration on September 23, 2017 was a Countdown to the Rapture event and the start of the 70th Week of Years or the 7-Year Tribulation Period.
ORDER ON AMAZON BOOKS

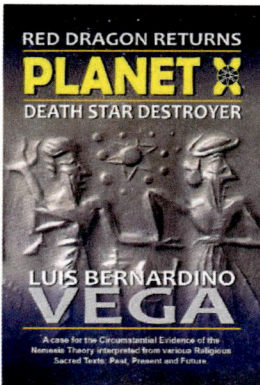

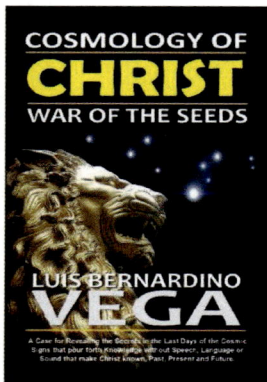

INSIGHTS INTO PLANET X
Red Dragon of the Revelation
The purpose of this Book is to present various insights for and against the Planet X Phenomena. The study will try to ascertain a comprehensive array of subject matter surrounding an allusive extra Solar System 2nd Sun.
ORDER ON AMAZON BOOKS

COSMOLOGY OF CHRIST
Divine Patterns of the Messiah
This Book seeks to unlock the Secrets of the Celestial Blueprint of the Last Days based on the 'Image and Likeness' of Jesus Christ; His Pattern of the Body Form and its Dimensions that occur on a Prophetic Scale.
ORDER ON AMAZON BOOKS

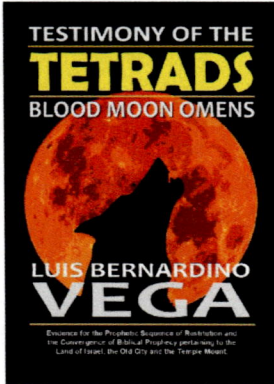

TESTIMONY OF TETRADS
Blood Moon Omens

The purpose of this Book is to provide a retrospective and comprehensive study of the Tetrad and Blood Moon Sequences that occurred since 1949 that suggest a Prophetic Reconstitution of Israel, the end of the Church Age, and start of Daniel's 70th Week.

ORDER ON AMAZON BOOKS-

Prophecy

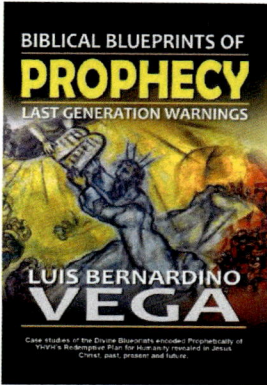

BLUEPRINT OF BIBLICAL PROPHECY
Divine Patterns of Christ
The Book will illustrate the various divine Patterns in the Bible whose theme and purpose is to testify of Jesus. These hidden divine Blueprints are what are seen and how the Bible speaks such Blueprints are yet to occur.
ORDER ON AMAZON BOOKS

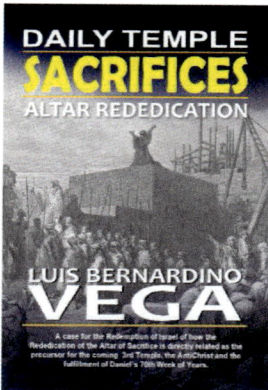

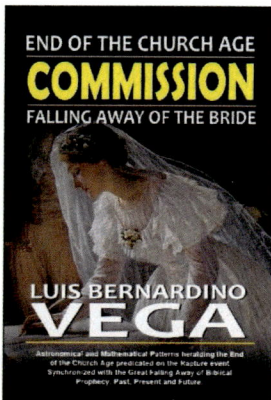

DAILY SACRIFICES
Rededication of the Altar of Sacrifices
The purpose of this Book is to present a case for the Redemption of Israel of how the Rededication of the Altar of Sacrifice is related as precursor for the coming 3rd Temple, the AntiChrist and fulfillment of Daniel's 70th Week.
ORDER ON AMAZON BOOKS

END OF THE CHURCH AGE
Conclusion of the Commission
A study of the Astronomical and Mathematical Patterns heralding the end of the Church Age and the coming transference of Testimony and the Witness of the Gospel of Jesus Christ. The 7-Year Sabbatical Cycle of the Church Age is about to conclude and transfer back to Israel.
ORDER ON AMAZON BOOKS

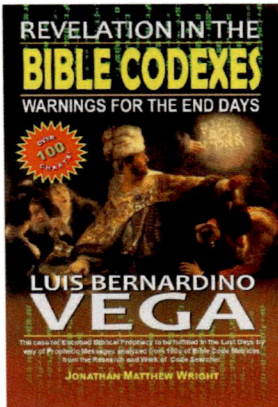

BIBLE CODEXES
Revelation for the Bride of Christ, Church and Israel

This Book suggests that ' Prophetic Warnings' or Messages in the form of 'Codes' are found within the Bible text or scroll itself. In part, these 'Codes' are what the Angel of YHVH told the Prophet Daniel what would be unveiled now as these Last Days to warn the Bride of Christ.

ORDER ON AMAZON BOOKS

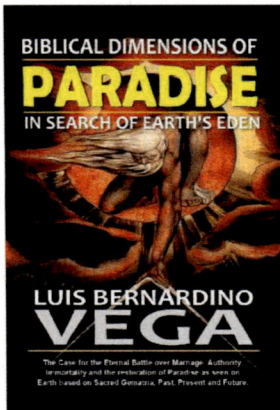

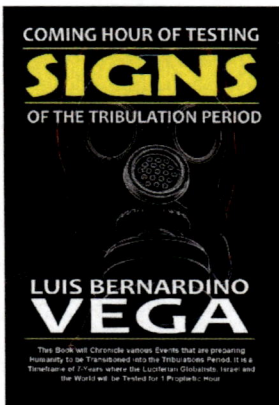

DIMENSIONS OF PARADISE
Garden of Eden's Location and Restoration

The purpose of this Book is to investigate and ascertain the possible Geographical Location of the Garden of Eden. The presumption is that certain locations have been built perhaps on the very Ley-Lines of the Dimensions of Paradise itself.

ORDER ON AMAZON BOOKS

SIGNS OF THE TRIBULATION
Coming Hour of Testing

The purpose of this Book will Chronicle various Events that are preparing Humanity to be Transitioned into the Tribulations Period. It is a Timeframe of 7-Years where the Luciferian Globalists, Israel and the World will be Tested for 1 Prophetic Hour.

ORDER ON AMAZAON BOOKS

NOTES

Made in the USA
Las Vegas, NV
02 December 2023